Daniela Carpi (ed.)

Property Law
in Renaissance Literature

PETER LANG
Europäischer Verlag der Wissenschaften

Bibliographic Information published by Die Deutsche Bibliothek
Die Deutsche Bibliothek lists this publication in the Deutsche Nationalbibliografie; detailed bibliographic data is available in the internet at <http://dnb.ddb.de>.

ISSN 0177-6959
ISBN 3-631-54133-3
US-ISBN 0-8204-7745-1

© Peter Lang GmbH
Europäischer Verlag der Wissenschaften
Frankfurt am Main 2005
All rights reserved.

All parts of this publication are protected by copyright. Any utilisation outside the strict limits of the copyright law, without the permission of the publisher, is forbidden and liable to prosecution. This applies in particular to reproductions, translations, microfilming, and storage and processing in electronic retrieval systems.

Printed in Germany 1 2 3 4   6 7

www.peterlang.de

Property Law in Renaissance Literature

ANGLO-AMERIKANISCHE STUDIEN
ANGLO-AMERICAN STUDIES

Herausgegeben von Rüdiger Ahrens und Kevin Cope

Band 28

PETER LANG
Frankfurt am Main · Berlin · Bern · Bruxelles · New York · Oxford · Wien

Table of Contents

Introduction   vii
Daniela Carpi

PART I   1

Nietzsche's Hermeneutics: Good and Bad Interpreters of Texts   3
Richard H. Weisberg

PART II   17

Comic Plots and Property Law in Plautus's Trinummus: 19
Humanistic and Renaissance Reflections
Ida Mastrorosa

Rational Animal by Participation. Images of Patriarchal Power from   41
Ariosto to Tasso
Marco Cavina

Property and Inheritance in the Renaissance *novella*:   51
from Arienti's *Porretane* to Bandello's *Novelle*
Luisa Avellini

Land Rhetoric and Ideology in Sir John Davies's Report   63
on the Case of Tanistry (1615)
Jean Paul Pittion

The King's Great Matter: Shakespeare, Patriarchy and the Question   75
of Succession
Ian Ward

To Have and *Have not* in Shakespeare: Patrimonial Questions in   91
"*As you like it*"
Giuseppina Restivo

Macbeth, or the Question of Dominion *Maurizio Pedrazza Gorlero*	105
Patrilineal Law and the Plays of Ben Jonson *Richard Cave*	117
Person and Property in Thomas Middleton's *A Chaste Maid in Cheapside* *Daniela Carpi*	131
From Law to Literature: Guillaume de La Perrière's Intellectual Path *Géraldine Cazals*	145
«De l'affection des pères aux enfants»: Sentimental Bonds and Juridical Bonds in Montaigne, *Essais*, II, 8 *Giovanni Rossi*	161
The Voice of Dominium - Property, Possession and Renaissance Figures in *The Cantos* of Ezra Pound *Adam Gearey*	179

APPENDIX 193

King James and an Obsession with *The Merchant of Venice* 195
Peter J. Alscher and Richard H. Weisberg

Introduction

The law historian who turns backwards to examine the evolution of the juridical system across the centuries cannot fail to realize that civil law, in comparison with the other juridical systems, has undergone few, and almost imperceptible, transformations, at least in some sections. That is to say that when one approaches, for instance, last century's penal law or administrative law or constitutional law one perceives that each institution has undergone such transformations that it is hardly recognizable. We may avow that theft is still theft, and Parliament is still Parliament, but the way of conceiving of legal institutions and cases is so changed that it is hard to draw a comparison with the past, even when the names of the offences and of the institutions involved have not changed.

On the contrary the civil law system challenges the flow of time. It may sound incredible to those who are not versed in law, but, even if everyday life and people's ways of thinking have so deeply changed and people's customs are "ictu oculi" so different from those of the past, the laws concerning succession, property and contracts, and the governing of the family, have remained stable. The French civil code, notwithstanding its many developments, has been valid for more than two hundred years. In the same way our concept of marriage is perfectly compatible with the definitions given by Modestino in the Roman sources (notwithstanding the great innovations brought about by Christianity!), and the definition of "usufruct" (right of user) in the Italian civil system still in use is provided by literally translating a passage from Justinian's Digest.

This is not to say that many sections of the civil law system itself have not partially evolved, especially in the laws concerning the equal rights of husband and wife within the family, or in the case of legitimate and illegitimate children. We must, however, acknowledge that most parts of the civil law system have undergone only very slight changes, especially in the sections dealing with property or real rights and most of the institutions concerning hereditary rights. For instance, the third book "On property" of the Italian civil code, in force since the 28th of October 1940, has never changed a single article since then. But even more than this, the Government Committee that in those days drew up the law was formed by a larger number of professors of Roman Law than of modern civil law.

These concepts are echoed in the history of the different juridical systems of the main European countries. The question of property was one of the principal preoccupations of all judicial systems of Roman inspiration (from Justinian to Napoleon) and also a central theme in political thought. At the beginning of the Renaissance, the question was revived by humanists owing to the return to the

Bible and the acknowledgement of the authority of Cicero and other classical authors such as Caesar. The evident analogies between the civil law systems of the continental countries stem from their being rooted in the "ius commune", that is in the Justian code, which, after being relaunched by the Bolognese School of law, formed the basis for legal regulations in the various countries. However these regulations, in their basic principles, were applied also in England whose "common law", even if it cannot be confused with the "ius commune", is not totally unrelated to the Roman code. The latter was imported into England by the English jurists who studied in Bologna and in the other continental universities. This is why, for instance, the main real rights (usufruct, servitude etc.), notwithstanding their being inserted into a fundamentally different legal background, retain the characteristics which are perfectly recognizable to a continental jurist. Hence the fact that the right of property valid in the English Renaissance was very similar to the rest of the continent, even if each country had undergone a different socio-economic evolution. This is an incontrovertible principle still valid in western civilization and culture.

The English Law of Property is largely feudal in origin and by the beginning of the 20th century it developed from comparatively simple beginnings into a highly complex and comprehensive system containing many anachronisms. The need for reform came to the fore in the 19th century and many Acts were passed bringing about some improvements. But it was only in 1925 that a real transformation in both real and personal property took place, when, for instance, feudal methods of transferring land were abolished. However, in the period under examination the law of property was still largely feudal in its arrangement.

The legal and social historian can therefore feel at ease when examining the panorama which the juridical sources, no less than the extra-juridical ones such as literary texts, offer him, and this even if he must face patent discrepancies in the different social evolutions presented by the different countries, for instance deriving from the superior mercantile development of England at the time (here let us consider the rise of the joint-stock companies in England which were also to pass into the other juridical systems).

Consequently, one could wonder how this fundamental conservatism, especially concerning real rights, can cope with the extraordinary transformations of social life. The answer should lie more with the sociologist or the psychologist than with the jurist. The man in the street is generally conservative or suspicious of all innovations: it is a sort of animal instinct of survival. The right to property is deeply felt by the whole of mankind and considered as intrinsic in the individual's self-identification, and this is why only with exceeding slowness and resistance can socio-economic changes take place and force any transformation from inside the field of acquired rights in terms of property. Any sudden alteration would represent a sort of estrangement or

Introduction

deracination for the individual's "das sein", which may explain the recurring failure of the ideologies that promise, through a sort of revolutionary catharsis, an unforeseen and violent change in the relationship between man and property.

The essays included in this collection all take into consideration a particular aspect of property law in English, French and Italian literatures, thus demonstrating how the European countries share such a common interest and how the security of the states rests on solid patrimonial laws. Literature once more serves the function of echoing what takes place in society, and it textualizes seeds of agreement or discontent with the law itself, which in turn appears as either inimical or friendly. All of the essays discuss the equity or inequity of juridical systems and how the common man tolerates juridical precepts willingly or unwillingly. The law may curb and force man into obedience and he may suffer from it, or he may enjoy particular interpretations of the law itself. In any case all the essays bring about a dialogue between law and literature, to which field this book belongs.

Weisberg's essay opens the discussion: he concentrates his argument on Nietzsche and on the problem of the interpretation of the law. He starts by referring to Nietzsche's 11th aphorism in *On the Genealogy of Morals*, where he cautions against using law as an end in itself: "It is always the anti-vitalistic means to the always vitalistic end of justice". So the way is paved for the importance of interpretation. But interpretation of the law is also what permitted the deformation of the law itself during the Vichy period and led to racial division. In this essay, part of a long-term study of the Vichy period, Weisberg asserts that racism stemmed from a hermeneutic approach. It was a question of retaining a sacred text (the Bible) while fundamentally altering its meaning. "Insistence on faithful readings is forever challenged as a hermeneutic method": this can be connected with Derrida's assertion of "the violence of the Letter". Weisberg closes his discussion, which is a perfect introduction to a book dealing with the interpretation of the law and its application to some literary texts, with an appeal to a recourse to flexibility in law, a flexibility which means not strict adherence to the text of the law, but which implies that the law must "be flexible, elastic, fluid, as well as definitive, clear and steadfast".

Alscher's and Weisberg's essay concludes the volume with an example of what results the comparison between law and literature can bring about. The essay concentrates on the diachronical study of the audience's and King James' reception of the *Merchant of Venice*, and in particular it analyses semitic or anti-semitic approaches to the play. Weisberg and Alscher take into consideration the so-called "majority report" and "minority report", that is to say, how the majority of critics reacted to the play, contraposing the majority attitude (mainly anti-semitic) with a minority group, viewing it in a tragic light of religious and legal violation. The *Merchant of Venice* has always been a central work in the law and literature field of research because of the patently legal elements that pervade the text. Weisberg and Alscher, though not centring their analysis of the property problem, still consider the fact that Shylock's spiritual and social annihilation has in itself strong financial innuendos, based on the supposition that Shylock might be seen as threatening a state grounded in the financial security of his citizens.

The topics of the several essays move between many different interpretations of the concept of property. Property fundamentally means anything that belongs to a person, or in other words, anything which is proper to that person, and therefore the law of property is centred on the relationship between persons and things. In pre-industrial societies this relationship entails more a social position than an economic function. In an agricultural society land conveys a different significance than in a society based on money exchanges: ownership of land in fact conveys a particular social status and does not merely give control on an important means of production. Moveables certainly lack this symbolic significance. The law of property sets the rules through which things belong to particular persons; but it may happen that a thing is possessed by someone who does not actually own it. When this relationship between things and persons becomes complicated, a set of rules must be fixed that regulates such transactions. This is when the distinction between moveables and immoveables is drawn.

In particular, English law recognizes two kinds of property: real property (that is freehold interest in land) and personal property (any other kind of property, including leaseholds in land). We must, furthermore, distinguish between ownership and possession, where the former is a legal concept, while the latter is a matter of fact. Possession was recognized by the law before property, so when in the old days there were cases of accusations for wrongful dispossession the plaintiff had only to prove that he was entitled to the possession of that property, and not that he was the owner.

Therefore the topics of this collection span from the property of land to the property by inheritance, from very special cases of ownership and possession to examples of usufruct and "usucapio", from problems of royal succession considered from the point of view of "acquisition of power", to struggles between generations over wealth.

Ida Mastrorosa in "Comic plots and property law in Plautus's *Trinummus*: Humanistic and Renaissance reflections" considers Plautus's work as a perfect exemplum of solutions regarding the *mandatum*, which in turn represents an engine of dramatic action. The text functions as a technical instrument capable of providing answers concerning legal problems, with the result of representing a typical effect of *contaminatio*. The text patently deals with issues concerning *mandatum*, guardianship and *patria potestas*. Both Plautus' *Trinummus* and Cecchi's *The Dowry* prove the vitality of the patrimonial motif: the legal theme is not so much to be appreciated as coherent with the juridical model of those

Introduction

days but rather as the proof that the law represents an unavoidably regulating element of reality.

Marco Cavina in "Rational Animal by Participation" centres his analysis on the figure of the servant ("famulus") within aristocratic families as part of family property. The individuality of the servant was lost within the unity of the "domus", clustered around the authority of the head of the family. The servant was a sort of "res" at the patriarch's disposal. The servants of noble families were legally protected because an insult to them was considered an insult to the nobleman himself. In literature – and here Cavina quotes Ariosto and Tasso – the servant reflects the good and bad qualities of his lord, in a sort of osmotic relationship.

Luisa Avellini, in "Property and Inheritance in the Renaissance novella: from Arienti's Porretane *to Bandello's* Novelle", concentrates her attention on wills in the world of Renaissance tales, observing how autobiographies *in limine mortis* are part of the rite of departure of Christian individuality and are connected to the final confession. This religious act becomes a means through which to proceed to an exchange between material and spiritual goods in the form of the will. The structure of the autobiography and consequent will is therefore the common one: "an initial confession, the redemption from sins, pious bequests, accurate burial prescriptions, the distribution of charity, suffrages, and so on". The will is a "passport to heaven" by means of the invention of a third purgatorial space that is somehow destined for the negotiation of salvation, and it is also an instrument for the rehabilitation of temporal and material possessions". The confession of sins, therefore, goes hand in hand with the necessity to set one's possessions in order. Through this act of will the individual has the impression of being able to control his wealth even from the world beyond. Patrimony seems also to direct one's acts of repentance and to guarantee entry into heaven through pious bequests. The Italian Renaissance "novella" best epitomizes the literary approach to the genre of the will.

Jean-Paul Pittion, in "The 'Case of Tanistry': Land Rhetoric and Ideology in Le Primer Report of Sir John Davies (1615)," stresses the fact that the Renaissance saw the emergence of new genres of legal writing. Of these, one is particularly significant: the genre of the arrêt and of the report, that is, narrative summaries of legal "cases" or "causes" worthy of recording, written in order to be published as collections of "Recrueils d'arrêts notables" in France and as "Law reports" in England. Even if they belonged to different legal traditions (Roman Law and Common Law) the texts share some fundamental characteristics: they are responsible for the development of the traditions which had produced them. On one hand, in fact, they bring about a continental jurisprudential law, that is, in the modern sense of the term, a jurisprudence which constitutes a subsidiary or complementary source of law based on interpretation. On the other hand, in the case of the English Common Law, they gave rise to a case-based law. Moreover, even if these writings were mainly addressed to lawyers, they were produced as autonomous texts and did not only represent commentaries, but – especially in the case of the arrêts and the reports – they had their origins in real judicial events considered to be exemplary. These texts abstain from commentaries but describe the cases objectively and neutrally. But it is precisely in this exemplariness that they reflected the value system they stemmed from.

These hidden assumptions are analysed in a law report, "The case of Tanistry", by Sir John Davies. "Tanistry" is a legal custom connected to the traditional land-based power in Gaelic Ireland, a society grounded on clans dominated by elected chieftains. The legal dispute described in "The case of Tanistry" regarded the transmission of an inheritance of land. Davies asserted that if land tenure in Ireland still caused political and social disorder, that was due to the Common Law not being fully applied. In this way Davies' rhetoric can be accused both of considering the recourse to Common Law as an instrument of policy and of trying to justify and legitimise this use. The case of tanistry seems to prove the failure of the Common Law to achieve the pacification of Ireland. Davies tries to defend himself against such accusations but in doing so becomes trapped in an ideological tangle.

Ian Ward, in "The king's great matter: Shakespeare, patriarchy and the question of succession", analyses how the related issues of patriarchy and patrimonial law find their symbolic and material apogee in the matter of royal succession. Sixteenth and seventeenth century England presented an intensely gendered and patriarchal society, in which women in general were thought to be a threat to social stability and it was widely supposed that women could not be good monarchs. And yet, attitudes towards women in general were slowly beginning to change by the end of the sixteenth century, influenced almost certainly by Elizabeth I's position as Queen of England.

Historically, the monarchy of England was described in terms of the corporeal body, which helped to distinguish Elizabeth's private female body from the public, irreducibly masculine, one. The potential disadvantage of a female monarch was subtly transformed by her into an advantage. She made herself into an icon, into a positive quasi-divine image which was both patriarchal and matriarchal.

Elizabeth was not the first queen of England but she was the first to make herself so authoritative and to imprint society with her image, and this opened up considerable questions of received ideas of patriarchal succession. Shakespeare's treatment of the question of succession, and, by implication, patriarchy and the crown, are very ambivalent. The question of illegitimacy occurs in many plays, such as in *King John*, for instance, where the ambiguous figure of the Bastard is more kingly than the king. In the famous speech between

Introduction xiii

John and Queen Eleanor we are told that succession depends not only on lineage, but also on the capacity to hold political power.

Concerning the question of gender and patriarchy Shakespeare once again proves ambiguous. Let us consider, for instance, the figure of Portia, who manages to redress wrongs committed against patriarchal authority only by dissimulation, and Lear's daughters who promote Lear's tortuous attempt formulate some rationale regarding the issue of succession.

Ultimately, all these questions of usurpation, illegitimacy, female magistracy and succession come together in *Henry VIII*, with its genealogical and providential arguments for legitimate succession. It is as if Shakespeare is striving to assert the unimpeachable legitimacy of the Tudor line because the legitimacy of the Stuart succession is dependent upon it. In fact, *Henry VIII* is about the politics of successive successions. Time and again the idea of patriarchy is both reinforced and subverted in Shakespeare.

Giuseppina Restivo, in "To Have and Have Not in Shakespeare: Patrimonial Questions in "*As You Like It*", observes how different patrimonial problems are highlighted in *The Merchant of Venice* and *As You Like It*. In the former we are witness to an evolution in society, with the increasing wealth of the middle class. Patrimonial and matrimonial conceptions are here fused together and the clash is between spendthrift Bassanio and Shylock, seen as the emblem of "thrifty" or "breeding" money. Very skilfully, Lawrence Stone describes the fluctuating situation of Elizabethan England, which was undergoing strong turnovers between the aristocracy and the bourgeoisie. The problem of primogeniture and of patrilineal descent, described in *As You Like It*, as well as the question of the younger brother's allowance and education, represents the core of the play and testifies to the accuracy of Stone's assertions.

Maurizio Pedrazza Gorlero's "Macbeth, or the acquisition of dominion" discusses the dichotomy between legitimisation and consensus and analyses that sort of power that is devoid of legitimisation. This is at the basis of the "neo-feudal" political pluralism of and between nations that makes the concept of power expressed in *Macbeth* actual and enduring. Gorlero's paper considers the various methods of acquiring power in *Macbeth*: from those more immediately connected to subjectivity and juridical property to those in which subjectivity and juridical property are translated into constitutive elements of modern states. *Macbeth* represents the tragedy of absolute power which feels the lack of a solid sense of legitimisation, and from the point of view of the history of juridical and political thought, the period described in *Macbeth* is characterized by the seeds of the birth of contractualism. "Contractualism is a doctrine that explains the origin of society through a contract according to which any individual surrenders his strength on condition of reciprocity, authorising the king to apply such a strength in order to preserve the right to life for everyone and to preserve the welfare of the political body." Power can be exercised only from within juridical legitimisation, which, conversely, can be realised only in consensus. Macbeth lacks both elements, so much so that he feels forced to seek legitimisation at all cost, which in his case entails a series of murders, in the attempt to attain a solidity of power which will never be his.

Richard Cave, in "Patrilineal Law and the Comedies of Ben Jonson", analyses the treatment of patrilineal law and the related issues of lineage and inheritance in some plays by Ben Jonson, such as *Every Man in His Humour* (1598), *Volpone* (1606), *Epicoene* (1609), *The Devil is an Ass* (1616), and *The Magnetic Lady* (1632). As a dramatist, Jonson reflects the impact of such issues on everyday life and focuses on the human consequences of legal theory. For instance, he considers the anxieties involved in safeguarding the patrimony to pass down to one's heirs; the worry of protecting the family lineage from the risks deriving from poor marriages or adultery (on the wife's part); the problems where the heir has not yet reached his or her majority, which requires a fit guardian to protect the patrimony; the troublesome question of cultural and often legal prejudice against minors, bastards and women; and the difficulty of determining a precise relation between a dowry and the patrimony.

According to Daniela Carpi, in "Person and Property in Thomas Middleton's *A Chaste Maid in Cheapside*" , property is strictly linked to the development of the self and to a person's growth, and to conceptions of freedom and of individualism. This idea is based on the principle that there is a strict relationship between the law and the cultural implications of property. The existence of laws regulating property relates to our judgement and evaluation of the justice or injustice of property itself. In a civil society, the protection of individual property interests lies at the foundation of economic organization. Property and contracts, and the security of acquisitions and of business, are the fields dealt with most extensively by the philosophy of law. Liberal property theory indeed states that property is strictly linked to individuality and freedom. From this perspective, the conflict between young and old generations concerning money in Thomas Middleton's "city comedies of London life" comes to represent a quest for maturation, for the acquisition of an independent identity in society. In particular, Carpi takes into consideration Thomas Middleton's comedy *A Chaste Maid in Cheapside*. This work is particularly emblematic of situations dealing with the concept of property, the transmission of wealth, and the distinction between "ownership" and "possession". The second scene of act one metaphorically stages some of the main points concerning the concept of property: a need for property in order to exist socially, woman as commercial property, the need to create a position in society through money, the duty to protect one's property and make it produce wealth, the uses to which personal property is put, the paraphrasing of a case of rental or one in which possession is separate from property, usufruct compared to bare ownership, the morality of possession, the social rites entailed by possession, and a final balance of costs and return.

Géraldine Cazals, in "From Law to Literature: Guillaume de La Perrière's intellectual path", considers the reversed intellectual development of a Renaissance jurist from Toulouse who "converted" to literature, abandoning any number of juridical technicalities in his texts. In his works *Du pauvre et du riche* and *Miroir Politique*, he asserted the idea that man's rule over things did not express some basic natural principles rooted in a universal order, but man's very nature. He asserted that God himself had ordered the division of property, considering Book of Joshua in the Bible where each tribe of Israel was attributed a portion of land. In this way, La Perrière demonstrates the existence of private property dating back to the Bible. Cazals refutes these assertions by observing that La Perrière cleverly avoided becoming involved in the scholarly quarrel that had been raging for more than a millennium. The other side of the debate, in fact, stated that the Holy Scriptures, on the contrary, demonstrated that the idea of communion was preferred by God and that the Gospels recommended a life of poverty to reach a blessed life in heaven. La Perrière stated that communion of rights could even generate popular sedition: community of rights was pure fantasy, like Plato's *Republic* and Thomas More's *Utopia*. However, La Perrière fell into contradictions because he also refused to consider that private property was beneficial to men. Therefore, on the one hand he recognized the necessity for private property, while on the other hand he rejected its beneficial influence.

Giovanni Rossi, in "'De l'affection des pères aux enfans': sentimental bonds and juridical bonds in Montaigne, Essais, II, 8", concentrates his analysis on the common preoccupation in Medieval Europe with the transmission of one's family wealth. The family's fortune should be safeguarded, kept undivided and handed down following the male line of succession. Several parts of Montaigne's *Essais* testify to such an overwhelming preoccupation in 16th century Europe. The originality of Montaigne's thought in comparison with the Middle Ages is his admission that family relationships should be based merely on an economic vision, and should also entail individual subjectivity. Inheritances should be distributed among the children not only *post mortem* of the *pater familias*, because children's lives should not be thus conditioned. Families should not be ruled despotically but in an atmosphere of relaxed unselfishness. Inheritance mechanisms should be complied with after having verified that they are in keeping with the criteria of equity and humanity. The rigid hierarchy that reigns in the family under the dictatorial rule of the *pater familias* is, according to Montaigne, at the basis of the social *malaise*. The side-effects deriving from such a custom are unjust results, placing the mother or the children in an unbearable condition of subjection. Therefore the power concentrated in the hands of the father should be limited by reason and common use.

Adam Gearey, in "The Voice of Dominium: Property, Possession and Renaissance Figures in *The Cantos* of Ezra Pound", asserts that Pound's aesthetic is strictly connected to issues of possession and ownership. In particular, Gearey concentrates his analysis on the concept of "manumission", or, in other words, the granting of freedom to slaves. He wonders, in fact, why such a doctrine should appear in *The Cantos* and realizes that the problems concerning ownership and possession become a sort of paraphrase of the relationship between poetry and law, in the imagining of a vision of law's correct order. In Canto VI, in fact, Cunizza's kindness in freeing her slaves gives form to a central theme which will pervade the entirety of the Cantos. The opening lines of the Canto draw attention to inheritance and from here the poem goes on to deal with the notion of lawful genealogy and the points at which that genealogy breaks down and has to be re-established. The narrative of Eleanor of Aquitaine is largely concerned with an attempt to found a dynasty, and to ensure the perpetuation of a name and property. The Canto celebrates the conjunction between law and poetry: Cunizza's kindness suggests a new beginning in the merging of an objective order of law and a subjective act. Her kindness allows those who had so far been considered things to attain the status of human beings.

PART I

Nietzsche's Hermeneutics: Good and Bad Interpreters of Texts

Richard H. Weisberg

Cardozo School of Law

How can the same thinker pervasively attack legal argumentation while equally consistently endorsing the law? *Genealogy*'s second essay famously accomplishes both. Nietzsche there displays his customary dissatisfaction with contemporary modes of legal interpretation – and by contemporary I mean from the Gospel writers to the legal sociologists of the late 19th century – while also endorsing law (if properly propounded and interpreted) as the sole pointer to justice-on-earth, as the sole if less-than-perfect means to that elusive end. Let us listen to this central text from *On the Genealogy of Morals*; in the 11th aphorism of the second essay, Nietzsche first disposes of the link between justice and kneejerk revenge or *ressentiment*, and then offers us this account of justice on earth:

> To what sphere is the basic management of law, indeed the entire drive towards law, most connected? In the sphere of reactive people? Absolutely not. Much more so in the realm of the active, strong, spontaneous, aggressive. Historically understood, the place of justice on earth is situated as a battle *against* the reactive emotions, a war waged by means of that active and aggressive power that here uses a part of its strength to quiet the ceaseless rumblings of *ressentiment* and to enforce a settlement.
>
> The most decisive move, however, made by the higher power against the predomination of grudge and spite, is the establishment of *the law*, the imperial elucidation of what counts in [the codifier's] eyes as permitted, as just, and what counts as forbidden and unjust. [...] From then on, the eye will seek an increasingly *impersonal* evaluation of the deed, even the eye of the victim itself, although this will be the last to do so.
>
> [...] [I]n welcher Sphäre ist denn bisher überhaupt die ganze Handhabung des Rechts, auch das eigentliche Bedürfnis nach Recht auf Erden heimisch gewesen? Etwa in der Sphäre reaktiven Menschen? Ganz und gar nicht: vielmehr in der der Aktiven, Starken, Spontanen, Aggressiven. Historisch betrachtet, stellt das Recht auf Erden [...] den Kampf gerade *wieder* die reaktiven Gefühle vor, den Krieg mit denselben seitens aktiver und aggressiver Mächte, welche,

ihre Stärke zum Teil dazu verwendten, der Ausschweifung des reaktiven Pathos Halt und Mass zu gebieten und einen Vergleich zu erzwingen. [...] Das Entscheidenste aber, was die oberste Gewalt gegen die Übermacht der Gegen- und Nachgefühle tut und durchsetzt – sie tut es immer, sobald sie irgendwie stark genug dazu ist –, ist die Aufrichtung des *Gesetzes*, die imperativische Erklärung darüber, was überhaupt unter ihren Augen als erlaubt, als recht, was als verboten, als unrecht zu gelten habe; [...] von nun an wird das Auge für eine immer *unpersönlichere* Abschätzung der Tat eingeübt, sogar das Auge des Geschädigten selbst (obschon dies am allerletzten [...])[1]

This is a remarkable passage because it at first seems so different from what post-modernists have made of Nietzsche. He is linking to social justice the most controversial and value laden aspect of his personal moral agenda: the ranking of nobility above *ressentiment*, of action above reaction, of the heroic Old Testament code above the rococo, privatized spiritualization of the Gospels.[2] The will to power emerges from the realm of self-perfection into the world of socialized humanity. The individual striver – think of Moses, the Revolutionary generation, or some recent feminists – *devotes some of her time to codewriting!* And, from the time of codification on, as the rest of this aphorism tells us, people's actions are gauged cooly and impersonally along the lines of their *duty*, as prescribed by the codifier.

Happy is the generation whose actions are regulated by such a code, and whose people share the same reverence for its codifier! But Nietzsche lived in a quite different era – or in his terms a more typically Christian era – in which people are overcome by *ressentiment*, so much so that (as he foregrounds in this Aphorism's attack on Duhring's interpretation of justice) they wilfully digress and distort the codifier's values; they lose sight of the greatness of the code. Consider the Umsturz der Werte – the Nietzschean upsetting of the table of values through *ressentiment* – that occurred in France during the Vichy period[3] Consider this exact moment in American constitutional law, where governments are interning citizens and others without due process and where legal academicians of some liberal repute are busy rationalizing torture.[4] Constitutions

---

[1] Friedrich Wilhelm Nietzsche, *Genealogie*, II, vol. 76, aphorism 11 (my translation).
[2] See, e.g. Friedrich Wilhelm Nietzsche, *Beyond Good and Evil*, aphorism 52.
[3] See Richard H. Weisberg,*Vichy Law and the Holocaust in France* (New York: New York University Press, 1996).
[4] See a variety of perspectives on, e.g., Alan Dershowitz, *Why Terrorism Works: Understanding the Threat, Responding to the Challenge* (New Haven: Yale University Press, 2002), by Sanford Levinson (in manuscript sent to this author) and by John T. Parry and Welsh S. White, "Interrogating Suspected Terrorists: Should Torture be an Option?", in *University of Pittsburgh Law Review* 63 (forthcoming).

codifying lists of human rights can be undone by interpreters who deliberately distort the text's meaning or, to put it better, manage to achieve sufficient power to undermine long held traditions of meaning and value instantiated in the text.

Aphorism 11 ends with cautionary words about law itself; law should not be understood, according to Nietzsche as an end in itself. It is always the anti-vitalistic means to the always vitalistic end of justice. To understand Nietzsche's view of the always possible and indeed already there linkage of law to justice, one needs (as I have done often in writings now spanning 20 years or so[5]) to step outside the Second Essay itself, although the first such baby step takes us along to the Third Essay, in which Nietzsche continues a lifelong love affair with the Jewish people – in their deep past as people of the book and in their present incarnations as one of Europe's "strongest, toughest and purest races".[6] (The unfortunate middle period, when the Jewish priestly class managed to produce the new Christian approach to heroic codes, is evoked in *Genealogy*, III #22, in which Nietzsche places these various periods of religious transition in comparative context:

> The reader may have guessed already that I have no fondness for the New Testament. [...] The Old Testament is another story. I have the highest respect for that book. I find in it great men, a heroic landscape, and one of the rarest things on earth, the naivete of a strong heart.

Could there be higher Nietzscehan praise, particularly towards the end of his genalogical tour through morals? What could naivete mean in this context? Perhaps the anti-resentful, vitalistic urge to justice, against all odds? But of course, that naivete is connected, always in Nietzsche, with the Book, with law, with the Code!:

> In the Jewish "Old Testament", the book of divine justice [von der goetlichen Gerechtigkeit], there are men and things and speeches in such a grand style that Greek and Indic literature has nothing to equal them. One stands in awe and reverence before these enormous remains of what man had once been [...][7]

Justice is a positive urge, as Nietzsche reminds us in the Second Essay. But it has been – and could be even in the degraded context of 19th century European

---

[5] From Richard Weisberg, *The Failure of the Word* (New Haven: Yale University Press, 1984) through "De Man Missing Nietzsche," in *Nietzsche as Postmodernist*, ed. Clayton Koelb (Albany: SUNY, 1990) to, most recently, "It's a Positivist, It's a Pragmatist, It's a *Codifier!*," reprinted from *Cardozo Law School* 18 (1996): 85 in *The Revival of Pragmatism*, ed. Morris Dickstein (Durham: Duke University Press, 1998), 312-33.

[6] Nietzsche, *Beyond Good*, aphorism 251.

[7] Nietzsche, *Beyond Good*, aphorism 52.

values – codified in a book. Such a text can guide a people through millenia, but to do so there are two execptionally rare pre-requisites: 1) the text must instantiate the vitalistic urge to justice of the codifier and 2) the text must be – as consistently as possible – *interpreted* from the perspective of that same set of positive values.

Now, in turning from the Book to its interpretation, we again have straightforward if unpost-modern guidance from Nietzsche in the legalistic aphorism with which we started, indeed throughout the *Genealogy*, which is as much about interpretive methods as it is about anything else. A recent account of this method by my colleague Peter Goodrich[8] stresses what I have mentioned often – the *need for patience* while reading, for what Nietzsche calls in fact "rumination"[9] – no leap to judgment but instead – time!, time being as fundamental for a sound act of reading as it is for a sound morality. Understanding and action both progress "as slowly as possible"[10] and are not distracted by current trends, by sophistry, by the newest methods of interpretive distortion; and again, for Nietzsche and unsurprisingly, "new" is a term of derogation that modifies almost all European interpretive techniques since the New Testament.

The word in the eleventh aphorism of Essay Two is "impersonally" [unpersoenlicher]; if the reader of the Code can only abstract himself from his own emotion (even in the face of having been traduced or criminally violated, Nietzsche's example here} and recapture the impulse of the codifier – and always insisting as we have that the original code strives towards justice and is hence free of *ressentiment* – then the Code will live and will resist the inevitable distortions of resentment, haste, violence, revenge, or what today we might encapsulate in one antithetical word: "emergency". From how many noble impulses, codes and books, has Western culture been distracted by "emergency", whether it is today's war on terror, World War II's reversal of human rights in Europe, or the early Gospel writers' prediction that the End of Days was approaching. Every time this happens, the Book suffers, a text is wilfully distorted, interpretive methods are directed towards sacred words with the aim of changing their meaning while still preserving the original language.

---

[8]See Peter Goodrich, "Europe in America: Grammatology, Legal Studies, and the Politics of Transmission," *Columbia Law Review* 101 (2001): 2033-2084, 2065.

[9]See Weisberg, *Failure* 1984, and Weisberg, De Man Missing 1990.

[10] Nietzsche, *Beyond Good*, aphorism 251. The statement is made in admiration of the Jewish people through the millenia. The Christian theologian, Franklin Littell, puts the thought only slightly differently: "In stubborn fashion, and in spite of flirtation with assimilation at different times and in different places, the Jews have clung to history, earthiness, concret events. And Israel, which came into existence as part of a specific series of historical events, cannot properly be judged by persons whose dominant thought patterns are ruled by a flight from history." Franklin Littell, *The Crucifixion of the Jews* (New York: Harper and Row, 1975) 95-96.

Nietzsche injects his most potent interpretive venom into those early Christian exegetes. In Aphorism 84 of *Morgenröte*, Nietzsche gives us all we need really to understand the relationship of interpreter to text – but will we heed him?:

> However much the Jewish scholars protested, everywhere in the Old Testament there were supposed to be references to Christ and only to Christ and particularly his cross. Wherever any piece of wood, a switch, a ladder, a twig, a tree, a willow, or a staff is mentioned, this was supposed to indicate a prophecy of the wood of the cross; even the erection of the one-horned beast and the brazen serpent, even Moses spreading his arms in prayer, even the spits on which the Passover lamb was roasted – all are allusions to the cross and as it were preludes to it! Has anyone who asserted this ever believed it? [...] [But] they were conducting a war and paid more heed to their opponents than to the need to stay honest.[11]

We are dealing here, of course, with a characteristic impulse within Nietzsche, with easygoing moves from normative to descriptive language. The *norm* is an impersonal absorption of the codifier's own noble values by the interpreter, and this takes rumination and considerable moral strength, particularly in law. Not only the victims but also judges are power players unlikely *in fact* to be impartial, rational onlookers. But Nietzsche merely describes – with scorn – such self-involved interpreters; he does not wish to suggest that the *temporary* control over hermeneutics of the resentful in Europe constitutes a norm.

So he begins the *Genealogy* with the hope that this text itself will (someday) be understood for what its author means by it, and this can be accomplished only by an unsparingly careful reader [einige Muehe dabei nicht gespart hat] through a rumination [das Wiederkauen] entirely untypical of modern readers. This is the norm of understanding of great texts; but the everyday practice so digresses from the norm that the New Interpreter – now finally in the Zarathustrean sense – will have to leap ahead of the (current) herd, become "reckless", interpret again in the ways of the un-moderns. [...]

Or, again, we might say today, such a reader will have to resist trends of understanding that have long developed – against older moralities, pagan or Jewish – in Christian Europe. In a recent article expanding on what my book-

---

[11] Friedrich Wilhelm Nietzsche, *Kritische Studienausgabe* ("Morgenröte", "Dawn of Day"), V/I, fragments 19/35. For a cogent view of Nietzsche's interpretive method in this sense – and one differing considerably from the way he is perceived by many post-modernists, see, e.g. Henrik Birus, "Nietzsche's Concept of Interpretation," *Texte: Revue de critique et de théorie littéraire* 3 (1984): 78-102.

length study[12] had previously called the "Vichy hermeneutic", I indulged a Nietzschean reading of the resentful depths to which Europe, left in the hands of the anti-semites, might dive; and then I associated with the early Gospel writers the ability of France to adopt quickly during Vichy to abject negations of their own great Code of Human Rights. Nietzsche stands as prophet of Europe's inability *to read*; and Catholic France, for which (with the exceptions of Napoleon and Stendhal, codifier and grand reader) Nietzsche had so little sympathy in the *Genealogy* – struck me as the best example of both the tragedy and of its sources in events several millenia previous.

My thesis there was and remains that a form of *flexible* deformation of ensconced textual understandings gradually permitted lawyers (and others) to overcome their native hostility to Vichy's racial scheme.[13] For French lawyers during World War II first needed to leap a hurdle not present in other countries victimized by Hitler. They had to reckon with their ingrained belief in *egalitarianism*, a staple of the French legal system since 1789 and one that endured throughout the 20th century, up to and including Dreyfus (which did not involve any statist racial legislation) and even the Vichy years, during which government lawyers consistently invoked the "rights of man" while contemporaneously ejecting the Jew from the circle of traditional protection. My findings firmly indicate that the *private* reaction to Vichy racial laws of most lawyers (even those in the Vichy bureaucracy) was one of aversion to such a fundamental and distasteful change in French legal tradition. Even among antisemites at the bar, for example, there was regret that Jews were being singled out, especially those many hundreds of respected colleagues who were not foreign-born. And, even as to the latter group, many felt that discriminatory legislation was simply "not French"; if the Nazis insisted on singling out the Jews, perhaps nothing could be done, but surely the French themselves would not initiate and then instantiate such a gross deviation from the basic egalitarian principle of French law.

To overcome this "gut" aversion to French statist anti-semitism, the entire legal community benefitted from a ready-to-hand hermeneutic of flexibility typical of – and being practised contemporaneously by – the French Catholic Church. They adopted a two-pronged strategy of a corrupting flexibility towards their foundational texts and of a total rejection of what lawyers and others called derisively the "Talmudism" of the thus-excluded group.

This flexibility derived in large part from a tradition of Catholic reading strategies that influenced even lay and largely anti-clerical professionals. As

---

[12]See Weisberg, *Vichy Law* 1996, particularly chapter 10.
[13]See Richard Weisberg, "Differing Ways of Reading, Differing Views of the Law: The Catholic Church and its Treatment of the Jewish Question During Vichy," ed. Maurice Levy, *Remembering for the Future: the Holocaust in an Age of Genocide,* (London: Palgrave, 2001): 509-30.

inbred as the story itself of egalitarianism, this strategy of manipulating foundational texts and concepts allowed lawyers during Vichy to work with the notion of equality and *at the same time* to develop an intricate four-year-long pattern of discrimination against Jews.

I thus suggested that Vichy antisemitism, and its acceptance among the masses of the people, was a hermeneutic – as much as it was a xenophobic, racist or even traditionally anti-Jewish – problem. The ability to shift one's ground – fairly quickly and without a sense of profound, seismic change – as to foundational ideas and texts originated, as I saw it, in the early Christian ability to distort the sacred text upon which Christians chose to base their vision: the Jewish Bible. Their contribution instantiated a way of reading that wove distortion into the very moral fabric of the emerging religion's followers. This hermeneutic, at its origins and as it continued into the 20th century – involved a rejection of close reading itself, a discomfort with textual fidelity masked in many of Christianity's founding texts as a rejection of Jewish law.

How was the Talmudic outsider, with his sin of a (Nietzschean) allegiance to Law and the careful reading it required – how was this Talmudist to be expunged from the prtotected circle of equal protection? This required an effort, and my archival sources indicated it was a struggle for the French, but one they failed to muster for the good. Even Marshal Petain, their octogenarian leader whose regime autonomously produced almost 200 antisemitic laws that often went beyond the Nazi precedents – even he asked his legal counsel at the Vatican in the Summer of 1941 to find out if the Holy See had a problem with his regime's laws? The answer Leon Berard received at the highest levels both apologized for the antisemitic laws and – again – rehearsed the Nietzschean observation of Christianity's hermeneutic of deformation of text.

As Berard's letter to Petain proceeds into theology, the flexible hermeneutic of Catholic Europe becomes explicit:

> E. [...] One could find in our legislation as a whole, as in that of many other states, and for example in our still very much extant Napoleonic codes, many statutes that would not be approved of by the Vatican. Also, [the Vichy] rule denying to everyone who might be baptized the status of Catholic is perhaps, from a theological point of view, not the most serious breach.[14] The Church has never ceased to practice an essential distinction, full of wisdom and reason: the distinction between thesis and hypothesis, the thesis, in which the principle is

---

[14] Perhaps Berard, by the Summer of 1941, had in mind arrests and encampments – in inhuman conditions eventually leading to the death of 3000 Jews on French soil – all under color of Vichy law, beginning with the antisemitic statutes of 3-4 October, 1940.

invariably affirmed and maintained, and the hypothesis, where practical considerations are comprehended [ou s'organisent les arrangements de la pratique.[15]

The Church thus both asserts an opposition to "racism" and– on the "realistic" plank it calls "hypothesis" – accepts it! Vichy, meanwhile and reciprocally, vaunts its constitutional retention of virtually every individual right proclaimed by the generation of the 1790's and also manages to exclude the Jew. The hermeneutic is ingrained and requires no clear articulation on such high levels of authority. Church and State, preserving their historical functions, can reach a détente. As Nietzsche does so often, so the lawyer fascinated by this process in Vichy can find the sources of this flexible hermeneutic in the Gospel writers.

1. The Pauline paradox: rejecting textualism
while retaining the text

Common to an otherwise highly variegated set of early Christian writers is a deep skepticism about the law. To the extent these writers perceived "legalism" in the Jewish traditions and also in the practices of some Jews who lived at the same time as Jesus, they often associated the law with an allegiance to textualism, that is to a kind of literalism that they felt sometimes overrode the spiritual or more essential elements of the Jewish relgion. Acoording to A.N. Wilson, a very comprehensive and sympathetic observer of Paul, many of these writers initiated

> the attempt to translate Hebrew ideas into a Gentile setting. [This involved] using words either with new senses or with great boldness.[16]

On this reading, Paul's rejection of the Jewish law and of its textual base carried with it a program of retention of Hebrew ideas and even a retention of the full material text of the Jewish Bible.

It is this paradox that I believe lies at the origins of the French Catholic hermeneutic exemplified tragically during Vichy. It may help to explain later developments – like Vichy – in which a Catholic culture based on Pauline "love" but nonetheless acting governmentally within the world, far exceeds in cruelty anything imagined by the original Jewish textualists against whom Paul rebelled.

I am very mindful, in speaking of Paul in particular, of the caution expressed by post-Holocaust Christianity's true prophet, Franklin Littell. This pioneer

---

[15] Berard letter in full, Centre de documentation juive contemporaine (CDJC) # CIX-102, p. 10 of letter, cited with rest of letter in Weisberg, *Vichy Law* 1996.
[16] Andrew Norman Wilson, *Paul: the Mind of the Apostle* (London: Pimlico, 1998) 28.

allowed that Christianity has much to answer for after the Holocaust ("the French Catholic community," he reminds us as just one national example, "has a long record of Antisemitism"[17]), and he did not hesitate to date virulent Christian theological antisemitism to as early as certain first century epistles;[18] he is more equivocal in pondering "the question whether the New Testament is necessarily antisemitic, an issue which is increasingly exercising the skills of exegetes."[19]

Littell observes that Paul needed to use "considerable skill" in order "to graft believing gentiles into an essentially Jewish history of salvation."[20] What seems at first to be an admirable, nay brilliant career of textual manipulation, must – in view of the thousands who followed Paul's hermeneutic example during the Holocaust – be reconsidered. To do this, I believe we must pass briefly through the more transparent window of the Gospel according to St. John.

2) The example of John: using the Hebrew text
while attacking the textualists at every turn

As Nietzsche observed, retaining a sacred text while fundamentally altering its meanings took some work, at least at the beginning of Christianity. By the time we get to John, the methodology is easier (even for an "outsider" like myself) to find, although still as paradoxical as it seems to some when handled by Paul's anti-platonic, chaotic but in every way remarkable soul.

Any set of verses from the Gospel according to St. John will reveal the bifurcated hermeneutic aim of re-interpreting the Hebrew Bible to make it fit Christian beliefs while also attacking wherever possible as legalists and textualists the non-accepting Jewish community. The first prong instantiates the Jesus-story – against all the textual odds –as having been "predicted" by the older text; but the second prong justifies sloppiness in the readings of those older texts by attacking, precisely, the "Jewish" reading strategy of textual legalism. John, so to speak, has his cake and eats it, too. In case – as for most knowledgeable readers of the Hebrew texts – the alleged allusions to Jesus-as-Messiah simply will not do – he attacks the very idea of sticking closely (label it, say, legalism) to a text altogether.

While John, perhaps in particular, has been the critical object of much commendable post-Holocaust Christian commentary – from all of which I have benefitted and will continue to learn[21] – I am not sure on the readings as yet

---

[17] Littell, *Crucifixion* 1975, 84-5.
[18] Littell, *Crucifixion* 1975, 26-7.
[19] Littell, *Crucifixion* 1975, 24.
[20] Littell, *Crucifixion* 1975, 29.
[21] See, for example, Henry F. Knight, "Facing the Holy Whole: Reading *John 8* with Chastened Eyes" (unpublished paper distributed at the Holocaust Scholars Conference, March 2000, Philadelphia); George Smiga, *Pain and Polemic: Anti-Judaism in the Gospels* (New

called to my attention that this twinned hermeneutic has been noticed as an essential contribution to antisemitism, as important as the increasingly discredited, more direct, anti-Jewish verses in the New Testament.

In John 7, Jews respond to the idea that Jesus might be the Messiah with some textualist skepticism. They nitpick (in verses 40-44), for example, about whether the Messiah was supposed to descend from David and come from Bethlehem. Opposition to Jesus is both textually derived and linked to the hermeneutic strategy of sticking to the text. Commentators call this a quibble: "there is a division among the people over superficial matters," says one.

Now the textual basis for Jesus-as-Messiah is usually given as a compendium of allegedly prophetic verses in such Hebrew texts as Isaiah, chs 52-53 or Psalms (e.g., 69:9); both of these are evoked in John. Yet any reader of these two texts must grapple with the long tradition of understanding – still (frustratingly?) adhered to by Jewish exegetes – that denies any plausible prophesy of someone like Jesus, however admirable, as the Messiah. Thus, in a superb and traditional commentary on Isaiah 53;3 ("he was despised [...]") and the surrounding verses, the traditional understanding is espoused that Isaiah is beuatifully rendering no single individual at some future time but instead "the Babylonians, or their representatives, having known the servant, i.e. exiled Israel idealized, in his humiliation and martyrdom, and now seeing his exaltation and new dignity, describe their impressions and feelings."[22]

John is annoyed that some Jews just could not see these sacred texts his way. But to take them with his understanding required more flexibility than they (or, I imagine, most reading communities up until then) were willing to show. These were, after all, sacred texts received not without creative variation but nonetheless within certain hermeneutic bounds that were being stretched to fantastical limits.

John needs, in the face of such opposition, to go further. Not only must the textual understandings be distorted; distortion as a hermeneutic principle must be ensconced and ratified. "By no means," Paul wrote, has G-d abandoned Israel (*Romans*, 21:1), but apparently all the time-honored rules of understanding Him have been changed in the twinkling of an eye. For most Jews, methods of

---

York: Paulist Press, 1992); Robert Kysar, "Anti-Semitism and the Gospel of John," in *Anti-Semitism and Early Christianity*, eds. Craig A. Evans and Donald A. Hagner (Minneapolis: Fortress Press, 1993).

[22]*Isaiah*, ed. Israel Wolf Slotki, (London: Soncino Press, 1949) 261 – the Soncino version being a respected commentary on the Tanakh – no Jewish reader, even after the long centuries of Christian interpretation (and surely not at the origins) would even imagine that this text has anything to do with a figure like Jesus. See e.g., Rabbi Albert J. Rosenberg, "So-called Christological Inferences," in the Preface to *The Book of Isaiah* (New York: The Judica Press, 1995) xiv-xv. Most Jews have not even thought about the idea. John, however, indicates that some had to in the days of the historical Jesus. He does not seem very sympathetic with their quite traditional and utterly mandated skepticism in the face of such uses of sacred texts.

reading are indistinguishable from ways of living life morally, so has there been no abandonment?

Perhaps impatient with the traditional Jewish mix, John goes on to pepper his account of the Jews with a kind of gratuitous distaste, mostly centered around the Law and people's textual allegiance to it. A reader coming fresh to the Gospels wonders why such verses as the following are necessary to John's mission:

> 5. 1. After this there was a feast of the Jews. and Jesus went up to Jerusalem. 2. Now there is in Jerusalem by the Sheep Gate a pool . . . which has five porticoes. 3. In these lay a multitude of invalids, blind, lame, paralyzed. [Jesus sees a man who had been lying there sick for 38 years.] [...] 8. Jesus said to him, "Rise, take up your pallet, and walk." 9. And at once the man was healed, and he took up his pallet and walked.

This is a beautiful story. But what follows is not:

> Now that day was the sabbath. 10. So the Jews said to the man who was cured, "It is the sabbath, it is not lawful to carry your pallet." 11. But he answered them, "The man who healed me said to me 'Take up your pallet and walk'. [Later] 15. The man went away and told the Jews that it was Jesus who had healed them. 16. And this was why the Jews persecuted Jesus, because he did this on the sabbath.

This gratuitous slur, difficult to believe in view of the original miraculous story, leads to a teaching of Jesus that articulates and forever ensconces the anti-Jewish anti-textual principle:

> 39. You search the scriptures, because you think that in them you have eternal life; and it is they that bear witness to me.

> In other words, Jews, you need to be more flexible in the way you interpret your own texts so that you will see me in them.

> 40. Yet you refuse to come to me that you may have life.

One way of reading these passages – and I think the way Nietzsche probably read them from boyhood on – is as a rejection not so much of the Jews as of their manner of reading the Law. Insistence on faithful readings is forever challenged as a hermeneutic method. Words can be used "flexibly" to suit the needs of the reader and his/her community. From now on, even if you cannot accept the new view of the old text, it has become immoral even to look to the text. The early Christian writers – or those Jews from whom Christianity emerged – felt they were in an eschatalogically new situation that mandated a distorted look at the old texts. More than this, it seemed to them to mandate a departure from text altogether.

Let me end briefly with a question and three brief answers: If Nietzsche's hermeneutic approach is as consistently text (and even author) oriented as I suggest here, and if he is opposed to faithless readings in the service of some new vision, is his hermeneutics agreeable to us as moderns and post-moderns?

First, as Constitutional lawyers, we might welcome the kind of interpretive flexibility shown, for example, by the Court in Brown vs Bd. of Education, where allegiance to text and intent is forthrightly disavowed in favor of America's needs in mid 20th century. Recall only that Nietzsche's insistence against Brown's methodology *only applies* when both the original text and the interpretation that follows it are non-resentful and constitute for that reason worthy (and occasionally sacred) texts. If Brown is re-instantiating (against Plessy, specifically) the true interpretive intent of the Framers as to equality, then it is interpreting superbly according to the Nietzschean hermeneutic.[23]

Second, is the tradition associated with the Talmud in fact any less flexible than the Pauline tradition that followed? This is the stuff of some of my current work and an enormously complex question. Recall that under Vichy, at least, the Talmud did clearly stand for an unyielding tradition based on the letter of the Law, and this view evoked a double-barreled legal strategy to rationalize the anti-semitic laws France promulgated. The Talmud both revealed the need for a special law to regulate a group that has defined itself as legally special and legitimated persecution of that group through loose, amorphous, and often incoherent readings of history, religion, and France's own sacred texts. If you're faced with a people whose insignia of "otherness" is their long-term allegiance to literal acceptance of law, what better way to condone getting rid of them than by interpreting one's own laws with sufficient flexibility to ignore the egalitarian principle imbedded in them?

I am indebted to Peter Goodrich for an argument articulating and agreeing with my historical perspective on the hermeneutic conflict in Vichy. Goodrich accepts that we must grapple with the fact that "there is a dimension of conflict between traditions and faiths", although such reminders "may not be popular".[24] He further accepts my data and thesis about Vichy anti-Talmudism. But – and

---

[23]For inquiries into the different "intents" we may say we are looking for – and sometimes trying to preserve – in Constitutional Law, see, e.g. Jefferson Powell, "The Original Understanding of Original Intent," *Harvard Law Review* 98 (1985): 885; Paul Brest, "The Misconceived Quest for the Original Understanding," *Boston University Law Review* 60 (1980): 204 ; Richard Weisberg, "Text Into Theory: A Literary Approach to the Constitution," 20 *Georgia Law Review* 20, (1986): 939.

[24]See Goodrich, Europe in America 2001, 2057.

this is to begin my third and concluding "answer" – Goodrich goes on to reject a related argument I have made (and continue to propound) – namely that certain modes of post-modernist reading strategies were both exhibited by Vichy lawyers and connect to the "flexible" hermeneutics that brought such violence to people – and to texts. Goodrich finds this argument untenable and even contradictory. This is because his article defends "grammatology", a system derived from Derrida's classic *Of Grammatology*[25], and defends it in part because of a richly nuanced approach to text that Goodrich in fact defines as being "Talmudic". I do not agree with that assertion. As a Nietzschean who has also studied Talmud, I of course allow that the Christians were not the first to embellish and perhaps even "improve" on texts through multi-faceted interpretive methods. However, I do not think deconstructionism is essentially "Talmudic", for all its wonderful readings, and I continue to feel that in establishing what Geoffrey Hartman calls the text's "nimbus of density" as well as in avoiding both the "grand narrative" and (perhaps for ethical reasons after the Holocaust, an irony I explore in my book) direct modes of speech linking sign to referent, some post-modernisms descend directly from Christian exegetical methods and, as Derrida himself puts it famously, posit "the violence of the Letter".[26]

Nietzsche at least would not have put "violence" together in the same sentence with the Letter. This is not to say that Jewish tradition abjures creative and, indeed, "flexible" readings, often embodied in the oral as opposed to the written tradition. To compare the imaginative embellishments of Jewish and Christian interpretation is the task of a lifetime. But it may well be quite fair to say that the work done by early Christian exegetes on the Tanakh, or Hebrew Bible, broke all the rules revered then – and now – by traditional exegetes.

Maybe Goodrich and I can agree to disagree for the moment, anyway, as we both might be able to endorse the following text by a respected thinker on the Talmud recently puts it:

> A viable system of law must not sacrifice either its spirit or its letter. Hasty compromises, unfounded alterations, and whimsical abandonment of legal traditions lead only to chaos. In order for a legal system to endure and flourish, it is necessary for the law to be flexible, elastic, and fluid, as well as definitive, clear, and steadfast.[27]

---

[25] Jacques Derrida, *Of Grammatology* (Baltimore: Johns Hopkins University Press, 1976).
[26] Derrida, *Grammatology* 1976, 101. And neither can I agree with Goodrich that Derrida has interpreted Nietzsche faithfully in his *Spurs*. See, for example, Weisberg, De Man Missing 1990.
[27] Samuel N. Hoenig, *The Essence of Talmudic Law and Thought* (New York and London: Aronson, 1967) 13. For a relevant related text, see Susan A. Handelman, *The Slayers of Moses: the Emergence of Rabbinic Interpretation for Modern Literary Theory* (Albany: State University of New York Press, 1982).

PART II

Comic Plots and Property Law in Plautus's *Trinummus*: Humanistic and Renaissance Reflections[1]

Ida Mastrorosa

University of Perugia

The work of Plautus, which is scarcely known, and then almost only because of its fortune in the centuries of the Dark Ages, finds its memorable date of revival, as has been agreed, in 1429, when a Humanist, Niccolò Cusano, discovered in the German library of Köln a manuscript containing twenty comedies of the Sarsinate, twelve of which had long been lost.[2] This discovery immediately appears to Poggius Bracciolini as an *ingens lucrum, neque parvo estimandum* as is testified in his letter, dated 26th of February 1429,[3] and sent to Niccoli to give him the news. However, this is only the beginning of a success that is destined to consolidate itself principally in this area, especially thanks to those who in the 15th and 16th centuries[4] intervened first of all on the redaction of important vulgarisations, often urged by meaningful events, for representations held in the

---

[1] Translated by Alice Bendinelli and John Scaggs.
[2] On the re-discovery and the diffusion of Plautus see Remigio Sabbadini, *Le scoperte dei codici latini e greci ne' secoli XIV e XV* (Firenze: Sansoni, 1905) 110; Sabbadini, *Le scoperte dei codici latini e greci ne' secoli XIV e XV: Nuove ricerche col riassunto filologico dei due volumi* (Firenze: Sansoni, 1914) 17, 241 (both volumes are now in *Edizione anastatica con nuove aggiunte e correzioni dell'autore*, ed. Eugenio Garin (Firenze: Sansoni, 1967); as far as the fortune and influence successively played on European dramatic production see also Karl von Reinhardtstöttner, *Plautus: Spätere Bearbeitungen plautinischer Lustspiele. Ein Beitrag zur Geschichte* (Leipzig: Friedrich, 1886; repr. New York: Hildesheim, 1980); Ettore Paratore, *Plauto* (Firenze: Sansoni, 1961) 100-123, and see in particular Ferruccio Bertini, *Plauto e dintorni* (Roma-Bari: Laterza, 1997).
[3] See Poggio Bracciolini, *Lettere*, I. *Lettere a Niccolò Niccoli*, ed. Helene Harth (Firenze: Olschki, 1984) 78-79, *epist*. 28: *Nicolaus ille Treverensis scripsit litteras cum inventario librorum, quos habet. In his sunt multa volumina, que longum esset referre [...] Habet volumen aliud, in quo sunt XX comedie Plauti. Hoc ingens est lucrum neque parvo extimandum [...]* (p. 78).
[4] For some insight in relation to this period see Alessandro Perosa, *Teatro umanistico* (Milano: Nuova Accademia Editrice, 1965); Antonio Stäuble, *La commedia umanistica del Quattrocento* (Firenze: Istituto Nazionale di Studi sul Rinascimento, 1968), as well as Vincenzo De Amicis, *L'imitazione latina nella commedia italiana del XVI secolo* (Firenze: Sansoni, 1897; repr. Bologna: Forni, 1979). As far as the influence of Plautus on English dramatic production is concerned, at the centre of much literature see at least the recent Wolfgang Riehle, *Shakespeare, Plautus and the Humanist Tradition* (Cambridge: D. S. Brever, 1990); Robert S. Miola, *Shakespeare and Classical Comedy: the Influence of Plautus and Terence* (Oxford, Clarendon Press, 1994).

most famous European courts of the period. It would be enough to mention the increased diffusion of Plautus' work in Rome as a result of the intervention of Pomponio Leto and the members of his academy, who were promoters of presentations such as the memorable one held in the Quirinal in 1483, or to mention the sequence of Plautine presentations recorded in Ferrara for three successive days at the beginning of February 1501 or, in conclusion, the collection of five comedies which were presented in 1502 during the celebrations for Lucrezia Borgia's wedding,[5] once more held in Ferrara.

Besides the creators of such initiatives, a more important role is played by those who drew from Plautine comedy in order to compose new comic *fabulae* in which the influences of the Latin source, rich *per se* in elements which are useful in shedding light onto property motifs,[6] is diffused further and it is felicitously accompanied by innovations and actualisations which allow an in-depth analysis of the property motif in the Humanistic and Renaissance period. In light of this, it is interesting to focus attention on the *Trinummus*, a comedy which dates to probably around 188 BC. This comedy is useful in order to obtain information regarding the economic reality of Roman society in the years immediately after the second Punic War,[7] and the revolution of moral values in the society of that time[8] which led young men to abandon the strict and

---

[5] See Bertini, *Plauto* 1997, 144-145.
[6] Among the studies on this topic see, above all, Pierre Brind'Amour, *La Richesse et la Pauvreté chez Plaute et Térence* (Strasbourg: Dissertation, 1968); Cesidio De Meo, "Appunti sull'uso del linguaggio del commercio e degli affari in Plauto" in *Mnemosynum. Studi in onore di Alfredo Ghiselli* (Bologna: Pàtron, 1989) 195-205; Monique Crampon, *Salve lucrum ou L'expression de la richesse et de la pauvreté chez Plaute* (Paris: Les Belles Lettres, 1985); Emilia Sergi, *Patrimonio e scambi commerciali: metafore e teatro in Plauto* (Messina: Sfameni, 1997). For an evaluation of the interest of Plautus for financial transactions see also George E. Duckworth, *The Nature of Roman Comedy: a Study in popular Entertainment* (Princeton: Princeton University Press, 1952; repr. Bristol: Classical Press 1994) 278.
[7] On these topics the conlusions of Gabba are fundamental, see Emilio Gabba, *Arricchimento e ascesa sociale in Plauto e in Terenzio*, already published in *Index* 13 (1985): 5-15, now in Gabba, *Del buon uso della ricchezza. Saggi di storia economica e sociale del mondo antico* (Milano: Guerini e Associati, 1988) 69-82, 78-80.
[8] Consider Megaronides' considerations on the violation of the *boni mores* and of the *fides* by Callicles, and also the tendency to sacrifice what is useful for the community in *Trin.* 23 ss.; 34-35: *nimioque hic pluris pauciorum gratiam / faciunt pars hominum quam id quod prosint pluribus*, a topic to which Desideri called our attention, see Paolo Desideri, *Parassitismo e clientela nel teatro di Plauto*, in *Plauto testimone della società del suo tempo*, eds. Luciano Agostiniani and Paolo Desideri (Napoli: Edizioni Scientifiche Italiane, 2002) 55-66, 60-62. More generally, on the influence of traditional morality on the comedy see also Pierre Grimal, "Analisi del Trinummus e gli albori della filosofia in Roma", *Dioniso* 43 (1969): 363-375; Erich Segal, "The purpose of the Trinummus", *The American Journal of Philology* 95 (1974): 252-264, 255; Gianna Petrone, "Il Trinummus, ovvero il valore dei soldi" in *Tito Maccio Plauto. Le tre dracme*, eds. Cesare Questa - Gianna Petrone - Mario Scàndola (Milano:

parsimonious customs of their fathers in order to embrace an enjoyable lifestyle consisting of ill-considered expenses. This comedy, furthermore, offers information about the juridical institution of marriage and, implicitly, about women's position within marriage, even if no female character[9] appears on the stage. Therefore, it seems useful to summarise, first of all, the content of this comedy, which is centred on the fate awaiting a young woman, deprived of a dowry because of the dissipate whims of her brother Lesbonicus who is ready to squander the family's assets[10] and to freely dispose of the paternal estate during the absence of his father Charmides, in favour of Callicles, a friend of Lesbonicus.[11]

Callicles, in turn, hastens the purchase in order to safeguard the estate from the heedless behaviour of the young man, and to protect in particular the treasure buried therein, a treasure that had been shown to him by Charmides himself,[12] as we gather from the confession of Callicles, a confession he is forced to make in order to dismiss the accusations of Megaronides, who was persuaded by evil gossips that he had betrayed the trust of the old man and had taken advantage of the situation (*Trin.* 39-222). In these circumstances, Lysiteles, willing, because of his benevolence towards his friend Lesbonicus[13] to marry his dowry-less sister, is then forced to test himself with the perplexities of his father Philto demonstrating skilful persuasive strategies.[14] At the beginning Philto refuses to accept a daughter-in-law with no money, and later he is willing to grant his consensus in order not to harm his son's feelings (*Trin.* 276-391). However,

---

Rizzoli, 1993), 61-90, 62-65, 80-83; Claude Pansiéri, *Plaute et Rome ou les ambiguïtés d'un marginal* (Bruxelles: Latomus, 1997) 551-552, 558-559.

[9] See Leo Peppe, *Le forti donne di Plauto*, in Agostiniani – Desideri, *Plauto testimone* 2002, 67-91, 84-87; but on this subject see also Elisabeth Schuhmann, "Der Typ der 'uxor dotata' in den Komödien des Plautus", *Philologus* 121 (1977): 45-65.

[10] See Plaut. *Trin. Prol.* 13: *Is rem paternam me adiutrice perdidit*; and on the importance given to patrimoni in the text see also Petrone, Trinummus 1993, 64 and ff.

[11] On the character and behaviour of Charmides see William S. Anderson, "Plautus' Trinummus: the absurdity of officious morality", *Traditio* 35 (1979): 333-345.

[12] See Plaut. *Trin.* 149-151:*Quoniam hinc est profectu<ru>s peregre Charmides / thensaurum demonstravit mihi in hisce aedibus / hic in conclavi quodam - sed circumspice! [...]*; 153-155: *Id solus solum per amicitiam et per fidem / flens me obsecravit suo ne gnato crederem / neu quoiquam, unde ad eum id posset permanascere [...]*

[13] On the meaning of the friendly attitude of Lysiteles towards Lesbonicus and on the moral choices characterising the two characters see Petrone, Trinummus 1993, 86-88; Sergi, *Patrimonio* 1997, 90-93; Renata Raccanelli, *L'amicitia nelle commedie di Plauto. Un'indagine antropologica* (Bari: Edipuglia, 1998) 107-110, 122-128; Lisa Maurice, "Amici et sodales: An Examination of a Double Motif in Plautus", *Mnemosyne* 56 (2003):164-193, 175-181.

[14] See Plaut. *Trin.* 223 ff. and see also Gregor Maurach, "Eine entlarvte Vortäuschung: Plaut. Trin. 301-401", *Gymnasium* 94 (1987): 298-306; Raccanelli, *L'amicitia* 1998, 19 and ff.; Mario Lentano, *Le relazioni difficili. Parentela e matrimonio nella commedia latina* (Napoli: Loffredo, 1996) 129-131.

Lesbonicus attempts to solve the situation by offering land which is still in possession of the family as his sister's dowry, as the future father-in-law discovers by listening to a conversation with the servant Stasimus.

Stasimus, worried by the prospect of seeing the only source of income left to the family lost, attempts to dissuade Philto from accepting the offer with an emphatic argumentative harangue (*Trin*. 517-561) in which he presents to the old man's eyes the ghosts and ill fortune which accompany the piece of land, which is a real and proper *hospitum calamitiatis* (*Trin*. 553).

Meanwhile, considering the obstinacy with which Lesbonicus refuses to give the dowry-less sister in marriage to Lysiteles (*Trin*. 627-728), maintaining that he wants neither to lose his reputation nor to see her compared to a concubine[15] because of the lack of a dowry, the only way out to safeguard the family estate is represented by the intervention of Callicles.

After having consulted Megaronides, Callicles decides to make up for the situation offering as a dowry the treasure hidden in the garden of the house he bought from Lesbonicus, but, willing to avoid the risks of a new dissipation of the wealth of the estate by the young man, Callicles prefers to leave Lesbonicus unaware of this, and hires a sycophant who, for the modest amount of three coins, from which the title of the comedy is derived, will pretend to be carrying a letter with the money necessary as a dowry[16] in the name of Charmides, the father of the girl (*Trin*. 729-819). But this offer arrives at the same time as the *mise-en-scène* of the false intermediary, and Charmides unmasks the impostor and forces him to reveal his identity (*Trin*. 843-1005) before receiving more information about the events from the servant Stasimus, who informs him in particular about the bankruptcy caused by his son (*Trin*. 1075-1087).

Nevertheless, even if Charmides is persuaded that Callicles is responsible for the situation and that he has contravened his moral duty to protect the sons entrusted to him, Charmides discovers from Callicles' words that, in buying a part of the property, he was in fact attempting to save it from the inconsiderate actions of Lesbonicus, thus neutralising the effects of the latter's behaviour on his sister (*Trin*. 1093-1102). In other words, thanks to the honest behaviour of

---

[15] See Plaut. *Trin*. 681-683: *Meam [vis] sororem tibi dem suades sine dote. Aha, non convenit / Me, qui abusus sum tantam rem patriam, porro in ditiis / esse agrumque habere, egere illam autem, ut me merito oderit*; 688-694: *Nolo ego mihi te tam prospicere qui meam egestatem leves, / sed ut inops infamis ne sim; ne mihi hanc famam differant / me germanam meam sororem in concubinatum tibi, / si sine dote <dem>, dedisse magis quam in matrimonium. / Quis me inprobior perhibeatur esse? Haec famigeratio / te honestet, me conlutulentet. Si sine dote duxeris, / tibi sit emolumentum honoris; mihi quod obiectent siet.*

[16] Thanks to a formally impeccable and juridically typical syntagm, the bond between Callicles ad the sycophant is qualified as a *locatio operis*: Plaut. *Trin*. 843-844: *nam ego operam meam / tribus nummis hodie locavi...*

the friend, who is vividly praised for his trustworthiness,[17] in the end the need for a dowry turns out to be not only preserved but even doubled by a double marriage: on the one hand, Lysiteles, who marries Charmides' daughter, and on the other, Callicles' daughter, who, being in possession of the same requisite (the dowry), can marry Lesbonicus. This said, the central role played by property in the plot outlined above should be noted. Such a role emerges clearly in the acrostic *argumentum* preceding the comedy (that probably is not really composed by Plautus, but by the rhetor Aurelio Popilio a century later):

> *Argumentum*: *Thensaurum abstrusum abiens peregre Charmides / remque omnem amico Callicli mandat suo. / Istoc absente male rem perdit filius, / nam at aedis vendit; has mercatur Callicles. / Virgo indotata soror istius poscitur. / Minus quo cum invidia ei det dotem Callicles, / Mandat qui dicat aurum ferre se a patre. / Ut venit ad aedis, hunc deludit Charmides / Senex, ut rediit; quoius nubunt liberi.*

In such a context, a strict connection is immediately established between the condition of Lesbonicus' sister as *virgo indotata* and the ruin which he has caused the *res familiaris*, taking advantage of the father's absence up to the point of selling the house to the old friend Callicles. Callicles is, in turn, the holder of the title of a sort of *mandatum*,[18] which the presence of the verb *mandare* in the *argumentum* seems technically to allude to: *remque omnem amico Callicli mandat suo*, which evidently echoes and explains the directions traceable in various passages of the comedy,[19] upon which, in reality, Roman juridical science focused its attention, proposing different interpretations since the end of the 19th century.

At the end of the twenties William Green[20] offered a meaningful contribution to the debate on the nature of the relationship between the two old friends, Charmides and Callicles. Such a debate is characterised, among other things, by

---

[17] See Plaut. *Trin.* 1125-1126: *Neque fuit neque erit neque esse quemquam hominem in terra arbitror / Quoi fides fidelitasque amicum erga aequiperet tuam.*
[18] In Roman law the *mandatum* is a contract in which a subject (mandatary, agent) assumes gratuitously the management of one or more businesses that another subject entrusts him with (mandant, principal), as we understand from a definition by Ulpiano: *procurator est qui aliena negotia mandatu domini administrat* (*Dig.* 3, 3, 1 pr.); the mandatary acts under his name but in the interests of the mandant (or of a third party), under the obligation of completing the task bestowed onto him and of directing any subsequent profit into the mandant's estate through specific juridical acts; see Giuseppe Provera, *Mandato (negozio giuridico - storia)*, in *Enciclopedia del Diritto*, vol. XXV, (Milano: Giuffrè, 1975): 311-321, 311-318, also for a wider bibliography on the topic.
[19] See Plaut. *Trin.* 117, 128, 136-138, 158, 956.
[20] See William McAllen Green, "Greek and Roman Law in the Trinummus of Plautus", *Classical Philology* 24 (1929): 183-192: 185.

the intervention of Emilio Costa according to whom this is "a general mandate, entailing, in addition to patrimonial issues, also merely moral issues", and which is characterised by a juridical nature founded upon *fides*.[21] This scholar, who was more generally interested in pointing out the incoherencies in the *Trinummus* between some references of juridical nature and the normative Roman system, thus hypothesizing that such references mirrored the Greek system, highlighted in particular the incompatibility of the juridical configuration of the *mandatum* with elements traceable from other Plautine textual evidence. The recurrence of the verb *mandare*, in fact, if taken technically, could have allowed an identification of Callicles with a *procurator omnium bonorum*, invested with the powers of a *pater familias*, whereas the development of the stage action shows the limits of his position. Green also proposes an analogous reservation about the technical use of terms with a juridical dimension regarding the entrustment of the sons' tutelage to the friend, terms which are directly mentioned in *Trin*. 138-139 when Megaronides accuses Callicles of having interpreted the authority/office entrusted to him by Charmides as an opportunity to serve his own interests, and reproaches him, among other things, with the claim that by buying his home he has thrown the friend onto the street.[22] Moreover, in keeping with Beauchet[23] and Lipsius,[24] Green remarks on the difficulty in clarifying Callicles' juridical condition in light of Greek norms, which were quite deficient and obscure on this matter. Finally, Green does not hesitate in relegating to the Plautine character the faculty of action in the guise of a mandatory, or an administrator,[25] entitling him with the main function of moral guidance in accordance with a perspective which was probably influenced by the indeterminacy in this matter of Greek law, given the fact that in Roman law there were punctual prescriptions back in ancient times, as it is testified by Cicero who on this topic refers to the discipline imposed by the *maiores* (*Rosc. Am.* 111). In this perspective, as Frederhausen

---

[21] See Emilio Costa, *Il diritto privato romano nelle commedie di Plauto* (Torino: F.lli Bocca, 1890, repr. Roma: L'Erma di Bretschneider, 1968) 390.
[22] See Costa, *Il diritto* 1968.
[23] See Ludovic Beauchet, *Histoire de droit privé de la republique Athenienne*, IV. *Le droit des obligations* (Paris: Chevalier-Marescqetc, 1897, repr. Amsterdam: Rodopi, 1969) 371-377.
[24] See Justus H. Lipsius, *Das attische Recht und Rechtsverfahren* (Leipzig: R. R. Reisland, 1905) 772.
[25] See Green, Greek and Roman 1929, 185-186: «We are still at loss when we attempt to find any Greek law to apply to the case [...] evidently this "mandate" was an extra-legal matter. Callicles was instructed to look after affairs, but found himself without any legal powers to act as agent or administrator, though his presence might carry some moral weight (166-72), and the young man might, on occasion, seek Callicles' advice (583-84). It may be that this situation conforms better to the absence of recognized powers of agency in Attic law than to the Roman conditions in which mandate was clearly defined, long before Cicero's time, at least».

has noted[26] Green could also confirm the problematic identification of the nature of the *mandatum* referred to in the Plautine passages thanks to the unclear juridical position of Lesbonicus, entitled to use the paternal estate so that he could squander it, and entitled even to sell the family house, regardless of the mandatory role apparently entrusted to Callicles. Therefore, Green overlooks Pernard's hypothesis,[27] according to which the faculty of the young man derives from Charmides' prolonged absence from home. In Roman law such an absence is, as a matter of fact, the equivalent of an already declared death. Green advocates against this the presence of numerous references in the text to a never fully abandoned idea of the possibility for a return,[28] thus preferring, in the end, to assess the young man's condition in relation to the Greek juridical praxis rather than in relation to Roman law, which was particularly careful to protect the interests of the absentees.

Greek law, although not well known on this matter, could offer Green useful comparative references to the cases of *divkh paranoiva"* concerning the opportunity granted to sons of depriving their fathers of the estates on the grounds of decrepitude or of insanity. According to this scholar these were opportunities that pointed at a scarce attention to protect the interests of the owner under certain conditions.[29] On the grounds of such evidence, and of a parallel case offered in the *Mostellaria*, Green maintains that the right, given by Plautus to Lesbonicus, to sell the house could somehow be justified (for example the son could have acted according to a quality of *negotiorum gestor* in order to manage the paternal interests), and it probably did not seem totally unlikely to the public.

---

[26] See Otto Fredershausen, "Weitere Studien über das Recht bei Plautus und Terenz" in *Hermes* 47 (1912): 199-249, 226-227.
[27] See Louis Pernard, *Le droit romain et le droit grec dans le théatre de Plaute et de Terence* (Lyon: Rey, 1900) 104.
[28] See Green, Greek and Roman 1929, 187: «[...] in neither country is there any evidence that a son, in the absence of his father, could dispose of the estate at will. If we could suppose that Lesbonicus had entered on his father's estate as heir, his conduct in the play would be fully explained. So Pernard, from the standpoint of Roman law, would explain the situation: "There has been no news of Charmides for a long time, one has the right to consider him as dead". But in the play all seem to regard his return as still possible, if not probable (106, 137, 156, ...), and in Roman law it would have been impossible for the heir to enter on his estate until it was known that the father was dead».
[29] See Green, Greek and Roman 1929, 187-188: «But Greek custom seems to protect the father less than does the Roman. The divkh paranoiva" gave sons a wide opportunity to remove their fathers from the management of their estates, on the ground of decrepitude as well as insanity. The Roman curatorship of *furiosi* and *prodigi* [...] was strictly limited to the insane (of any age), and those squandering the estate which they had themselves inherited. This might suggest that the Athenian law would be less careful than the Roman to protect the interests of an absent father».

In more recent times, from an observation by E. Karakasis,[30] we gather a further confirmation of the difficulty in clarifying in a sufficiently probative way the singular position of Lesbonicus, who was *de facto* authorised to make use of the paternal estate before a regular succession by *mortis causa*. Inclined to believe that, on the example of D. M. MacDowell,[31] Plautus had been influenced by the possibility of transferring onto a third party the aspect of *patria potestas* concerning the consensus to marriage in the case of absence (of the father), as it was enforced in Greek law and from which, as the scholar maintained, the *mandatum* agreed between Charmides and Callicles derived. Thus, he interpreted the pact as an adaptation of Roman law in function of which he proposed to understand the verisimilitude of the Plautine reference to such an institution.[32] With regard to the singular *potestas* granted to Lesbonicus which enables him to sell the *paternal* assets, Karakasis takes inspiration from the analogous faculty given by Plautus to the son Theopropides in the *Mostellaria*, although in the context of an imaginary *emptio-venditio*. Following Green, Karakasis traced the role of the young man in that of a *negotiorum gestor*,[33] which is in principle admissible although he is subject to *patria potestas*, and although it disrupts the meaning of such a institution since Lesbonicus' profession is, in fact, guided by the need for money and is not aimed at safeguarding his father's interests. After all, the perplexities about the possible return of Charmides, manifested by the other characters on the stage, implicitly attribute the faculties typical of an heir to Charmides' son, and, therefore, they invalidate his father's mandate agreed with the friend Callicles.[34]

In light of these hypotheses, which are technically plausible *per se* but not sufficiently binding to solve the ambiguities of Callicles' juridical role, the conclusions of Bechmann, who, at the end of the 19th century, was ironically ready to offer a prize to whomever could clarify the incongruence in the

---

[30] See Evangelos Karakasis, "Legal Language in Plautus with special reference to Trinummus", *Mnemosyne* 56 (2003): 194-209, 198-204.
[31] See Douglas M. MacDowell, "Love Versus the Law: An essay on Menander's Aspis", *Greece & Rome* 29 (1982): 42-52, 44, n. 5.
[32] See Karakasis, Legal Language 2003, 199: «The Athenian legal possibility for somebody to make a third person temporarily *kyrios* of a woman in his family is altered by Plautus so as to fit the context of Roman law, and thus he presents Charmides and Callicles as having agreed to a *mandatum*».
[33] On the management of somebody else's estate see Aldo Cenderelli, *La negotiorum gestio. Corso esegetico di diritto romano, I. Struttura, origini, azioni* (Torino: Giappichelli, 1997).
[34] See Karakasis, Legal Language 2003, 202: «Although at the end of the play he appears on stage, it seems that during the play some of the *dramatis personae* on stage have doubts about his safe return [...] and this is very important, because in this way Lesbonicus could be regarded as the heir of his own father, and the mandate of his father would not be valid any longer».

Trinummus[35] on the basis of Roman law, seem still valid. However, I believe that such incongruence helps us to better understand in which measure the analysis of the relationships between law and literature in the Plautine comedy is a slippery surface; and, such incongruence induces us, first of all, to suspect that one of the merits of the art of this ancient playwright lies precisely in the wilful indeterminacy of certain technical aspects. He was a playwright who was not unaware of the impact of the law on a sufficiently realistic staging of comic plots, which drew from daily life, and who, perhaps, was more interested in ensuring the effects of generic verisimilitude rather than the precise representation of juridical facts.

On these grounds, besides a greater or smaller admissibility of the different above-mentioned solutions regarding the *mandatum*, chosen by Plautus in the *Trinummus* as an engine of dramatic action, the propensity of the critics to attribute to the text the function of a technical instrument capable of providing confirmations and deductions concering legal institutions and foresights cannot be denied. However, in my opinion, a clear knowledge of such topics cannot be accredited, in principle, to the ancient playwright.

In the light of the previous considerations, I would rather believe that an analysis of the juridical clarity of certain passages of the play allows us to attribute to Plautus the tendency to mix, consciously or not, heterogeneous juridical elements together, with the result of a typical effect of *contaminatio* and of the overlapping of different institutions. It is in this light that we should posit the discussion concerning the *mandatum* between Charmides and Callicles beginning with *Trin.* 137-138. In particular, in this context, the problem of the juridical value of the verb *mandare*, perhaps, can be explained by placing the emphasis on the fiduciary relationship that was in any case presupposed and subtended to the mandate contract,[36] since it can hardly make reference, as we have said, to a mandate in a technical sense, which is prevented by the availability for the spendthrift Lesbonicus of a part of the patrimony and, as Alan Watson observed, is also prevented, on the other hand, by the lack of any testimony of such a form of contract in Plautus's day.[37] The justification that Callicles gives to motivate the acquisition of his friend's house seems to lead us to such a contract, as he explains how the contract of sale represented only a

---

[35] See August Bechmann, *Geschichte des Kaufs im römischen Recht* (Erlangen: Deichert, 1876, repr. Aalen: Scientia, 1965) 507.

[36] See D. Nörr, *Mandatum, fides, amicitia*, in *Mandatum und Verwandtes. Beiträge zum römischen und modernen Recht*, eds. Dieter Nörr and Shigeo Nishimura (Berlin: Springer, 1993) 13-37 in which, within the juridical institution of the mandate, the roles of *fides* and that of *amicitia* – deriving from the former – are underlined.

[37] See Alan Watson, *Contract of Mandate in Roman Law* (Oxford: Oxford University Press, 1961, repr. Aalen: Scientia, 1984) 11-16; the statement of the British scholar is peremptory: «First of all, we can have no doubt but that he uses mandatum and mandare in a non-technical sense, since the contract in his day could not be legally enforceable» (p. 11).

functional stratagem for ensuring the safeguarding of the treasure hidden therein, which, on the other hand, from the very first moment he had intended to give back to Charmides, thus complying with the juridical praxis of a trust, especially in the particular case of the hypothesis of *fiducia cum amico*:[38]

> *Trin.* 156-159: *Nunc si ille huc salvos revenit, reddam suom sibi; / siquid eo fuerit, certe illius filiae / quae mihi mandatast habeo dotem unde dem, / ut eam in se dignam condicionem conlocem.*

In regard to this, some specifications of Megaronides also appear meaningful. Megaronides is ready to remind Callicles that in the event that he wanted to personally supply the girl with a dowry *ob amicitiam patris*, he would inevitably incur the accusations and the insinuations of people, since to their eyes he would give the impression of having been munificent with goods that were not *de facto* his, but which he had rather received from her father for that very task, and he would even give the impression of returning them after keeping a part for himself:

> *Trin.* 736-743: *post adeas tute Philtonem et dotem dare / te ei dicas; facere id eius ob amicitiam patris. / Verum hoc ego vereor nec istaec pollicitatio / te in crimen populo ponat atque infamiam. / Non temere dicant te benignum virgini: / datam tibi dotem ei quam dares eius a patre; / ex ea largiri te illi, neque ita ut sit data / incolumem sistere illi, et detraxe autument.*

In light of these clarifications I would not exclude after all that Megaronides plays in the plot of the *Trinummus* the role of Plautus' alter ego, as he is interested in focusing the attention of the public on the violation of the contractual institutions and forms in which the characters of the play are involved due to their conduct. I believe also that an initial passage of the play should be interpreted in such a direction; here Megaronides accuses Callicles of having misunderstood the meaning of guardianship and to have had it transformed into an advantageous opportunity for himself (*Trin.* 139: *crede huic tutelam; suam melius rem gesserit*), and therefore he implicitly seems to consider him as chargeable for an *accusatio suspecti tutoris*.[39]

---

[38] The explicative formula employed by Gaio enounces clearly its finality: *Sed fiducia contrahitur aut cum creditore [...] aut cum amico, quo tutius nostrae res apud eum sint* (Gaius *Inst.* 2, 60). See. Giuseppe Grosso, *Fiducia (diritto romano)* in *Enciclopedia del Diritto*, vol. XVII (Milano: Giuffrè, 1968): 384-388.

[39] On the bonds related to the institution of *guardianship* in general see Alan Watson, *The Law of Persons in the Later Roman Republic* (Oxford: Clarendon Press, 1967, repr. Aalen: Scientia, 1984) 102 and ff.

In the final of the play Callicles' behaviour seems, in my opinion, equally eloquent in reinforcing the hypothesis of *fiducia*. Here Callicles, remembering his moral responsibility towards the young sons of Charmides,[40] wards off the praises of the latter, underlining that he simply did his duty. After all, it should not pass unnoticed that, from the very beginning, Callicles declares himself to be ready to return the treasure that he came into possession of, maintaining that he considers it as his friend's property (*Trin.* 156: *Nunc si ille huc salvos revenit, reddam suom sibi*), while precisely underlining the amicable bond according to which he is involved in the story (*Trin.* 153: *per amicitiam et per fidem*). On the other hand, once again at the end of the play, Callicles affirms that while both a *donatio* or a *cessio bonorum* imply the loss of the goods, the attribution by loan leaves to the owner the faculty of claiming the *res* back whenever he likes, confirming in this way that Callicles never perceived himself as the real owner of his friend's goods, and also demonstrating this time an unsuspected juridical expertise:

> *Trin.* 1129-1131: *Non videor meruisse laudem, culpa caruisse arbitror. / Nam beneficium homini proprium quod datur, prosum perit; / quod datum utendumst, id repetundi copiast, quando velis.*

In conclusion, the ambiguity of the juridical status of Callicles, to whom Plautus attributes both the entitlement of a *mandatum* and of *guardianship* (*Trin.* 136-139) without being concerned about limiting the patrimonial faculties of Lesbonicus as a consequence of the latter, might be considered as the price paid by the Latin playwright in order to offer some space to the legal sphere in texts generically alien to it, rather than being classified among the incongruence to be necessarily explained in relation to Greek praxis. As far as the violations of *patria potestas*, which can be attributed both to Lesbonicus and Lysiteles, are concerned, and in contrast with the Roman juridical regime, far from necessarily offering us a portrait of the Greek model, as Green[41] had hypothesised, they could rather be read as a tangible proof of the upheaval in the normative system,

---

[40] See *Trin.* 612-613: *Flagitium quidem hercle fiet, nisi dos dabitur virgini, / postremo edepol ego istam rem ad me attinere intellego.*

[41] See Green, Greek and Roman 1929, 189-190, according to whom the wide-ranging power, conceded to Lesbonicus who did not substitute the father in the role of acknowledged guardian, of disposing of his sister's marriage at will, does not mirror the hereditary Roman system, which gives the brother the authority of providing for the sister's marriage only in the case of an absence of their father which exceeds three years or in the case of death of the father. On the other hand, the young man's total lack of interest in respecting his sister's will probably draws inspiration from Greek customs. According to Green, the autonomous management of his own engagement granted to Lysiteles, in detriment of his father Philto, is also traceable back to Greek law, rather than to the Roman juridical system in which the condition of the son *in potestate* would have required first of all the consensus of the father.

which, at the close of the play, Stasimus stigmatises *a voce*, lamenting the sad fate awaiting the laws that will be obliged to surrender to bad habits:

> *Trin.* 1037-1044: *Mores leges perduxerunt iam in potestatem suam, / magisque <is> sunt obnoxiosae quam parentes liberi<s>. / Ea<e> miserae etiam ad parietem sunt fixae clavis ferreis, / ubi malos mores adfigi nimio fuerat aequius /* [...] *neque istis quicquam lege sanctumst; leges mori serviunt, / mores autem rapere properant qua sacrum qua publicum.*

Broadly speaking, it is still evident that this play has the value of reflecting the juridical *Realien* of the ancient world, but only if we bear in mind the filter represented by the intervention of the author, that is to say, his cultural patrimony and the goals he aims at.[42] This literary genre, if it is intended as a product destined for an immediate fruition in the theatre, was conceived in view of a communication that, although bearing in mind the evolution of the juridical model enforced in the represented society due to reasons of verisimilitude, neither entails nor demands, on the other hand, a possession of technical knowledge for a proper understanding of its modules and contents.[43]

On the contrary, the reinterpretation of the Plautine plot, certainly more knowing and attentive under the profile of the juridical mechanism subtended as it is proposed by Giovanni Maria Cecchi (1518-1587), who was not a secondary figure in the panorama of the Renaissance comic production within which his work has been too long overlooked, manifests clearer traces of a self-conscious technical virtuosity.[44] Cecchi is ready to exploit the plot of the *Trinummus* in order to obtain, around the mid-16th century, material for a comedy which denounces from the very prologue its debt to classical traditions, and in

---

[42] On the meaning and finality of the legal references in Plautine work and on a «juridicisation» of a typically Roman matrix of the motifs imported from the tradition of Greek comedy, see Netta Zagagi, *Tradition and Originality in Plautus. Studies of the Amatory Motifs in Plautine Comedy* (Göttingen: Vandenhoeck & Ruprecht, 1980) 106-131.

[43] For a synthetic and panoramic view on the various positions taken by the scholars on the value to be attributed to Plautus' comedy as a source of juridical matters, see Giuseppe Rotelli, "Ricerca di un criterio metodologico per l'utilizzazione di Plauto", *Bullettino dell'Istituto di Diritto Romano* 65 (1972): 97-132; Gianfranco Lotito, "Usi e funzioni del diritto. Qualche osservazione su Plauto e la Commedia Nuova", *Per la storia del pensiero giuridico romano. Dall'età dei pontefici alla scuola di* Servio. Atti del Seminario di S. Marino, 7-9 gennaio 1993, ed. Dario Mantovani (Torino: Giappichelli, 1996): 185-208.

[44] For a biographical introduction see Claudio Mutini, *G. Maria Cecchi* in *Dizionario Biografico degli Italiani*, vol. XXIII (Roma: Istituto della Enciclopedia Italiana, 1979): 263-267; for further considerations on the relationship with classical sources see also De Amicis, *L'imitazione latina* 1979, 124-128.

particular to Plautus.[45] He seems, in fact, inclined to bring up-to-date some elements of a juridical matrix using a vivid realistic sense, in my opinion since he was influenced by his personal exercise of the notary profession, and, what is more, in the meaningful context of a family of notaries. It would suffice to focus first of all on the unequivocal efficacy of the title *The Dowry* in order to verify Cecchi's full perception of the meaning acquired in the plot of the ancient model of the patrimonial motif, and to confirm his intuition on the important necessity for the woman's family to provide her with a dowry, as had already been envisaged by the Roman discipline and confirmed also in Renaissance time.[46] Cecchi does not hesitate to transfer in a more explicit way the central function invested by the dowry in the whole story to the title, insisting on it also in the prologue, while complying with the Latin plot, centred on the treasure necessary to solve the difficulty in providing a dowry to Charmides' daughter, and certainly establishing a debt to the Greek original, *Thesauros* by Philemon.

> *Imitating, and, in this way, adapting to today's time [Plautus' Trinummus], when we are speaking of some marriage the dowry is always mentioned first; and it is here that all the disputes derive from: this is the beginning which spoils and styles everything nowadays; all the other things that we nevertheless look for mean nothing: which are the qualities of your wife-to-be? who was her father? Is she similar to her mother?, with whom was she was brought up? and what are her manners like? All these are fables, things that nowadays can be resolved in a few words: let the dowry be comfortable, since all the other things are not of such a value that they cannot be compensated with some money.*[47]

In such a context, the prologue of the Trinummus, which was morally focalized on the symbolic transference of Lesbonicus' custody from *Luxuria*,[48] guilty of having helped him to squander his patrimony, to the daughter *Inopia*, is replaced in the Florentine rereading, thanks to Cecchi's resolution of assuming an up-to-

---

[45] See Giovan Maria Cecchi, *La Dote*, in *Commedie di Giovan Maria Cecchi*, Preface by Olindo Guerrini (Milano: Sonzogno, 1883): 17-71, in part. *Prologue*, p. 21: «Let this Dowry be a new comedy/ drawing in a good measure from Plautus. / This is said because none should think that the author wants to be similar to certain thieves who steal, if not the subject, complete comedies [...]».
[46] On the nature, characteristics, and finalities of the dowry in the Middle Ages and in modern times see Manlio Bellomo, *Dote (diritto intermedio)* in *Enciclopedia del Diritto*, vol. XIV (Milano: Giuffrè, 1965): 8-32.
[47] See Cecchi, *Dote* 1883, 19-20.
[48] On the moral tones which characterise the prologue see above all Peter Stein, "Morality in Plautus' Trinummus", *The Classical Bulletin* 47 (1970): 7-13; Richard Hunter, "Philemon, Plautus and the Trinummus", *Museum Helveticum* 37 (1980): 216-230, 216-227.

date position, and by the author's confession of having intended to realise his imitation by adapting it to the customs of his time, according to which the dowry represented an inescapable issue when discussing a marriage, and it is also replaced by the observation that many disputes arise around dowries, so that the possession of other moral or physical requirements becomes of secondary relevance in respect to patrimonial contributions. Moreover, in a modernising perspective, the specification on the quadruple destination of the comedy is particularly incisive too. The comedy, according to Cecchi, is directed not only towards those who are already married and have already come to terms with this issue, but it is rather directed towards young *nubendi*, thus acting as advice to avoid any inconsiderate act; to priests; and, what is more, to those who think they glimpsed in the dowry offered by the family of the wife-to-be an instrument useful for paying their own debts, to consolidate their patrimonial status through the acquisition of immovables, and also to obtain the ability of being able to spend money when needed. On these grounds, which demonstrate the interest of the author in highlighting both the Plautine echoes and also the fully Florentine setting of the story, several passages from the text deserve to be analysed, not only for their dialogic structure, but also because in these parts Cecchi's realistic intention and the juridical competence subtending this modern rereading can be revealed.

The technical precision in a passage from Act I[49] is particularly meaningful. Here, Cecchi introduces old Manno. Drawing from the model of Callicles in Plautus, Manno appears on stage as the guardian of Federico, the son and of the daughter of Filippo Ravagnani, and also as the mandatory of all the possessions (*he wanted to remit to me merely everything*). Manno is preferred to any other relative for the exercise of this task, which is expressly related to that of *custody* on the basis of a mandate which does not appear problematic under a technical profile. Considering the hypothetical and presumed death of Filippo, which is explicitly formulated in the text (*as far as I know he died*), Manno's duty is not, after all, irreconcilable with the faculty of the young Federico to put the paternal house on sale. In this sense the impasse looming over the *Trinummus* by Plautus, in which the idea of Charmides' possible return was, in my opinion, never fully abandoned, seems to be finally resolved in *The Dowry*.

Undoubtedly, in Cecchi's comedy, the insistence on the necessity of a dowry appears verisimilar. This was a burden which in the Florentine reality must have

---

[49] See Cecchi, *Dote* 1883, *Atto I, scena I*, 24: MAN.: *Was he out of his mind when he left the city, a year ago, to go to London (and during the journey shipwrecked and, as far as I know, he died) since he left me as the guardian of his son Federigo and of his daughter, and of everything he possessed? Didn't he maybe want to remit to me just everything, although I was not family-related to him in any way, rather than one of any of the relatives? Would you think that these were not signs of benevolence? Or issues that could be entrusted to someone who were not a real friend?*

seemed heavy to carry even to those who enjoyed a good economic situation: *Don't you know that nowadays it is difficult to get Florentine maidens in possession of a large dowries married, since they are hardly ever wealthy enough?*[50] It is particularly interesting to observe that Ippolito's generous temperament, ready as he is to renounce the dowry and interested in giving a beneficial lesson of parsimonious moralilty to the spendthrift Federigo, encounters the opposition of Fazio, the father,[51] who is, after all, averse to the hypothesis of a marriage with a dowry-less girl. In front of his son, who is persuaded that good manners are a more important feminine requisite than a dowry, and whose good manners are conversely accompanied by a frequently excessively disdainful attitude, Fazio, in fact, does not hesitate to deny explicitly his consent to the marriage of his son with a girl devoid of an adequate patrimony, as is understood from Act II, Scene iv:

> -- FAZ. *If she were more beautiful than the sun, nobler than nobility, and the daughter of the Venetian Doge, I still don't want you to take a wife with no dowry [...] I do not live on favours, nor on pure air: [...] And imagine that if you want to stay here where I am, you mustn't take a wife as a gift.* -- IPP. *I thought that wives were something other than an issue of money.* -- FAZ. *Something other than that? Do you maybe think that to take a wife is a fable? Don't you know how expensive it is to have a wife? [...]* -- IPP. *My father, I think that good manners are the real dowry, and that often under the other great dowries torments and the ruin of a family are hidden; rarely a woman is rich in herself without also being proud.* -- FAZ. *What good reasons! Where did you study them? [...] seen, or unseen, enamoured or not, this does not interest me. Be persuaded that I don't want you to take a wife if she does not possess at least 3000 golden ducats as her dowry [...] Can you hear me, I don't want you to take her as wife if she does not have 3000 ducats as her dowry? And if you do otherwise, I will show your error to you: clear your ears.* -- IPP. *I want to do what you want.*[52]

Inspired by an authentically chrematistic mentality, Fazio's statements reveal a certain distance from the Plautine character Philto, who in the *Trinummus* appears mainly interested in exhorting the son Lysiteles to respect ancient

---

[50] See Cecchi, *Dote* 1883, *Atto I, scena I*, 25.
[51] See Cecchi, *Dote* 1883, *Atto I, scena II*, 28: IPP. *As far as your sister's dowry is concerned, did I not say that I will marry her, and that I do not wish that we speak of a dowry? Stay in Florence, and enjoy it, and I will have the dowry I desired. You know that I have already told you this many times and thus I will keep my word; and if my words did not sort any effect until now, I am left with nothing but with the observation, not of a wish to do it, but of not having found the right words to persuade my father to give us his consent.*
[52] See Cecchi, *Dote* 1883, *Atto II, scena IV*, 32-34.

customs[53] and to demonstrate a constant and natural good behaviour,[54] beside being persuaded, on the other hand, that the economic defeat of Lesbonicus represents a punishment rightly inflicted on someone who dared to venture into the exercise of lucrative commercial activities.[55] Notwithstanding the limited moral that inspires his discourses aimed at the search for individual profit,[56] the Plautine character ends up pleasing the son Lysiteles and complying with his wishes,[57] up to the point of offering him his unconditional consent,[58] which he will offer again on more occasions.[59]

Besides all the differences between the model and its appropriation, Cecchi generally appears more consciously inclined to represent the versatile faceting of patrimonial ethics of the humanity he puts on a stage. A passage from Act II, scene i is particularly interesting. Here the young Federigo, who is responsible for a financial ruin which certainly does not betray a full perception of the liability of the *res patrimonialis* and who is concerned about his sister's fate, assumes effortlessly the role of the moralist stigmatizing the conduct of the old friend of his father with a brilliant linguistic *boutade*,[60] in which he reconnects this man's name with an already proven tendency to be concerned only with his own interest and with the accumulation of wealth to his own advantage: *he*

---

[53] See Plaut. *Trin.* 279-280: *Feceris par tuis ceteris factis, / patrem tuum si percoles per pietatem*; 283-286: *Novi ego hoc saeculum moribus quibus siet; / malus bonum malum esse volt, ut sit sui similis; / turbant, miscent mores mali, rapax, avarus, invidus; / sacrum profanum, publicum privatum habent, hiulca gens*; 291: *Nam hi mores maiorum laudant, eosdem lutitant quos conlaudant*; 295-299: *Meo modo et moribus vivito antiquis; / quae ego tibi praecipio, ea facito. / Nil ego istos moror faeceos mores, / turbidos, quibus boni dedecorant se. / Haec tibi si mea imperia capesses, multa bona in pectore consident.*

[54] See Plaut. *Trin.* 320-323: *Is probust, quem paenitet quam probus sit et frugi bonae; / qui ipsus sibi satis placet, nec probus est nec frugi bonae; / qui ipsus se contemnit, in eost indoles industriae. / Benefacta benefactis aliis pertegito, ne perpluant.*

[55] See Plaut. *Trin.* 331-332: *Qui eam perdidit? Publicisne adfinis fuit an maritumis negotiis? / mercaturam, an venalis habuit, ubi rem perdidit?*

[56] See Plaut. *Trin.* 335-337: *Edepol hominem praemandatum ferme familiariter! / Qui quidem nusquam per virtutem rem confregit atque eget. / Nil moror eum tibi esse amicum cum eius modi virtutibus*; 349: *De magnis divitiis si quid demas, plus fit an minus?*

[57] See Plaut. *Trin.* 347-348: *Multa bona bene parta habemus, bene si amico feceris, / ne pigeat fecisse, ut potius pudeat, si non feceris*; 350-352: *[...] sed civi inmuni scin quid cantari solet? / «Quod habes ne habeas et illuc quod non habes, habeas, malum, / quandoquidem nec tibi bene esse pote pati neque alteri».*

[58] See *Trin.* 382-384: *Verum ego, quando te et amicitiam et gratiam in nostram domum / video adlicere, etsi adversatus tibi fui, istac iudico. / Tibi permitto, posce, duce.*

[59] See *Trin.* 442-445: *Meus gnatus me ad te misit, inter te atque nos / adfinitatem ut conciliarem et gratiam / tuam volt sororem ducere uxorem; et mihi / sententia eademst et volo*; 499: *sine dote posco tuam sororem filio.*

[60] The pun used in the text in Italian is unfortunately lost in the translation into English, and it plays upon the assonance between the Christian name, *Manno*, and the verb, *ammannare*, to accumulate (translator's note).

turned out to be a Manno, a man only *concocting for himself.*[61] In this perspective we should not forget to mention some words pronounced by the servant Moro, real past master of expressive sententiousness, according to whom Manno's nefarious deeds derive from the good faith of his master, who has the defect of having left *the ducks guarding the lettuce.*[62] Whereas, the young Federigo is ironically defined as a valorous man, considering his capacity for squandering the patrimony.[63] From this point of view, the servant turns out to be the occasional spokesman for a patrimonial ethics which frees the individual person from any sort of bond, an ethics on the grounds of which the servant defends his young master with misleading arguments, claiming to have induced him to face onerous expenses to cure himself, arguments which are grounded on the assumption of the aleatory nature of the patrimony that should be considered an instrument in service of men rather than a source of servitude, as we read in Act Iv, scene ii:

> MOR. *I promise you, trust me, that this young man regretted all that squandering, which was getting worse, and he was tormented inside by it; and if I had not comforted him inducing him not to think about it (telling him that men build a patrimony and not the contrary, and that a patrimony was made to be spent when necessary and that he should have tried to recover so that he would be able to recover the patrimony as well, and in this way I would distract him from that fantasy) otherwise he would have become crazy. Oh, my God! I have never seen a young man praising the patrimony more than he did.*[64]

Finally, it is not a negligible detail that at the end of the comedy, once the attempts at concealing the fate which awaited the ancestral estate, which lead the old man to believe that the house was only rented and not in possession of Manno, and once the fake messenger, who had been sent to deliver the money necessary for the dowry of the girl in the name of Filippo Rovagnani,[65] are unmasked, the clarification between the father and the young Federigo becomes for Cecchi an opportunity to weave a limpid apology for the instrumental function of patrimony. Giving that the squandering of a patrimony does not only imply an infringement of the frugal customs of those who built it with great effort, but, above all, it implies an alternative choice of a dissolute lifestyle, the correct management of the *stuff*, rather than its entity, becomes a pragmatically

---

[61] See Cecchi, Dote 1883, *Atto II, scena I*, 30.
[62] See Cecchi, Dote 1883, *Atto II, scena V*, 35.
[63] See Cecchi, Dote 1883, *Atto III, scena III*, 43: FAZ. *Therefore, he must be a valorous man, indeed!* MOR. *Valorous indeed, since he consumed whatever he possessed.*
[64] See Cecchi, Dote 1883, *Atto IV, scena II*, 54.
[65] See Cecchi, Dote 1883, *Atto V, scen. I-V*, 63-68.

discriminating principle (Act V, scene vi):

> FIL. *Now, my son, that we are alone, I do not want to restrain myself from saying what is in my heart. If I said that I did not regret the stuff that you ruined, do not trust me; since I made efforts to earn it, and I know with how many difficulties and dangers. But I will clearly tell you that what hurts me more is the honour that you valued so little, keeping the life you kept, and the little judgement you demonstrated to have, and the blame that you acquired with so many expenses [...] And remember, my son, that a few faculties are more profitable to those who can use them wisely than many faculties to those who use them badly.*[66]

From this point of view, it is also necessary to underline that the conclusion proposed in the comedy, that is, the possibility of providing the girl both with a dowry and, therefore, with a marriage, seems, under certain aspects, of secondary relevance in respect to the educative exemplum given by someone who knew how to forgive a spendthrift son, and aimed, first of all, at teaching him the vacuity of deceit.

On these grounds, notwithstanding the debt inherited with the plot of the *Trinummus*, Cecchi's theatrical work seems to be drawing from medieval mental paradigms which differ from Plautus' ones. The ancient playwright, sensitive in perceiving the threats to the maintenance of property arising from the absence of wise custody in owners who were more interested in the exercise of trading (the real economic and social pole of attraction in a society in evolution in the years following the first Punic war[67]) appears, in fact, basically interested in defining, with an apparent technical plausibility, the network of bonds and obligations existing between the characters of the story narrated in his comedy. As far as the Florentine notary is concerned, in contrast with a view which was common in 16th century society, according to which the possibility for a woman to bring a congruous sum to the husband-to-be in the event of a marriage represented, as it is well known, a burdensome and an inevitable duty which was directed to the constitution of a familiar nucleus[68] given its expressed finality *ad sustinenda*

---

[66] See Cecchi, *Dote* 1883, *Atto V, scena VI*, 69-70.
[67] See Emilio Gabba, "Ricchezza e classe dirigente romana fra III e I sec. a. C. ", *Rivista Storica Italiana* 93 (1981): 541-558, now in Gabba, *Del buon uso* 1988, 27-44, 29 and ff.
[68] On the preponderant importance of the necessity to dower maidens and on the consequent economic difficulties deriving from the involution of such an institution in the Dark Ages and in early-modern times, see, within the vast literature on this subject, Manlio Bellomo, *Ricerche sui rapporti patrimoniali tra coniugi. Contributo alla storia della famiglia medievale* (Milano: Giuffrè, 1961) especially 61-130; Julius Kirshner and Anthony Molho, "The Dowry Fund and the Marriage Market in Early Quattrocento Florence", *Journal of Modern History* 50 (1978): 403-438; Christiane Klapisch-Zuber, *La famiglia e le donne nel*

onera matrimonii, in the final instance Cecchi seems to call attention to the perils, both for the family and for the instauration of harmonic relationships between its members, which derive precisely from the *res patrimonialis*.

The decisive function played by the acquisition of the dowry, especially in the Plautine plot of the *Trinummus*, a function which is valorised by Giovanni Maria Cecchi in a realistic manner accordingly to the Florentine praxis, constitutes, if we look at it more closely, a narrative pivot that is cleverly exploited also in previous Humanistic comic production. In this production such a theme appears equally fruitful and functional on a narrative level too. It will suffice to consider the role this theme plays in three more texts produced in the Veneto region around the end of the 15th century, starting with the *Epirota*.[69] In this play, dedicated by the Venetian noble Tommaso Mezzo to Ermolao Barbaro, which was praised by Pico and was edited for the fist time in Venice in 1483 and reprinted many times in Germany, the lack of a dowry represents the main impediment to the marriage between Clitofonte and Antifilia, who, after her father's death, was hosted in the house of the young man's uncle.

This impediment can be removed only by the arrival at Siracusa, the theatre of the action, of Antifilia's uncle from the Epiro, who has the necessary money to make her worthy of such a marriage. The fact that a dowry represents an unavoidable requirement results clearly also from the plot of the *Stephanium*,[70] written by Giovanni Armonio Marso, native of Abruzzo but Venetian by adoption, and which was presented at around 1500 in the refectory of a convent of the Eremitani of Santo Stefano. In this comedy the uncle of the young girl once again has to intervene, providing her with a sufficient dowry for the consent to marriage to the Athenian Nicerato. This is a marriage that not even the attempts of the servant Geta, who was ready to steal the treasure of Egio, the father of the young man and an exemplar figure of a miserly man, clearly influenced by Euclione in Plautus' *Aulularia*, were of any avail. Beside the debts to the ancient model, the risks implied in a behaviour that attributes too much

---

Rinascimento a Firenze, trans. Ezio Pellizer (Roma-Bari: Laterza, 1988); Anthony Molho, *Marriage Alliance in Late Medieval Florence* (Cambridge (Mass.): Harvard University Press, 1994) 27-179; Maria Fubini Leuzzi, *«Condurre a onore»*. *Famiglia, matrimonio e assistenza dotale a Firenze in Età Moderna* (Firenze: Olschki, 1999).

[69] On the *Epirota*, that can be read in Thomae Medii *Fabella epirota*, ed. Ludwig Braun (München: Fink, 1974), as well as in *Il teatro umanistico veneto: la commedia*, ed. Graziella Gentilini (Ravenna: Longo, 1983) 19-69, see also Stäuble, *La commedia* 1968, 106-110; Graziella Gentilini, "Appunti su Tommaso Mezzo e la sua commedia Epirota", *Atti dell'Istituto Veneto di Scienze, Lettere ed Arti* 129 (1971): 231-248; Giorgio Padoan, *La commedia rinascimentale veneta (1433-1565)* (Vicenza: Neri Pozza, 1982) 28.

[70] For an interpretation of the *Stephanium*, that can be read in Ioannis Harmonii Marsi *Comoediae Stephanium*, ed. Walther Ludwig (München: Fink, 1971), as well as in Gentilini, *Il teatro umanistico* 1983, 79-141, see Stäuble, *La commedia* 1968, 111-116; Padoan, *La commedia* 1982, 29-30.

importance to patrimony, whose growth by any means is the cause of a mean and base conduct, surfaces once again from this text.

Finally, the case of the *Dolotechne*[71] is interesting, a play that was edited in 1504 by the Venetian chancellor and notary Bartolomeo Zamberti, in which the plans of the servant Sfalero, who is engaged in the search for the money necessary to dower the slave Rodostoma for her marriage with her master, seem to be resolved by the arrival of the father of the girl, who was believed lost, and by her *agnitio* as an Athenian citizen in possession of a rich dowry. Apart from the formal differences (that is, the use of prose and the lack of a division in acts in the *Epirota*, the preference for the verse in the *Stephanium* and in the *Dolotechne*, respectively, divided into 5 acts in the former and articulated by the division into scenes with no numeration in the latter), it is still significant that the dowry is considered by the three authors as a subject useful to establish a narrative plot which is influenced in setting and characterisation by the characters of the ancient tradition, and especially of Plautus's comedies.

On the other hand, the unknown author of the *Aetheria*[72] also seems to be drawing from Plautus's comedies. The *Aetheria* is an anonymous comedy that survived in a single manuscript, and it can be traced back to a period between the end of the 15th and the beginning of the 16th century. In this play the old Paurea, a nobleman hostile to marriage, seems willing to accept it in order to secure for himself the dowry of the young Clarimena, who is the daughter of the merchant Claridemo. In this way he would also seize the only opportunity left to him to rescue a family possession with a mortgage on it. However, Paurea is, in the second instance, also ready to renounce the marriage in exchange for the same amount of money as the dowry, which is offered to him by the young Archite, who was in love with the girl, and to whom the ploys of Carite, Paurea's servant, who is in search of the money, are beneficial.

It is relevant that the end of the story, which is enriched by the manoeuvres with which Falisco, Carite's friend, attempts in turn to ensure a marriage with Aetheria, the sister of Carite, is marked by the double marriage of the two dowry-less couples and, conversely, by Paurea's acquisition of the money he needed, which, from the very beginning, is placed as the key factor for the action. In conclusion, in the plot of the *Aetheria* the dowry, which in the other examples provided was conceived according to a correct traditional concept, is here defrauded of its structural function as the economic source of sustenance

---

[71] On the *Dolotechne*, that can be read in Gentili, *Il teatro umanistico* 1983, 151-271, see also Stäuble, *La commedia* 1968, 116-120; Graziella Gentilini, "L'ultima commedia umanistica veneziana: la Dolotechne di Bartolomeo Zamberti", *Atti dell'Istituto Veneto di Scienze, Lettere ed Arti* 137 (1979): 587-609; Padoan, *La commedia* 1982, 30-31.

[72] On the *Aetheria*, which is edited in Ezio Franceschini, "L'Aetheria: commedia umanistica d'ignoto", *Memorie della Reale accademia di scienze, Lettere ed Arti in Padova* 36 (1939-40), trans. in Italian by Perosa, *Teatro* 1965, 219-264, see also Stäuble, *La commedia* 1968, 132-139.

for the new family that is formed by a marriage.

The dowry rather seems almost identifiable with a typical and autonomous form of acquisition of goods, and it is explicitly intended as such by Paurea from the very first lines of *Act I*. In such a context, as if observing an ethic which was considered common and incontrovertible, Paurea does not hesitate to affirm that an eventual renunciation of the dowry would be the equivalent of being judged as a stupid person, since he needs a dowry and not a wife in order not to lose his ancestors' property. Paurea, persuaded that a dowry represents not only a consubstantial element of a matrimonial contract, but also, under certain aspects, a preliminary condition necessary for its existence, claims it immediately, willing to accept, only for the sake of it, the marital union that is certainly a carrier of litigation, and he professes himself ready for marriage only after having received the money.

Nourished by a misogynistic vein that authorises the correspondence between marriage and a total renunciation of freedom in favour of a servile condition, in this respect Paurea is coherent with a common line of thought that was typical in Humanistic times.[73] His speech documents, on the other hand, the interpretation according to which the vicissitudes of patrimony are necessarily reflected on interpersonal relationships, influencing them in a decisive way. It is meaningful in this respect that an initial passage from *Act III* in which Paurea notes that he had been abandoned by his friends because of his poverty, while observing how the same sad condition had made him wiser. Willing to renounce his freedom in order to ensure, through the nuptial dowry, the only opportunity to rescue his plot of land, he does not, however, ignore how at the origin of his financial difficulty lies a too generously munificent behaviour towards friends, who were assiduous in securing for themselves his gifts, but evidently are absent in times of need. He derives from this reasoning unfortunately belated considerations. In a few words, the dowry becomes in his eyes an instrument to face an imprudent administration of his patrimony, whose management is full of incognitos and dangers that the anonymous author of the play is well aware of.

In conclusion, in light of the previous observations, it seems to me that the Humanistic-Renaissance comedy testifies to the vitality of the patrimonial motif, which is particularly valorised, in the example of the *Trinummus* by Plautus – as

---

[73] This mysogynistic vein, which was already overtly attested to in the *Corbaccio* by Giovanni Boccaccio, is fully expressed in the 16th century in works such as the treatise by Giovanni Della Casa, *Quaestio lepidissima an uxor sit ducenda*, conceived by the author as a stern closing argument against women and against marriage, in the year immediately after 1529; see *Prose di Giovanni della Casa e altri trattatisti cinquecenteschi del comportamento*, ed. Arnaldo Di Benedetto (Torino: Utet, 1970): 47-133; for more general observations on the not always gratifying judgements on women expressed in renaissance texts, see Ida Mastrorosa, "Modelli femminili fra tardo Medioevo e prima età moderna: l'eredità classica", *La donna nella civiltà occidentale dall'epoca greco-romana ai nostri giorni*, ed. Chiara Vasta (Ragusa: Provincia Regionale di Ragusa, 2003) 77-134.

we have seen – and in *The Dowry* by Giovanni Maria Cecchi. As far as juridical norms are concerned, which are invoked more or less explicitly in the Latin original, and are reinterpreted, in general, in a more precise and correct manner by the Florentine notary, they should not be appreciated in function of a coherence with the juridical model coeval, but in order to perceive the value of the allusiveness to juridical data that, besides the level of preparation of the authors in legal matters, developed in any case from the attempt to photograph the whole complexity of reality, therefore, and to bear in mind also the law which represents an unavoidable regulating element of reality itself.

Rational Animal by Participation. Images of Patriarchal Power from Ariosto to Tasso

Marco Cavina

University of Udine

"The servant is hence a rational animal by participation, in the same way that the moon and the stars are luminous by the participation of the sun, or that the appetite, by participation of the light of reason, becomes rational: thus, just as the appetite retains those forms of virtue which reason has impressed upon it, so the servant retains those forms of virtue which the teachings of his master have impressed upon his soul":[1] with these words from a dialogue written around 1580, Torquato Tasso took up the threads of patriarchal literature, a literature firmly rooted in Aristotelian tradition whose meaning has been widely investigated by historiography.[2] This so-called Hausväterliteratur consisted in a series of highly successful precepts which rationalized and, shall we say, acculturated a code of ethics, a taxonomy of values, and a system of operative models, produced by and functional to aristocratic culture.

The issue of domestic servitude from the middle ages to the modern era has already received much attention on the level of social history,[3] but the complexity of its juridical implications perhaps also merits an in depth analysis:[4] the present paper offers several observations in this sense. Over the last two centuries, after the fall of classist, familistic society, this institution lost much of its social depth and juridical relevance. However, that was not the case during the ancient regime, when household servants were a stalwart of aristocratic families from both political and patrimonial perspectives.

The domestic servant was a *famulus*, or an integral part of the family as a community of people living 'under the same roof', family meant above all in its patrimonial dimension of *res familiaris*.

The individuality of the servant dissolved into the unity of the *domus*, clustered around the authority of the head of the family. Even Bartolo da Sassoferrato emphasized that in the running of the household, a *paterfamilias*

---

[1] Torquato Tasso, *Il padre di famiglia*, in Torquato Tasso, *Prose*, ed. Ettore Mazzali (Milano-Napoli: Ricciardi, 1959) 101-102.
[2] See in particular Daniela Frigo, *Il padre di famiglia. Governo della casa e governo civile nella tradizione dell'«Economica» tra Cinque e Seicento* (Roma: Bulzoni, 1985) [also for the bibliographical references].
[3] Here I refer to essays by Raffaella Sarti.
[4] Several interesting observations can be found in Nino Tamassia, *La famiglia italiana nei secoli decimoquinto e decimosesto* (Roma: Multigrafica, 1971, first published in 1911).

was entitled to *aliquid iuris regalis*, or a specific *iurisdictio* in regard to his spouse, children, and servants.[5] Such authority was exercised in respect to the three different categories of dependants: Coluccio Salutati noted that a *paterfamilias* commanded over his children royally and affectionately, over his wife politically and according to the dictates of the law, and over his servants despotically like over any other possession.[6] Under such profiles, patriarchal power is inscribed into provocative historical-juridical issues, which Diego Quaglioni[7] has already investigated quite keenly.

Thus the figure of the servant blends with that of the master, by no means in the guise of a child – *pater et filius eadem persona* – but instead as a patrimonial asset, *res*, at the patriarch's disposal. Between fathers and sons partial identification could occur – with several modest juridical effects – in dual directions, meaning from father to sons and from sons to father,[8] but in the context of patriarchal power, the passage is exclusively one-way, meaning from master to servant.

Ferrarese nobleman Ippolito Bonacossa[9] states this explicitly when he asks himself *an servus repraesentat personam domini?* – does a servant perhaps represent his master in person? – and answers *sic, sed famulus est as dominum, non econverso* – yes, but the servant is of his master, and not vice versa.[10] Noblemen's servants were considered by common law as better off than the servants of plebes and were thus rewarded with greater legal protection.[11] In the same way, the servants of ambassadors from enemy countries could not be insulted, just like their 'domini'.[12]

---

[5] See Diego Quaglioni, *Politica e diritto nel Trecento italiano. Il "De Tyranno" di Bartolo da Sassoferrato (1314-1357). Con l'edizione critica dei trattati "De Guelphis et Gebellinis", "De regimine civitatis" e "De tyranno"* (Firenze: Leo S.Olschki, 1983) 42.

[6] See Coluccio Salutati, *Il trattato "De tyranno" e lettere scelte*, ed. Francesco Ercole (Bologna: Zanichelli, 1942) 9 [I.7].

[7] See Diego Quaglioni, " "Quilibet in domo sua dicitur rex" (in margine ad alcune pagine di Francesco Calasso) ", *Studi Senesi* 89(1977): 344-358; Quaglioni, *Politica e diritto* 1983, *passim*.

[8] See Manlio Bellomo, *Profili di diritto familiare nell'età dei Comuni. Beni paterni e "pars fiii"* (Milano: Giuffrè, 1968) *passim*.

[9] Born in Ferrara in 1514, he died in 1591; he was a doctor 'in utroque' and taught at the university of Ferrara. He also collaborated with the Dukes of Este and cultivated an interest in literature, writing a volume of rhymes in vernacular. He authored several legal texts, the *Tractatus de servis vel famulis*, as well as the edition used here. In particular, there were three in the Germanic field (Coloniae 1590, 1620; Giessae 1663). For information about him see Gianmaria Mazzuchelli, *Gli scrittori d'Italia* II.4 (Brescia: G.B. Bossini, 1763): 2303-2304; Enrico Narducci, "Giunte all'opera "Gli Scrittori d'Italia" del conte Giammaria Mazzuchelli", *Atti della R. Accademia dei Lincei* III – 12 (1884): 117.

[10] Hippolytus Bonacossa, *De servis vel famulis, Tractatus Universi Iuris* VI.1 (Venetiis 1584) [q. LIIII] f. 124rb.

[11] See Bonacossa, *De servis* 1584 [q. XXXII] f, 123vb.

[12] See Bonacossa, *De servis* 1584 [q. XXXV] f. 123vb.

As it expressed a condition that many wished had its foundations in nature,[13] the Aristotelian conception of the servant/tool was revised and updated by advice book writers. And in a return to peripatetic models, Tasso put this conception at the base of his definition of the servant as a "tool for actions, living and separate". The servant was the living tool that made the inanimate tools in the house operative. It was a 'separate' living tool, different from the hand connected to the master's body: it was a sort of bizarre, physically disconnected hand, all the same controlled by its master's will, intellect, and powers. Different from a spade, knife, or harquebus, different from the master's hand, the domestic servant was also different from a craftsman, who was not a "tool for action', but an actual maker who produced 'wares' by way of his own professional autonomy.[14]

In legal terms, configuration of the servant as a tool belonging to his master emerged on various levels: in terms of earnings, but also in regard to the creation of family strategies for feud and vendetta. Just think of the issue – exquisitely typical of the renaissance – of insults, where an insult directed at a servant constituted an insult to the master, in turn bound by a code of honor to seek amends from the master of the offender.

Let's look at a famous case in the science of sixteenth century honor which saw two Neapolitan gentlemen, Cesare and Fabrizio Pignatelli, at odds over an abuse – a 'knuckle-wrapping' – which Cesare suffered by hand of one of Fabrizio's servants. When the time came for the duel, Fabrizio took exception to, among other things, the indeterminacy of the challenge inasmuch as the servant had not been identified. Claudio Tolomei, a famous man of letters and courtier with quite a solid knowledge of the law, objected to this, citing the Aristotelian conception of servant/tool: the offence was still to be considered and attributed to the master, whoever the serving agent happened to be.[15] For the purposes of an offence, a servant is a simple, nameless tool "moved here or there by the commanding will of his Lord: and as such the servant (as the Philosophers rightly stated) is a living tool belonging to his master. For this, he is not directly considered in the things he does, as these things were ordered and driven primarily by his master [...] It is as if a man on horseback purposely caused his horse to kick another rider who, were he to feel insulted, would not be obligated to tell the story or name the horse, the horse is not considered in the offence, if

---

[13] See Tasso, P*adre* 1959, *passim*.
[14] See Tasso, P*adre* 1959, *passim*.
[15] On this subject see Marco Cavina, *Il duello giudiziario per punto d'onore. Genesi, apogeo e crisi nell'elaborazione dottrinale italiana (sec. XIV-XVI)* (Torino: Giappichelli, 2003) *passim*.

not as a living tool. Hence it would seem that in our case there is no need to clarify the name of the servant, as he is to be considered purely a tool".[16]

In literature the servant reflects the good and evil of the master, his excellence or his low ranks: this is due no doubt to imitation, but above all it is due to a common social perception of a sort of osmotic, one-way process from the master to the servant/tool. In Pietro Aretino's comedy *Cortigiana*, a servant is insulted because he is the *servant of students, attendant to courtiers*.[17] In *Cassaria* by Ludovico Ariosto, Fulcio exclaims: "You can see whose servant he is, he imitates the haughty ways of his master quite well".[18]

In regard to the morphology of the relationship, Tasso – in a typically sixteenth century approach – went about identifying the dynamics that, in his opinion, had caused a differentiation in the figure of the household servant from ancient to modern times.

The decline of slavery was decisive. The master/servant relationship in ancient times was expressed pathologically through the practice of a trenchant punitive/correctional power, and physiologically through the performance of total servitude. In this respect, maintaining of the servants appeared not as a contractual exchange, but as fulfillment of a biological necessity.

Where physical punishment was appropriate for slaves, modern servants had to be corrected first by warning and then, if necessary, by dismissal. What's more, in addition to service, maintenance, and warning/dismissal, yet another element had become essential: pay. As Tasso said, "Still something else was left behind in ancient times, something that with slaves was inappropriate, but that with freemen is not only appropriate but necessary: and that is pay".[19]

Ippolito Bonacossa too made several observations as to the distinctions between ancient and modern, between servant in the strict sense – meaning slave – and servant in the broad sense, meaning someone who performed a service for pay, known as a *famulus*. The servant was he who lived at the expense and at the home of another, and who made himself entirely available for service on a daily basis: hence, a freeman who for indigence was forced to become servitor to others.[20]

The conceptual configuration was however anything but distinct. The fleeting identity of the domestic servant in ancient times was reflected in the difficulty encountered by lawmakers when attempting to pin down the master/servant relationship between reality and personality. This obvious

---

[16] Claudio Tolomei, "Allegationi", *Pareri, allegationi, discorsi, et lettere di diversi illustri Signori et eccellenti Cavalieri et Dottori sopra il duello et cartelli occorsi fra i Signori Cesare et Don Fabritio Pignatelli* (Fiorenza 1548). s.p..
[17] Pietro Aretino, *Cortigiana* [atto III, sc. 6].
[18] See Ludovico Ariosto, *Cassaria* [atto V, sc. 1].
[19] Tasso, *Padre* 1959, 100-101.
[20] See Bonacossa, *De servis* 1584, Preface, f. 121va, [q. I] f. 122rb.

ambiguity, also underlying the Aristotelian idea of living tool, was however explicitly accepted by the very same sixteenth century legal treatise[21] as well as by literary scholars like Girolamo Cardano.[22] The issue of domestic servitude held fatally strong analogies with that of serfdom, which has been closely analyzed by legal historiography in the last decade.[23]

Jurists' difficulty in pinpointing serfs within the *figurae* of the legal science are quite well known as far back as the marked *dissensio dominorum* seen during the glossators era, which was characterized by widespread perplexity in admitting to a perpetual *locatio operas*.[24] The relationship was deeply imbued with principles foreign to scholarly tradition. Just think of the usual lack of explicit reciprocity or of a just cause for taking on the momentous commitment to *fidelitas*, to a generic and global availability for service whose limits lay almost exclusively in habit and which ended up coming close to an unnerving and illicit *datio libertatis*.[25]

Such problems reemerge partially but from a different perspective with the servants of the first modern era. Common opinion prohibited perpetual serfdom, while at the same time recognizing perpetual tenancy for specific works that could also be performed by substitutes and thus without any dangerous assonance to a sort of voluntary slavery.[26] Moreover, the master/servant relationship did not foresee a need to be put into writing, and in fact testimony was admitted as the preferred probative tool.[27]

Contracts were usually drawn up when two parties needed to agree upon something in part unusual. In "Cene", Grazzini tells of a peasant girl ceded by

---

[21] See Bonacossa, *De servis* 1584 , Preface, f. 121vb.
[22] See Hieronymus Cardanus, *De prudentia civili*, in Hieronymus Cardanus, *Opera Omnia* I (Lugduni, Sumptibus Ioannis Antonii Huguetan & Marci Antonii Ravaud, 1563) [c. XXXVII] 377.
[23] See Manlio Bellomo, "Il lavoro nel pensiero dei giuristi medievali. Proposte per una ricerca", *Lavorare nel Medio Evo. Rappresentazioni ed esempi dall'Italia dei secc. X-XVI (Convegno Todi 1983)* (Todi: Centro Studi sulla Spiritualità Medievale – Benucci: Perugia 1983): 169-197; Carmelo Elio Tavilla, *Homo alterius: i rapporti di dipendenza personale nella dottrina del Duecento. Il trattato De hominiciis di Martino da Fano* (Napoli: Edizioni Scientifiche Italiane, 1993); Emanuele Conte, *Servi medievali. Dinamiche del diritto comune* (Roma: Viella, 1996).
[24] «An liber homo operas suas in perpetuo locare possit? - Differunt. Dicunt quidam quod si liber homo locavit operas suas in perpetuum, quod non valet talis locatio, sed tantum illa locatio valet, quae ad tempus fit. Hoc ideo quia perpetua locatio speciem servitutis obtinet, quum non liceat ei recedere, ut arg. D. de libero homine exhib (D. 43.29) l. 2 Yr. et Plac.. Alii dicunt locationem valere, sive sit perpetua sive sit temporalis, quoniam semper potest recedere, si voluerit praestare interesse et sic non obtinet speciem servitutis. Iob.» (*Dissensiones Dominorum*, ed. Gustavus Haenel (Leipzig: 1834, rist. Aalen 1964) [§ 81 cod. chis.] 181. For this source, see the reference cited in the previous note.
[25] See Conte, *Servi* 1996, *passim*.
[26] See Bonacossa, *De servis* 1584, [q. LXXXV] f. 126ra, [q. CVI] f. 126va.
[27] See Bonacossa, *De servis* 1584, [q. CXLIII] f. 127vb.

her parents to her master, who was formally obligated to treat her well and provide her with a dowry once she reached a marriageable age: marriage would mark the end of her servitude.[28]

Modenese chronicler Iacopino Bianchi published the text of a servitude contract from 1502 which was exceptional for its formal limit to a one month period. The duties of service were purposely left generic: "with this condition the servant shall perform the will of the master and his family, for the use and honor of the master and his home".[29]

Indeed, the extremely generic nature, to some degree customary, of the duties of domestic servitude represented a tendency towards a temporary ceding of freedom for the benefit of others. In theory, anything, in accordance to customs and circumstances, can be requested of the servant. Niccolò Machiavelli wrote that Castruccio Castracani "upon seeing one of his gentlemen being laced up by one of his servants, said: - I pray to God that you have him hand feed you as well".[30]

A decisive element in defining the master/servant relationship was that of the domestic servant's right to pay, which as previously seen, Tasso considered essential. Legal doctrine debated as to whether or not this right should be considered unavoidable, upholding its total or partial fungibility with room and board, while clothing was to be considered in usufruct and to be returned upon termination of the relationship. Echoing Virgilio, Bonacossa wrote that the servant bore clothing as an ass bore a saddle.[31] Girolamo Cardano advised lords to allot their servants, especially the young ones, with mere maintenance and little or no salary.[32]

In Aretino's comedy "Lo Ipocrito", servants are defined as 'salary-stealers',[33] when in reality they found themselves in need of stealing their salary, which had been agreed upon but which the master then refused to actually pay. A clearly endemic situation when considering that lawmakers theorized the servant's right to withhold his lord's property for a value equal to the unpaid salary.[34]

In the second act of Grazzini's "La Spiritata", Guagniele imagines turning the tables and suddenly going from servant to master. He then lists all the benefits that he would bring to the sad condition of domestic servants, stating

---

[28] See Antonfrancesco Grazzini, *Le cene*, ed. Carlo Verzone (Firenze: Sansoni, 1890) [cena II, novella X] 227.
[29] See Jacopino Bianchi, *Cronache modenesi* I (Modena: Fiaccadori, 1861) 267. Some contracts are also published in Gian Ludovico Masetti Zannini, "Servi e padroni bolognesi (da documenti inediti romani del sec. XVI)", *Strenna storica bolognese* 34 (1973): 217-234.
[30] Niccolò Machiavelli, *Vita di Castruccio Castracani* [65].
[31] See Bonacossa, *De servis* 1584, [q. LXXIX] c. 125vb.
[32] See Hieronymus Cardanus, *De prudentia civili* [c. XXXIX] p. 386.
[33] See Pietro Aretino, *Lo Ipocrito* [atto 1, scena 1].
[34] See Bonacossa, *De servis* 1584, *passim*.

first off that he "would give them a good salary, pay them on time [...] Where these masters do the exact opposite".[35]

And Lena, in Ariosto's comedy bearing the same name, exclaims that "Because Fazio didn't keep all his promises, I'm going to do like those servants whose masters always owe them and who trick, rob, and murder them".[36]

Maintenance of a servant thus corresponded to a rigorously classist vision of society. Rosso, a servant in Aretino's "La Cortigiana" compared the kitchen – where servants habitually ate – to a sort of prison: "And if you've seen the prison in Corte Savella when it's full of prisoners; you see the kitchen full of servants when it's time to eat, because they look like prisoners, they who eat in the kitchen, just like the kitchen looks like a prison".[37]

Lords, for their part, sensed the delicacy of choosing domestic servants: advice book writers expatiated highly detailed practical rules on how to choose servants by gathering information, requiring trial periods, subjecting candidates to insidious inspections, and even assessing them physiognomically.[38] Girolamo Cardano urged his readers to opt for very young servants, no doubt less suited to heavy toils or to armed protection of the master, but more devoted, less cynical, and easier to control by threats and whippings.[39] If the servants were numerous, it was then necessary to set up a hierarchy according to their duties, so that emulation, careerism, and power mediation made punctual performance of the master's will more certain: the model was that of a royal Court.[40]

Female domestic servants faced yet other problems. In respect to woman servants, charwomen, and chambermaids, legal doctrine went so far as to partially admit the possibility of carnal trading more or less imposed by the master, practically assuming that "domestic maids are usually meretricious" - *plurimum istae ancillae sunt meretrices*. The need for proof was reversed: in the case of seduction of a free woman, it was the seducer who if necessary had to give proof of the woman's bad behavior. In the case of seduction of a chambermaid, the contrary was instead assumed, and it was the seduced who had to prove the unshakeable purity of her body and soul.[41]

Manuals for the heads of good families, just like civic charters and moralists' sermons, did at least urge unmarried women not to serve in the home of a

---

[35] Antonfrancesco Grazzini, *La Spiritata* [atto 2, scena 2].
[36] Ludovico Ariosto, *La Lena* [atto 2, scena 2].
[37] Pietro Aretino, *Cortigiana* [atto 5, scena 15].
[38] For all, see Giacomo Lantieri, *Della economica trattato* (Venetia 1560) *passim*.
[39] See Cardanus, *De prudentia civili* 1563, 378 [c. XXXVII].
[40] See Frigo, *Padre* 1985, 75-91.
[41] See Bonacossa, *De servis* 1584, [q. CCXLVII] f. 130ra. Not in regard to the issues covered here, but more generally for a detailed study of the issue of female consent in the ancient regime, see Giovanni Cazzetta, *Praesumitur seducta. Onestà e consenso femminile nella cultura giuridica moderna* (Milano: Giuffrè, 1999).

bachelor.[42] However, class law was implacable: in the case – recurrent in literature as well – of carnal relations between a nobleman and a servant, there would be no loathed and shattering marriage between the two social ranks. In the best of cases, the nobleman would simply be obligated to provide a dowry for the seduced girl, a dowry – let it be clear – in line with the class level of a servant.[43]

One last aspect that keenly expresses the ambiguity of the master/servant relationship between reality and personality is the master's punitive power. While, as seen earlier, Tasso was against any sort of physical punishment, legal doctrine was much less drastic, limiting itself to setting weak bounds for a certain sort of moderation.[44] As such – in respect to this aspect – children of the family and servants, or rather parental and patriarchal power, were united by this parameter.

Bonacossa reports a common opinion. I shall translate: "A servant has stolen something of little value from his master, for example a flask of wine, some salt, some salted meats, or other food. Should he be punished by an ordinary judge? No. It is his master who shall punish him, beating him mildly with whips, staffs or the like. However, if a servant steals something of little value today, something else again the next day, and so on, he must be hung. Indeed, what penalty should be applied to men of lowly conditions, servants or villains? They must be burned or hung".[45]

Girolamo Cardano claimed that the power to perform physical punishment should be particularly extensive with adolescent servants. He warned that when punishing young servants, the master needed to take care against delegating execution of the punishment to their parents at the price of seeing his own authority greatly reduced. The master's power was to prevail inexorably over that of the father.[46] Such power extended indiscriminately over the entire family heritage, down to even its smallest human appendages: the master had the right to whip even the servants of his colonies.[47]

Within such absolute asymmetry of powers, characteristic of the master/servant relationship, lay a harsh need not to succumb, from which arose in comedies the trait most typical of the servant: cunning. In "La Lena" by Ariosto we read "what we need is the cunning of a servant, like the ones I sometimes see in comedies".[48]

---

[42] For several observations, see Tamassia, *Famiglia* 1971, *passim*.
[43] See Bonacossa, *De servis* 1584, [q. CCXLIX] f. 130ra, [q. CCL] f. 130ra, [q. CCLII] f. 130rb.
[44] See Bonacossa, *De servis* 1584, [q. XCIIII] f. 126rb.
[45] See Bonacossa, *De servis* 1584, [q. CXII] f. 126vb, [q. CXXV] f. 127rb.
[46] See Cardanus, *De prudentia civili* 1563, 383 [c. XXXIX].
[47] See Bonacossa, *De servis* 1584, [q. CLXXVII] f. 128vb.
[48] Ludovico Ariosto, *La Lena* [atto 3, scena 1].

Perhaps what has been said here, along with this jumble of powers, passions, abuses, and frustrations, will make it easier to understand this telling remark by Pietro Aretino in "l'Ipocrito": "a wise man who had always lived without servants replied to those who criticized him for never having gone to confession: he who is without servants is without sin".[49]

---

[49] Pietro Aretino, *Lo Ipocrito* [atto 3, scena 11].

Property and Inheritance in the Renaissance Novella[1]: from Arienti's Porretane to Bandello's Novelle[2]

Luisa Avellini

University of Bologna

As part of a literary enquiry into the theme of "inheritance", it can be observed how one of the most recurring icons is the will, or final testament, either staged directly or referred to as an element of the plot.

As it appears in the world of Renaissance tales, the autobiography *in limine mortis* revolves around a will, which often accompanies another rite of departure of Christian individuality, another symmetric conscious settling of accounts: the final confession.

To these introductory remarks, which have only an indicative function here, we will return punctually in the conclusion, where they will also be supported by the studies of Philippe Ariès and Michelle Vovelle.[3] Meanwhile, in light of such a preliminary observation, it is not by chance that Boccaccio in the *Decameron* inaugurates his arcadian and contrastive narration of his party of speakers with the Machiavellian Ciappelletto's *mea culpa* after the plague's bleak *ouverture* that disrupts the normal order of life and death in the city and erases precisely the normal liturgies of departure with fear of contagion. This cunning moribund Italian confesses a false but edifying autobiography to his friends in a foreign land and thus he can leave the illusion of a halo of holiness as a spiritual inheritance to his guests who are uneasy witnesses to his real diabolic nature.

The reference to the foundational monument of the Boccaccian experience, an inescapable antecedent of the form of the *novella* of the 15th and 16th centuries from which we draw the sequence of literary examples of the patrimonial theme, is appropriate not only to evoke the influence of the "black death" in 1348 on habits and on the Western imagination, and, consequently, on the literature of the early modern age, but precisely to verify the socio-historical legitimacy of the choice made in favour of a literary medium that belongs to an intermediate kind of popular entertainment.

---
[1] Translated by Alice Bendinelli and John Scaggs.
[2] "Novella" ("novelle" is the plural) is the Italian word for a tale in prose as a specific literary genre. The Italian word is thus maintained in English.
[3] Philippe Ariès, *L'homme devant la mort* (Paris: Editions du Seuil, 1977), Italian translation *L'uomo e la morte dal Medioevo ad oggi* (Bari: Laterza, 1980) in particular 225-230; Michel Vovelle, *La mort et l'Occident de 1300 à nos jours* (Paris: Gallimard, 1983) abridged Italian edition, *La morte e l'Occidente*, ed. Giovanni Ferrara degli Uberti (Bari: Laterza, 1986), Chapter IX: *Le nuove strategie dell'Aldilà*, in particular 130-133.

In reality, it seems obvious that the *novella*'s social success, which is rooted in a meaningful peninsular topography during a chronological span of a few centuries, acts as a guarantee that legitimates it as the most trustworthy instrument for assessing the addressees' opinion and imagination in relation to the institutional forms and customs affected by it: in particular, in our case, the disposition of those patrimonial issues that are connected to family relations. Furthermore, the original affinity of the Italian *novella* with the coeval discursive activities of chronicles and homilies - real institutional foundations of municipal customs of the peninsula - is by now fully recognized by philologists and historicists of medieval ideas who, on this matter, expressed themselves in an exhaustive and decisive manner during the Caprarola conference (1988).

In fact, as Carlo Delcorno maintains, it has been proved that from the 13th century onwards "every form of tale tends in a more or less explicit way to build *exempla*, and, therefore, is subjected to the influence of hagiographic models"[4] both in their traditional communicative function and, primarily, in ideological configurations that are determined by epochal shifts, such as the translation into the vernacular of Cavalca's *Vitae Patrum*, in the context of the conquest of hegemony that the Dominicans' specific spiritual program proposes within a religious sensitivity of the Italian cities.

On the other hand, following Alberto Varvaro,[5] it can be similarly noted that in the relationships between the genres of the chronicle and of the *novella* what matters is the shared tendency to establish the selection of the events recorded "according to the memorability of the cases", along with the shared difficulty, over a long period, to "identify in the human vicissitudes intermediate organic processes between the single fact and the grandiose horizon of the history of salvation". Since there is no doubt that – as the most recurring formula of wills precisely demonstrates over the centuries - for those men we are speaking of, writing between chronicles and *novelle*, the general macro-history as well as the personal micro-history of the individual (who, however, is an individual only as long as he belongs to a class, to a definitive associative body) are paths towards salvation. We are dealing with the tips of narrative and anecdotic icebergs, which emerge from vast and submerged constellations of customs, of representations, from visionary and imaginative interpretations and mentalities that constitute an anthropological reality and offer valid and precise sources of investigation. In order to better clarify this connection we can affirm that, following Massimo Miglio,[6] a chronicle, no less than the *novella* especially at

---

[4] Carlo Delcorno, *Modelli agiografici e modelli narrativi tra Cavalca e Boccaccio*, in *La Novella italiana*, Atti del Convegno di Caprarola, 19-24 settembre 1988 (Roma: Ed. Salerno, 1989), 337-363, 337.

[5] Alberto Varvaro, *Tra cronaca e novella* in *La Novella italiana* 1989: 155-171, 157 and 159.

[6] Massimo Miglio, *La novella come fonte storica. Cronaca e novella dal Compagni al Pecorone* in *La Novella italiana*, 1989: 173-190, 174.

the foundational stage of the genre, is
> A tale of vices and virtues, entwined with sayings and gestures and narrated with a strong exemplary tension, in which the vicissitudes of the individual are naturally conjugated in society... a tale of events, and therefore, [it has] a total prevalence of reality in respect to other elements of narrative invention. In the illusion of the chronicler for the reader these events should be a complete book of human behaviour, in which the textual criticism of history is fully realised.

We should bear in mind the overall carefulness of the scholars quoted above (to which we could add at least André Sempous, Odile Redon and many Italian medievalists, from Fumagalli to Cherubini)[7] regarding the ways of approaching the literary genre under consideration as if it were, in one way or another, a primary source. Such a carefulness still manifests itself in the Nineties.

On the other hand, less than ten years ago even Lauro Martines moved on this perspective and printed his work *An Italian Renaissance Sextet: Six Tales in Historical Context* (1994), in Italy but in English. Here he declared his plan to "allure" readers through fiction in order to transport them into "a real historical world",[8] the historical world of the Italian Renaissance. As every reader can verify, after each novella translated into English there was an essay on its historical context that aimed to imperceptibly transform the text, replacing it as a tessera in a mosaic in the web of sensibilities and mentalities of the period, creating a document *sui generis*, that was capable of giving an individual body and a specific form to a survey made on groups, classes or complete urban communities from a socio-historical perspective.

In order to pass from the general to the tangible singular in this sequence of methodical observations that we are making on the "documentary" function of narratives also in our case it is worth making a direct quotation. In the fifth *novella* of the *Porretane* by Sabadino Arienti[9] the vicissitudes of the young Bolognese Carlo degli Ansaldi clearly represent the case of negative inheritance – in this case a bill of exchange signed by his father who had died 20 years

---

[7] André Sempoux, *La Nouvelle* (Turnhout: Brepols, 1973) in the series *Typologie des sources du Moyen Age occidental* ed. Leopold Genicot, in particular Chapter II: *La nouvelle, miroir d'une société et d'une mentalité*; Odile Redon, *Le corps dans les nouvelles toscnaes du XIV siècle*, in *Faire croire. Modalités de la diffusion et de la réception du message religieux du XII au XV siècle*, Romes, 22-23 juin 1979 (Rome: Ecole française de Rome, 1981): 147-163; Giovanni Cherubini, *Il mondo contadino nella novellistica italiana dei secoli XIV e XV. Una novella di Gentile Sermini*, in *Medioevo rurale. Sulle tracce della civiltá contadina*, ed. Vito Fumagalli and Gabriella Rossetti (Firenze: La Nuova Italia, 1980): 417-435.

[8] Lauro Martines, *An Italian Renaissance Sextet. Six Tales in Historical Context* (New York: Marsilio, 1994) 7.

[9] Giovanni. Sabadino degli Arienti, *Le Porretane*, ed. Bruno Basile (Roma: Edizioni Salerno, 1981) 37-42.

before – that determines a legal issue at the moment he comes of legal age.

Existent family archives and jural acts clearly parallel similar cases in which the rights of the lender, the guardianship of the underage heir and the prescription of the bond clash in various ways.

But the repetitive and, in fact, merely quantitative documentation of the phenomenon will never return what we could define as the historical energy determined by a tale of a juridical case rendered as represented events. In this way, to the clever transgressive reaction of the defendant, who interrupts the procedure with acrobatic pirouettes and avoids imprisonment thanks to a stone-fight with the jury, the *novella* adds a series of bordering details of historical relevance in an organic staging: the rivalry between opposing families - an inextinguishable social and political inheritance – perpetuating itself through generations in all the opportunities for possible conflict; the "rude and crass" wit of the judge that actually becomes the central theme of the narration; and, finally, the role of guardianship that an outstanding member of the city *élite*, Romeo Foscari, can exert as the real and proper godfather and patron of Carlo, lying outside any form of juridical norm and praxis.

This is a scene from ordinary city life, a picture of the administration of justice with regards to patrimonial issues, which acquires particular communicative emphasis given the specific nature of the genre of the "*novella*". In keeping with the most recent literary-historical synthesis on this matter as portrayed by Asor Rosa (in the 3rd volume of the encyclopaedic work on the novel edited by Franco Moretti), we can underline a "fabric" and a "rhythm" that denounce "a narrative vocation nourished by great practical experience".[10] On its basis "we still individuate the trace of 'public narration' that remains... a stereotype of Italian relational life" also in virtue of the visualisation imposed by Boccaccio of "the mechanisms of the relationship between narration, listening, and reading" recorded in the device of the narrative framing in the *Decameron*.

From this point of view, the *Porretane* do not constitute a clear sign of the passive reception of the decameronian scheme in a late Bolognese imitation, as we might superficially believe, but rather a sign of the participation in a historic-anthropological shift in urban life in the early modern age. This is an age in which – although in temporal dyscrasia but with similar conditions in the dialectic between classes and problems of institutional stability – the "listening society", the urge to narrate that coagulates in oral modality, starts to become a "reading society", while vindicating its origin and therefore the parallel possibility of receiving the voices that narrate on the written page and of making a strong, successful, structural and theatrical element of these voices.

It should however be added that the urge to write, the drive to transform "narratable" memory in an "achievable" document - an evolution that entails, or

---

[10] Alberto Asor Rosa, *La storia del "romanzo italiano"? Naturalmente, una storia anomala* in *Il romanzo*, ed. Franco Moretti, *Storia e geografia* (Torino: Einaudi, 2002): 255-297, 258.

better, produces chronicles and family diaries but also the collection of *novelle* because of the multiplying effects of custom – derives from the need for testimony which directly proceeds from juridical culture. According to Thomas Kuehn[11] (in his recent work *'Memoria' and Family in Law*, published in the miscellaneous book edited by G. Ciappelli and Patricia L. Rubin for the Cambridge University Press), in the second part of the 14th century the jurists underlined the risk of the transience of memory of events and of contracts. They spread the common sense idea that rights, which are nor recorded in a written form, can be lost. Even more so, as Franco Sacchetti uneasily reminds us in the *Trecentonovelle*, in the past, but also in the present, due to catastrophic events, from black death to famine, "many populations and families were reduced to poor and unhappy conditions".[12] The frailty of fortune is the other dreaded side of the transience of individual life against which an ordered memory of the self and of the lineage can defend. The continuity of the masculine hereditary line, sealed by the persistence of the family name, is therefore made concrete in the sequential form of the Book of Remembrances, which is inherited along with the obligation to continue it.

Once the general modelling power of such a defence is received by the stability of writing, even the grandiose Florentine monument to the oral tale, elevated by Boccaccio, takes on connotations that are even more coherent with this setting. Returning to our direct extracts, we will testify that the incurable distance between Boccaccio's and Arienti's styles in the literary and narrative voices does not affect the analogy between their communicative mechanisms. As we can clearly verify with reference to another *novella* in the *Porretane*, the eighth,[13] which is articulated on the same poles of the above mentioned rites of departure from Christian life, with regards to Master Ciappelletto: namely, the confession and the final will. This is not a spiritual will in this case, but rather a factual legacy of a house, although it is modest and there is only one.

Salvetto the Siennese, dying "of a very serious disease", makes a confession to his parish priest who, in this way, has a chance to reveal his "false opinion" about the resurrection of the body. Persuaded not to doubt the Last Judgement and its consequence by the insistences of his confessor, Salvetto is invited to write his will and to leave his house to the parish as redemption for his sins. But the Siennese, cunning in his ignorance, reminds the priest that, if he believed in the resurrection, he should hold tight onto his poor house in order to avoid, once resurrected, having "to rent a house".

As has been suggested above, in this case, with a less intense artistic result

---

[11] Thomas Kuehn, *'Memoria' and Family Law* in *Art, Memory and Family in Renaissance Florence*, eds. Giovanni Ciappelli and Patricia Lee Rubin (Cambridge: Cambridge University Press, 2000): 262-274.

[12] Franco Sacchetti, *Il Trecentonovelle*, ed. Antonio Lanza (Firenze: Sansoni, 1984) 1.

[13] Sabadino degli Arienti, *Le Porretane* 1981, 56-60.

than the Boccaccian *novella*, the common theme of the confessional dialogue and of testamentary pacts is mimicked, combining the perspectives according to a use, by then imposed for more than two centuries, of pious devotion but this time with a humorous symmetry of valuable narrative results. It is precisely upon the relationship between confession and will that it seems appropriate to dwell in order to access its effective documentary value that, in our opinion, has not been completely revealed by the scholars of the *Porretane*. If we look at Salvetto's character from a lay and juridicial-civil point of view, we realise that we are confronted with a representative of one of the most modest classes which was ascending in the municipal structures. This is a class that Harold Berman considers to be a daughter of the reorganisation of Western law, which had been initiated by the "pontifical revolution". As a matter of fact, among the relevant innovations in a civil context that "unlike Roman, Islamic and Oriental cities which believed in an organic growth of their own political, social and economic institutions across centuries and generations", in the civic law *in fieri* of the 11th and 12th centuries a reorganisation of certain aspects of the attributions of property emerged. Quoting Berman again:

> ... it was typical of civic law that a citizen could legally buy land and buildings through a sort of possession [that was] in clear contrast with possessions in clan and feudal regimes... [it] entailed the right to dispose of the possession by testament, to sell it, to place a mortgage on it, to rent it or in general to enjoy rights similar to those that in the 18th century will be called "property".[14]

In particular, since the model of such social mobility is obviously located by tradition in the important icon of the aristocracy that is, in its turn, artificer of an ineluctable development from feudal to hereditary possession, the property profile of the *homines novi* established itself in the space of the *domus*. This was a *domus* that was more and more detached from a concept of lineage, but that seems to underline, in the mirror of its possession, the projection of the Aristotelian *bios*, the representation of the "pure animal life" of the individual (*zoè*) integrated and elevated in a social enclosure by virtue of its public presence.

At this point it would be worth making reference to Leon Battista Alberti's reading of *Family Books* that is in keeping with a perspective delineated a few

---

[14] Harold Berman, *Law and Revolution. The Formation of the Western Legal Tradition* (Cambridge (Mass.): Harvard University Press, 1983) trans. into Italian *Diritto e rivoluzione. Le origini della tradizione giuridica occidentale* (Bologna: Il Mulino, 1988) 376-378, my translation.

years ago by Massimo Danzi.[15] The *domus* – as this Humanist's parallel interests for the "economic" dimension (in an Aristotelian and Senofontean sense) and for architectural forms of the family home demonstrate – becomes *oikos* in the Renaissance city (metaphorically a *polis*). It becomes the core of an existence that is civic and familiar, public and private at the same time, up to the point that its image and the house as possession coincide. In this way, Salvetto, once obliged to have faith in reincarnation regardless of his doubts, cannot imagine a self devoid of a home, which he acquired with great efforts.

But if we widen the horizon of our enquiry, combining a lay perspective with an unrelinquishable and devout point of view, the so-called "constitutional manifestation" of the relationship between the confession and the final will comes to the fore once again. Or we should better call this relationship a manifestation of the connection between liturgies of departure, redesigned in a juridicial-canonical order that the Italian 15th century still mirrored in its organic function.

From the seminal works of Philippe Ariès and of Michel Vovelle, who between the 70's and the 80's inaugurated and analysed this specific aspect of social history, we know that testamentary use, resurfacing in the 12th century in Europe, is not simply an act of private law aimed at the regulation of the succession of property as it was in Roman times and as it will be again in the 18th century. The will is rather an act that comes to acquire the chrism of a sacrament, controlled for a long time more by priests than by notaries, as, ultimately, Salvetto's *novella* fully proves:

> ... at the end of their life, believers confess their faith, acknowledge their sins and redeem themselves with a public act, written *ad pias causas*. Reciprocally, the Church, through the obligation of the will, masters the reconciliation of the sinner and puts a toll on death with a tithe of the inheritance, which nourishes its material wealth and spiritual treasure at the same time.[16]

The ritual and religious complexity of the operation of the control of collective consciousness and of the procedure of exchange between material and spiritual goods in the form of a deeply rooted common sense are mirrored persistently in the formulaic register of the "genre" of the will. In regard to this, without repeating quotations from the rich list of documents provided by Ariès (the wills of a Parliamentary President in 1413, of a Parisian baker in 1560, of a vintner in

---

[15] Massimo Danzi, *Fra oikos e polis: sul pensiero familiare di Leon Battista Alberti* in *La memoria e la città. Scritture storiche fra Medioevo e Età moderna*, eds. Claudia Bastia, Maria Bolognani, Fulvio Pezzarossa (Bologna: Regione Emilia-Romagna, Il Nove, 1995): 47-62.

[16] Ariès, *L'uomo* 1980: 217. See also Sharon Strocchia, *Death and Ritual in Florence* (Baltimore-London: Johns Hopkins University Press, 1992), passim.

Montreuil in 1628, and so on), it is useful to make reference to the analysis of a text with a provenance that is perfectly homologous to that of the *Porretane*. This text is the will of a Bolognese notary, Cesare Nappi – one of Arienti's storytellers – recently reprinted by Leonardo Quaquarelli along with his *Memoriale Mei*.[17] The scheme of the Bolognese document is not far from the formula highlighted by the French historians:

> primo idem ser Cesar testator, sciens se peccatorem et comittendo ac omittendo cogitando et loquendo maiestatem divinam diversimode offendisse propterea animam suam ipsi Deo trino et uni optimo maximo comendans et de suis peccatis ab eodem veniam humiliter orans, reliquit iure legati pro male ablatis incertis cui de iure debentur solidos quinque bononinorum. Item iure legati pro ipsius testatoris anima reliquit idem testator ecclesie S. Antonini eius parochie unum cereum cere nove...

Other legacies of the same nature follow this one: legacies to churches to celebrate masses for his father and mother, charity bequests for orphans and, finally, the bequest to the Dominicans for his own burial (in a well crafted coffin) in the Church of their convent. The structure is therefore the common one: an initial confession, the redemption from sins, pious bequests, accurate burial prescriptions, the distribution of charity, suffrages, and so on. However, the obsessive repetition after each element of the subject «ser Cesar testator» places the dramatic dialogue between individuals and their own death at the forefront.

Therefore, using a well-known definition by Jacques Le Goff, the will is a "passport to heaven" by means of the invention of a third purgatorial space that is somehow destined for the negotiation of salvation, and it is also an instrument for the rehabilitation of temporal and material possessions, which in a rigorous perspective would otherwise be suspicious. In both cases, what strikes our attention is the correlation between "the behaviour towards richness and towards death". To leave all one's temporal possessions in order is a religious obligation like the confession of one's own sins. Like possessions, that is, the richness acquired in lifetime that is felt as a part of one's self as if it were branded by the print of the individual who took possession of it, death, too, which by definition should be the same for everyone, is somehow personalised by the mediation of the will and in the attempt to prolong a personal portrait in a timeless way. This is a portrait in which patrimony represents one side of the coin whereas the guarantee of heaven built upon pious bequests represents the other.

---

[17] Cesare Nappi, *Memoriale Mei-Ricordi de Mi* with the appendix of the *Memoriale secondo*, ed. Leonardo Quaquarelli (Bologna: Archivio Umanistico Rinascimentale Bolognese (ARUB) - Instituto Italiano per gli Studi Filosofici di Napoli (EdG), 1997): xxxi-xliv, xxxii.

Behind an apparent *longue durée* of testamentary forms an evolutionary movement that cannot avoid the multiple approaches of an efficient social historian should be noted. Such an evolution is confirmed by our literary investigation in the field of *novelle*, particularly in those of the 16th century. The reference to the vast collection by Bandello is, from this point of view, a carefully considered option since it represents a *summa* of Italian short narrative forms. From the points of view of setting, of class, and of destination this collection is also placed in a perspective of European reception which is in conformity with a diffused and homogeneous courtly context of the period and which no longer has organic connections with either Boccaccio's real communal times nor with the late urban municipality of Arienti's and Bentivoglio's Bologna. In Salvetto's insistent doubts this city was already pointing to the fracturing of a total ecclesiastic control of collective consciousness (provided that such a totality could be fully realised and not only *in potentia*) under the power of a naïve plebeian materialism and under the eschatology of good common sense, which is not far from the conclusions of Menocchio, a miller brought to celebrity by the history of the Inquisition by Carlo Ginzburg.[18]

The fact is that central to the European 16th century were the fundamental questions of living well and dying well in relation to a Christian celestial judgement and a civic-religious order, which were materially devised by the Church on these grounds and were violently unsettled by a series of cultural, political and religious contestations that, it can be said, destabilised beliefs and behaviours, especially in regards to salvation. Undoubtedly, indulgences, purgatorial negotiation, and religious bequests were for a few decades at the heart of the fiercest dogmatic quarrel between Rome and the reformed Church since they were evident manifestations of a theory of redemption not by the means of grace, but by virtue of deeds. Such a theory was always subject to lapses in the commercial exchange of crypto-simony.

After all, the triumph of humanistic classicism in the 15th century, the discovery of new worlds, and, after a long phase of relative autochthonous balance, the irruption from the outside on the Italian scene of a period of great military and political dynamism that overwhelms even the papal charisma with the sack of Rome in 1527 are all elements of an uneasy transition that necessarily affects the ultimate questions of human life.

Even if these symmetric orthodoxies, the catholic and the reformed, will soon reorganise their art of well dying, interlacing liturgies of the *exitus* with the treatment of temporal inheritance, they will only achieve a partial restoration of the *status quo*. But it is not our duty to depict the situation following the mid-16th century, that is, after the watershed represented by Bandello to whom it is better to dedicate some considerations precisely because of the rare presence of

---

[18] Carlo Ginzburg, *Il Formaggio e i vermi. Il cosmo di un mugnaio del Cinquecento* (Torino: Einaudi, 1976).

the themes of inheritance and of the final will in his sequence of tales.

A systematic survey of the immense narrative archive of this Dominican friar from Lombardy signals on only two occasions a precise declaration of the question of inheritance, mentioning it in its initial outline. These lines link the real and proper *novella* with the respective dedicatory letter, which was used, in its turn, to pay attention to the individual voice and to the courtly occasion which Bandello, as he tells us, is "describing", transferring events onto writing. In the *Second Part of the Novelle* (we make reference here to the recent edition by the Centro di Studi Matteo Bandello),[19] the twenty-fifth *novella* recounts the tale of an "abnormally jealous" and rich Provençal gentleman who, with his obsessive surveillance of his young and lively wife, ends up inducing her to commit adultery.

Thinking of confirming his suspects with the ruse of a fake business trip and with the complicity of a servant – who in reality is devoted to the wife to whom he is a secret informer – the imprudent man hides himself in a granary which he will end up being confined in and which will be burnt down by a fire that the woman orders to be lit. In order to escape the flames he jumps out of a window and is almost killed, which obliges him to think about the salvation of his own soul. He makes his confession and will compile his last will in favour of his unfaithful wife.

In the *Fourth Part of the Novelle*, on the other hand, the fifth tale[20] is dedicated to the infamy of the Duke of Gheldria's son, who, unable to wait any longer for succeeding him in power, has his father captured and imprisoned with harsh treatment and various discomforts. Once freed by Carlo di Borgogna, who arrests and sends to jail the heartless son, the old duke "seeing that he was close to death, writes his will and, in order to reward the benefit granted to him, makes of the Duke Carlo his legitimate heir, having first juridically deprived the son of his succession".

If in this second case we are confronted with the will of a prince that interrupts the dynastic line because of the unworthiness of the natural heir, investing, out of gratitude, a third party with the succession, then considering the events of the previous *novella* it is legitimate to underline some points worthy of consideration.

In this case, the will and the confession are posited in a natural ritual parallelism. However, the promptness to leave "the wife as the universal heiress of all possessions" locates the protagonist coherently within the general view of the tale, with a "masochistic" obtuse man who deserves to be cheated, or better, a man who is doubly cheated because of the use of the inheritance by his wife,

---

[19] Matteo Bandello, *La seconda parte de le novelle*, ed. Delmo Maestri (Alessandria: Edizioni dell'Orso, 1993), novella XXV, 203-209.

[20] Matteo Bandello, *La quarta parte de le novelle*, ed. Delmo Maestri (Alessandria: Edizioni dell'Orso, 1997), novella V, 49-52, 52.

who, once remarried to her lover, will use it to "have good fun" for the rest of her life.

Looking at it more closely, we are on the level of a mere retaliation that is founded upon an ethic that we could carefully define as mundane, but which, bringing the reasoning to its extreme consequences, it would not be daring to consider as hedonistic. This is an ethic also sustained by the idea that to enjoy life and good fortune is a sort of must and that if we fail to do so the price to pay will be high. A "gentleman copiously wealthy of a good fortune", who, in addition, had the chance to have in his wife "a young, very beautiful and affluent gentlewoman" is therefore punished for his absurd inability to make his good luck bear fruit.

The critical consensus is that the implicit conviction that the events articulated in Bandello's collection of stories (mostly formed of love stories, sometimes tragic ones, but more often coloured with a play upon adulterous adventures) is embedded with vital passions. We are led to believe that the sparse frequency of the testamentary theme, although in a narrative context that always pays attention to render the often elevated social setting and to stage this affluent society while listing patrimonial riches, originates precisely from the abovementioned realistic-mundane perspective. The patrimony should be used and enjoyed while alive. The benefits of fortune, such as fulfilled passions, belong to the world, to a short and uncertain span of existence. Those who on the point of dying of a serious disease want, like the protagonist of the first *novella* of the *Third Part*,[21] to bring the lover, in that case Pandolfo del Nero, into their own grave in the illusion of prolonging the amorous process towards eternity, are mistaken.

In this *novella*, the dying woman, calls the young man to her bedside, takes advantage of the arrival of her old consort, and then obliges her lover Pandolfo to hide in a casket that cannot be opened from the inside. She then obtains her husband's promise to bury by her side the same casket, which contains objects and jewels she is intensely attached to. This is what follows: poor Pandolfo would have been doomed to suffocate if the husband's nephews, unwilling to lose a part of the inheritance, had not organised a night raid to the sepulchre, fleeing terrified upon seeing Pandolfo emerging with loud cries from the finally opened casket.

The miraculously freed young man will, in his turn, be able to take possession of the jewels buried with him. This is a sort of unexpected inheritance, recovered along with the right to corporeal and material life, which seems more and more emphatically represented as the most precious of all possessions.

---

[21] Matteo Bandello, *La terza parte de le novelle*, ed. Delmo Maestri (Alessandria: Edizioni dell'Orso, 1995), novella I, 9-15.

In the uneasy dialectic between being rich and being mortal, Matteo Bandello, as a "secretary of the world"[22] of the 16th century, chose the pleasure of living in the world, to chisel the narrative mosaic with fragments of life in a great summarising horizon of his time, a horizon that according to Stendhal, as it is known, seemed to be the best instrument to reconstruct the historical characteristics of the century.

---

[22] Salvatore S. Nigro, *Rinascimento fantastico* in Matteo Bandello, *Lettere dedicatorie* (Palermo: Sellerio, 1994) 9-34, 26.

Land Rhetoric and Ideology in Sir John Davies's Report on the Case of Tanistry (1615)

Jean Paul Pittion

Centre d'Études Supérieures de la Renaissance, Tours

The period of the Renaissance is a period when new styles of legal writing emerge. Among the genres of legal literature which come to the fore during the period, one in particular, stands out for its historical importance, the genre of the *arrêt* and of the report, i.e. narrative summaries of legal "cases" or "causes" deemed worthy of being recorded, and written for publication in collections of *Recueils d'arrêts notables* in France and as *Law reports* in England. Seen from the perspective of the history of the Law, Arrêts and Reports are important for the way they contributed to the development of the traditions out of which they emerged. In France, *arrêts* encouraged the growth of jurisprudence in the modern continental sense of the term, i. e. of a subsidiary or complementary source of law. In England *reports* were instrumental in consolidating the Common Law as judge-made and case-based law.

Considered as legal literature *arrêts* and *reports* broke new ground for though composed out of trial material, they were written as autonomous texts. This new way of writing the Law broke away from the tradition of jurisprudential writing illustrated by the learned commentary. In that tradition the Law was treated as a "scientia litteralis": the exposition of doctrine took precedence over the history of cases. In the legal literature which characterised it and which retained its dominant position during the Renaissance, texts were developed around and derived from other source-texts which functioned as their referents. On the contrary, *arrêts* and *reports* stand on their own legal and literary two feet and not on the shoulders of textual and legal authorities. The case i.e. the legal entity which constitutes their proper object, is a reconstruction of what took place during a trial.

Like the imaginary cases used as *exempla* in harangues or as *casus perplexi* in commentaries, the cases featured in collections of arrêts or reports were those of which the writers thought that they had a significant bearing on questions of law. But unlike the former, the cases presented in *arrêts* and in *reports* are based on actual trials. Out of the many singular events which had occurred during a given, the writers needed to select those which sustained the momentum of the case and which could be woven together into a structured and coherent narrative. In French *arrêts* the narrative focuses on significant stages in the course taken by the trial. The structure of an *arrêt* resembles that of a novella. In Common Law *reports* the narrative follows the main stages of the argumentation. This gives *reports* a dramatic structure reflecting the thrusts of legal duelling. In both *reports* and *arrêts*, selection and condensation reinforced the exemplarity of the case and added suspense and tightness to the text. Represented in the way just outlined, legal processes could be made accessible and even attractive to readers familiar with other genres using similar rhetorical strategies, and this despite the specialised, even hermetic character of legal language.

Though written from within different legal traditions, therefore, *arrêts* and *reports*, as a genre, share literary characteristics and their literariness is what made them attractive reading for a broad cultured audience not limited to a professional readership. No doubt the widespread interest that members of the social elite of Early-modern Europe showed for such texts was largely motivated by self-interest. But a pragmatic wish to be «in the know» did not exclude on the part of lay readers, a genuine literary taste for the way the Law was represented in the genre.

The emergence of the new genre changed lawyers' expectations about which trial material should be recorded. Manuscript collections of such material existed long before the period of the Renaissance, and the practise of note-taking by lawyers during proceedings or of making extracts from court records, was not new. In England, earlier trial transcripts known as the *Livres de Termes* and published as *Year Books* were soon to be perceived as deficient in this respect. They were concerned essentially with pleadings and legal fencing, often omitting altogether to mention judgement.[1] The need for fuller reporting gradually led to the emergence of the new style of Law reports, such as those written and collected first by Plowden and by Dyer, where pleadings and opinion with decision were presented separately. In France where less importance was accorded to advocacy and more to the decision of the court, the publication of the first collections of *arrêts notables* led to demands that the grounds for a decision should also be reported. As Guillaume de Lesrat wrote of his own *Arrests Notables* in 1581, had this been the case in the past, "nous aurions plusieurs difficultez esclaircies, desquelles encore nous ne sommes bien résolus".[2]

The inclusion of aspects of the trials not previously included made the new *reports* and *arrêts* more balanced in content, but did not make them less biased in approach. Nowadays the use of the impersonal mode of enunciation is the norm for legal reports and is seen as a sign and a guarantee of objectivity in the reporting. But Early-modern readers of legal texts did not expect objectivity or

---

[1] See Theodore Frank Thomas Plucknett, *Early English Legal Literature* (Cambridge: Cambridge University Press, 1958) 100-104.

[2] Guillaume de Lesrat, Arrests notables donnez en la Court de Parlement de Bretagne, et prononcez en robbe rouge, par messire Guillaume de Lesrat,... président en ladicte Court, Paris, Nicolas Cherreau, 1581, *Espitre Liminaire*.

neutrality on the part of the reporter, nor were such ideas prominent in the minds of the lawyers who wrote these texts. To consider *arrêts* first, those featured in most collections published during the Early-modern period, were written with the aim of drawing a moral as well as a legal lesson. The writers chose the structure best suited to their aim: Papon or Du Fail start with a statement of the point of law and follow with a narrative of the case, Ayrault's or Lesrat's proceed from concrete narration to argumentation and generalisation.

As compared to French *arrêts*, the structure of English *reports* of the late Tudor and Early-jacobean period is more uniform. The writers appear to stand at a distance from the cases they record contrary to their French counterparts. The subject matter of English *reports* of the period is more detailed and more technical than that of French *arrêts*. *Reports* look as if they are written in the first instance primarily for lawyers, and appear less literary and more restrained in their rhetoric. Their use of an impersonal voice creates the impression that the writers adopt a neutral stand. Yet those involved in the writing of reports sought to promote themselves as legal authorities and in the context of the period, this meant a sensitivity to the problems associated with the constitutional role played by the Common Law. During the period writing and above all publishing Law reports was not a politically neutral act.

To further examine this point, I want to consider the writings of Sir John Davies, one of the outstanding lawyers and Law-reporters of the Early-jacobean period. Sir John Davies was sent by James I to Ireland as Solicitor-general in 1603 and became Attorney-general in Ireland in 1606. Before coming to Ireland Davies had had a chequered legal career, but he achieved some fame as a poet and won the patronage of the Lord Chancellor, Egerton. Ever since the publication in 1985 of a study on him by Hans S. Pawlish, Davies is seen as the Crown official who was instrumental in bringing about the anglicisation of land tenure and who succeeded in changing the structure of land ownership in Ireland.[3] In his ground-breaking study, Pawlish analysed the political impact of some cases amongst those reported by Davies. The cases Pawlish selected come from a collection entitled *Primer report des cases & matters en ley resolues & adiudges en les courts del roy en Ireland* which was first published by Davies in 1615. This first edition was written in Law French but was later anglicised in a new edition, entitled *A Report of Cases and Matters in Law Resolved and Adjudged in the King's Courts in Ireland* which was published in 1762.[4] *A*

---

[3] Hans S. Pawlish, *Sir John Davies and the Conquest of Ireland. A Study in Legal Imperialis* (Cambridge: Cambridge University Press, 1985).
[4] Full title: *Primer report des cases & matters en ley resolues & adiudges en les courts del roy en Ireland. Collect et digest per Sir John Davys. Printed by Iohn Franckton: Dublin, 1615.* For convenience, quotes are from the second anglicised edition, entitled *A report of cases and matters in law: resolved and adjudged in the King's Courts in Ireland: now first translated into English / collected and digested by Sir John Davies. Dublin: Printed for Sarah*

Report of Cases contains ten reports, together with a summary of «The Resolution of the judges touching the *Irish* custom of gavelkind» and opens with a long Preface. Pawlish argued that the cases showed that Davies used the Law to achieve the anglicisation of native customs in Ireland and to open the way to conquest.

Three years before *A Report of Cases* was first published in Dublin, Davies, wrote a tract entitled *A Discovery of the True Causes Why Ireland Was Never Entirely Subdued (1612)*. Davies main point in the tract was that "if we consider the nature of Irish customs, we shall find that the people that doth use them be of necessity enemies of all good government".[5] Several of the reports published in *A Report of Cases* deal with cases which have a bearing on the question of the nature of Irish land customs as presented in *A Discovery*. One is led to ask, therefore, whether the reports are part of the same project as *A Discovery*, viz. to produce, in the words of the historian J. G. Crawford "a theoretical justification for the lawful expropriation of Irish land after 1603".[6]

To ask this question is to consider the reports not so much, as Pawlish does, as evidence of Davies's actual policies, but as testimonies on how Davies wanted his policies to be understood. It is in this perspective that I want to analyse one of the ten reports published by Davies which is entitled the "Case of Tanistry".[7] Earlier on, I reviewed the main characteristics that *arrêts* and *reports* as a new genre of legal literature, pointing out the use their writers made of rhetoric and drawing attention to the writers' commitment to a moral or political viewpoint It is this interplay between rhetoric, in the sense of a set of writing strategies, and ideology, in the sense of a set of political values, that I want to further explore in analysing the report. I need only say to justify this particular choice that the case in question concerned customary land tenure, and that rhetoric, according to Cicero was first taught as an art to be used in the defence of property rights.[8] Davies was a master of rhetoric which he had previously used with great effect in a long poem entitled *Nosce Teipsum* which stages a philosophical debate in verse on the nature of the soul. Did Davies use the report on tanistry to frame a debate about customary tenure, and if so which rhetorical strategies did he apply to the construction of the case in the report of tanistry what were the hidden ideological assumptions which lay behind his presentation

---

Cotter, under Dick's Coffee-House, in Skinner Row,1762, hereafter abridged as *A Report of Cases*.
[5] Sir John Davies, *A Discovery of the True Causes Why Ireland Was Never Entirely Subdued...161*(Washington: The Catholic University of America Press,1988, p.163.
[6] Jon. G. Crawford, *Anglicizing the government of Ireland: the Irish Privy Council and the expansion of Tudor rule, 1556-1578* (Blackrock,Co. Dublin: Irish Academic Press, 1993) 244.
[7] "The Case of Tanistry" occupies pages 78 to 115 in the 1762 edition from which we quote.
[8] Aristotle is quoted by Cicero in the *Brutus* as having said that rhetoric, viz. that it was first taught as an art in the city of Syracuse and used by its citizens in the recovery of their property seized by tyrants.

Before I consider how Davies constructs the case in his report, it is necessary briefly to recall the nature of traditional land tenure in Tudor Ireland and restore the case into its historical context. Gaelic Ireland, during that period, was a society of clans made up of dominant and subordinate lineages, ruled over by chieftains. Succession to the chiefry was by election within a four generation grouping descended from a common ancestor, the sept. The successor was elected during the chieftain's life time. This was the custom known as tanistry. Land – its possession and transmission, was at the heart of this traditional power structure. Land passed from subordinate to dominant sept, by pledge or as tribute. One crucial custom concerned the redistribution of the land between members of a sept on the death of one of them. The division was usually made by the head of the clan or by the eldest co-heir. This custom, also known to Wales, was that of gavelkind.[9] As Davies's Reports show, in the eyes of an English Common lawyer, gavelkind and tanistry were linked the one to the other to form the the Irish custom law of tenure. Indeed the *Resolution* of the Irish judiciary dating from 1604 stated «all the possessions [in Irish lands] ...ran either in the course of *tanistry* or in the course of *gavelkind*. Every seignory or chiefry...went without partition to the tanist...but all inferior tenancies were partible between the males in gavelkind»(*A Report of Cases* p. 134)

From 1540 onwards, land and tenure became an essential element of English policy in Ireland. After a rebellion by the great Earl of Kildare, the English Crown, abandoned its attempts at ruling by «aristocratic delegation» in Ireland and began a policy of direct government.[10] With the passing of an «Act for the Kingly Title», by the Dublin Parliament in 1541, and under the English Vice-Roy Saint-Leger, a new policy began to emerge which was focused on land and designed to bring about the assimilation and integration of the Gaelic chieftainry. The Court of Chancery issued letters–patent whereby chieftains surrendered their properties and rights to a new "Irish Sovereign" constitutionally subordinate to the English Crown, to be received back as subjects and regranted their properties as estates at Common Law.[11]

To transform native tenurial customs into Common Law practises however was no easy matter. Gradually it became apparent that a policy of anglicisation from the top, i.e. directed mostly at the main chieftains did not produce the expected results. The power of these chieftains depended on their right to

---

[9] See Kenneth W. Nicholls, *Gaelic and Gaelicized Ireland in the Middle Ages* (Dublin: Gill & Macmillan, 1972).
[10] See Hiram Morgan, *Tyrone's Rebellion, the Outbreak of the Nine Years Wars in Tudor Ireland* (London: The Historical Society, 1993).
[11] On this and related issues, see Ciaran Brady "Court, Castle and Country: the Framework of Government in Tudor Ireland" in *Natives and Newcomers, Essays on the Making of Irish Colonial Society*, eds. Ciaran Brady and Raymond Gillespie (Bungay: Irish Academic Press, 1986) 16-25.

interpret and apply custom. The policy of surrender and regrant exacerbated rivalries between them. It also created resentment amongst the lesser chieftains as it appeared to consolidate the power of senior lords over lesser ones. From the late sixties onwards, there was a change towards a more interventionist policy by the Crown. An Act of 1571 (12 Eliz C 5) renewed and further extended the policy of surrender and regrant. Plantation schemes were introduced in Ulster and the Crown began to deal with the lesser chieftains by negotiating recognition of their titles against the payment of an annual tax, a strategy known as "ëcompositioni".

The history of the Crown's attempt at anglicising land tenures forms the background to the dispute known as the "case of tanistry". Ithe case concerned the right to possession of an estate in the province of Munster. The plaintiff was one Murrough McBrian and the defendant one Cahir o'Callagan. The two were members of an extended kin group belonging to the same clan. The dispute originated with the creation some decades before the case came to the Court of King's Bench, of an estate at common law The estate was made up of lands and of a castle originally held by one Donogh McTeige O'Callaghan. It seems that at some point McTeigh made a gift of the lands and of the castle to his son Conogher O'Callagan and that on the death of Conogher, they passed into the possession of Conogher's own son.

Exactly how and when this happened is not clear. The Court of King's Bench where the case was finally heard in Dublin, considered the original transfers by McTeige as gifts in tail, i. e. limited to a person or his heir and due to revert to the donor or his heirs. What is certain is that in 1576, according to the narration of the case given in the *Case of Tanistry,* Donogh McTeige having survived both his son and grandson, settled the estate on his great grandson, «remainder to the right heirs of the feoffor» (*Case of Tanistry*, p. 79).

McTeige's great grandson died, perhaps in infancy, though the *Report* is not very clear on this or other details. According to Common Law, in the absence of any direct male heir, the estate was to revert to O Callagan's daughter, Eleanor and at her death to her male descendants. But Eleanor would not have inherited under the custom of tanistry, as was argued by counsel for the plaintiff according to the *Report*.

On the death of McTeige, «another» O'Callagan, known as Conoghor of the Rock, claimed and took possession of lands and castle "as the oldest and most worthy of the blood and surname of O'Callagan", i. e. by tanistry. Counsel for the plaintiff also argued that the Act of 1571 (12 Eliz c5) enabled those who had come into possession of land by tanistry, to surrender and be regranted that land as an estate at Common Law. To do this Conoghor O'Callagan had obtained letter-patents. Land and castle then passed into the possession of one Brian McOwen who by the time the dispute occurred, had leased them to Murrough McBrian, the plaintiff. His counsel argued that because Conoghor O'Callagan had lawfully come into possession of the land by tanistry, the estate and the lease were lawful.[12]

This was not the view of Eleanor's descendants. Eleanor had married to an O'Keefe and they had a son named Manus. After his parents' death Manus «entered and enfeoffed» Cahir O'Callagan. The report does not specify the nature of the blood ties between Cahir and Donogh McTeigh, but it is clear that he was a member of the sept. Claiming his right of possession by virtue of the common law settlement, Cahir forcibly seized the castle and ejected the lessee who started proceedings against him.

There is no doubt that the case itself had to do with the legal and political muddles created by years of attempts at anglicising Gaelic tenures. That the policy failed to achieve its objective and needed to be overhauled had been made apparent to Davies, when he took up his office, by the machinations of two Northern chieftains, the Earl of Tyrconnel and the Earl of Tyrone. The two earls had formed a confederation and waged a war, known as the Nine Years War, against the Crown. In 1603, having been pardoned, they used the restored property rights under the policy of surrender and regrant, to despoil some of the lesser chieftains. Clearly in these early years, Davies's main task was to try and establish the Crown's policy on land tenure on a firm legal basis. Thus in 1604, the Irish judiciary was prompted to adopt a Resolution registered as an Act of the Council which declared the custom of gavelkind void; and in 1606, Davies formed a Commission to investigate titles to land, including those gained by tanistry. The case of tanistry came to the Court of King's Bench some time after the Commission was set up and it is most likely that the eviction which led to the case of tanistry was in anticipation of the results of this investigation.

In the eyes of Davies, the case must have highlighted the sort of legal problems relating to title which arose out of the anglicisation of tenure as it had been conducted until then. The policy created more conflicts than it resolved, particularly regarding the relative priority and validity of the processes by which parties claimed to have obtained title. It was precisely such a conflict that the Court was asked to resolve, viz. "whether the title of the heir at common law [to the estate] which the defendant hath, or the title of the *tanist*, which estate the lessor of the plaintiff hath, should be preferred." (*Case of Tanistry*, p. 80). This however raised the question of the extent to which the granting of letter-patents under the 1571 Act applied to tanistry, Specifically, as Davies states in his

---

[12] cf. *Case of Tanistry*, p.80: "...As to the third point it was objected (by counsel for the plaintiff) that Conoghor o'Callaghan the last tanist gained a good estate by Queen Elizabeth's grant. For admitting that he who holds the custom of tanistry for admitting that he who holds land by the custom of tanistry hath not any estate by the common law, which he can surrender, yet the Act of 12 Elizabeth c. 5 enables him to surrender...then the grant made to Conoghor o'Callaghan shall be good and effectual, altho' he doth not surrender a good estate at common law...".

report, one of the main points of the issue was "whether Conoghor O Callaghan, who entered as *tanist*, after the estate tale (sic) was determined, *gained a better estate by his surrender to Queen Elizabeth, and the regrant made to him by letter patents*" (*Case of Tanistry*, p. 80, my emphasis). In other words behind the dispute, there lay the possibility of a damaging conflict between Royal prerogative and Common Law, an issue which in England was becoming politically very sensitive at the time.

In the event, the Court in Dublin resolved that "that the said custom of tanistry was void in itself and abolished when the Common Law of England was established" (*Case of Tanistry*, p. 86). The resolution adopted by the Court, had no direct bearing on the case though, for we learn from the *Report* that the case was ended by the two parties reaching an agreement on sharing the estate. On the other hand the resolution had the effect of removing any legal status that tanistry may have had in the past, and thus of making sure that constitutional issues similar to the ones in England would not arise in Ireland. Cutting the gordian knot in this way was expedient in relation to Ireland, but Davies must have been well aware well aware that the resolution of the Court could not be seen as having any bearing whatsoever on how the question of the relationship between Royal prerogative and Common Law was perceived in England. A sense of propriety and also, no doubt, a sense of self-protection led Davies in the *Report* to shift the ground of the case. Writing the *Report* offered him the opportunity to produce an argument designed to establish that Irish customs and the Common Law had nothing in common.

This becomes apparent when we examine the way the report is designed and how Davies proceeds in his analysis. Though Davies's uses the impersonal mode of enunciation in the *Case of Tanistry*, he adopts for the report a format different from the one which was gradually becoming the norm after the publication of Plowden's reports in 1571. Davies in the Preface to the *A Report of Cases* (p. 11) emphasises the important role played in the Common Law by what he calls "arrests of judgement". Clearly, Davies wanted the case of tanistry to be seen as belonging to that category of special verdicts, and this is partly why in the *Report*, he dispenses with following the normal sequence of declaration, pleadings and opinion. One would expect nevertheless that the *Report* would reflect the argumentation as it progressed towards a final resolution. But this is not how Davies structures the text. His report is divided into two parts, each with an apparently separate set of arguments. This dual structure is closer to that found in reports of Exchequer cases resolved by an assembly of judges. Davies's *Report* reminds one of other judicial consultations, for instance Calvin's case. It is as if Davies intended to give that kind of solemnity to his report.

The dual structure adopted by Davies also aims at giving the impression that the case is debated *in utramque partem*, and that Davies acts as the moderator during the case. The demonstrative mode of presentation he choses, however, conceals the fact that he acted as counsel for the defendant, a fact one learns, as if incidentally, only at the very end of the report. As one progresses into the text, it becomes clear that the *dispositio* adopted turns the report into a form of academic *disputatio*. In the academic disputations of the period, though, the thesis to be defended is first stated; it is then opposed and finally it is reaffirmed by means of a series of distinctions. In contrast the *Report* starts by a set of distinctions used as objections against the thesis, i.e. that the custom of tanistry was abolished by the Common Law. The objections are themselves refuted point by point, the refutations being introduced by the phrase "as to the first"...(or "second" or "third") "it was objected etc".

This sequence of objections cum refutations is then followed by a second part introduced by "but on the other part, it was answered...".There Davies as author conducts a rigorous examination of the nature of customs. That examination leads to the conclusion not, as one would expect, that the custom of tanistry was abolished by the Common Law but "that this custom was unreasonable and void ab initio" (*Case of Tanistry*, p. 92). Starting the report with the counter-argumentation of the losing side gives a sense of fairness, but reversing the order of the debate also gives the advantage to the point of view presented last. Above all this way of proceeding creates the space where Davies, having disposed of the arguments directly relevant to the case, can shift the debate onto a different plane. Thus in three deft steps, Davies has moved from the concrete to the general and from the legal to the political. The first step offers a quick summary of the dispute. The second reproduces the arguments for and against on the issue of which of the two estates by tanistry or by Common Law is valid. The final step he examines tanistry from the perspective both of the nature of customs in general and of their history.

The manner in which Davies conducts this examination of tanistry is complex, but the thrust of the argument is clear. Tanistry, so Davies argues, must be judged qua custom, and he proceeds to give a quasi-Aristotelian definition of the essence of custom. Custom is said to have "four inseparable qualities": "(1) It ought to have a reasonable commencement. (2) It ought to be certain and not ambiguous. (3) it ought to have had an uninterrupted continuance time out of mind. (4) It ought to be submitted to the prerogative of the king and not exalted above it" (*Case of Tanistry*, p. 86). From these Davies deriveds two "general rules" of custom by which any particular custom must be judged, viz. that it must be reasonable and recognised as such *ab initio*. The reasonableness of a custom is to be assessed by its positive effects on polity.

Though in the *Case of Tanistry* Davies restates the view that he expressed in *A Discovery* about the deleterious effects of tanistry, generally he refrains from dwelling on particular examples taken from the recent Irish context. Davies's tone is dispassionate and in the report there is no mention of the Earl of Tyrone who in *A Discovery* is presented as exemplifying the lawlessness which Irish customs contribute to bring about. With this important difference, Davies methodology, though more detailed, is similar to the historical he uses in *A Discovery*. He proceeds by reference to and comparison with aspects of similar existing or past customs, in particularly that of gavelkind in Wales. Thus Davies quotes the *Statute of Rutland* (12 Ed. c 1) which established that in specific circumstances, women should not be excluded from inheriting contrary to what obtained in Wales "where (before the Common Law was introduced), the true Irish custom of *Gavelkind* was then in use, by which custom the bastard inherited with the legitimate, and the females were utterly excluded from inheriting". And "...as in this case, it was ordained *quod hæreditates remaneant partibiles inter hæredes masculos, sicut esse consueverunt...hoc excepto quod bastardi de cætero non habeant h æreditates...et si forte hæreditas aliqua extunc oro defectu hæredis masculini descendat ad legitimas mulieres... volumus de gratia nostri speciali, quod mulieres legitimæ habeant propartes suas inde sibi in curia nostra assignandas, licet hoc sit contra consuetudinem Wallensicam ante usitatam*. And this ordinance agreeth with the divine ordinance in the case of Zelaphaad, Num[bers], cap. 27..." (*Case of Tanistry*, p. 95).

Davies's historical arguments are learned and very precise, and the precision of the learning has the effect of insulating the critique of tanistry from the immediate political context of policy. To elevate the debate by elevating the style, Davies, also occasionally quotes *sententiæ* from Virgil's *Æneid* or from Ovid's *Fasti*.[13] This use of such maxims also has the effect of placing the discussion at a general level of jurisprudential thinking. And when he defines tanistry as a custom by which land "have time out of mind used to descend, *seniori & dignissimo viro sanguinis & cognominis* of such person who so died seized..." (*Case of Tanistry*, p. 78, my emphasis), the use of the Latin phrase from the *Institutes* (Bk II, tit xv), to suggest that tanistry is a form of "jus substitutionis", also participates in this process of political distancing.

Davies's historical arguments against tanistry do not however fully match the criteria that he enounced regarding the qualities which should be found in custom, in particular that "it ought to have a reasonable commencement". In *A Discovery*, Davies dealt only in general terms with the question of conquest, in other words with that of the origins of the Common Law and of the legitimacy of its introduction in Ireland. He appealed to the example of the Romans as a nation who extended the protection of its laws to the people that it had conquered. He also stated that though the Common Law had been introduced in England by the Norman conquest, William the Conqueror did not "deny any Englishman that submitted himself unto him the benefit of that Law..."(p. 142). It is different in the *Case of Tanistry*. For in order to show that tanistry did not

---

[13] For instance "Scinditur incertum studia in contraria vulgus", *Æneid*, 2, 39; or "Unde data leges ne firmior omnia posset", *Fasti*, 3, 279,(misquoted).

Land Rhetoric and Ideology in Sir John Davies's Report 73

have "a reasonable commencement", Davies needed to stress that Irish land customs originated in spoliation. Tanistry, he wrote, "...appears plainly to have commencement by the usurpati[on] and tyranny of those who were most potent amongst them"(*Case of Tanistry*, 94). But could not the same be said of the origins of the Common Law and of its imposition on English natives? Indeed French jurists, in particular Jean Bodin and René Choppin, had argued the introduction of the Common Law in England had been possible only by the wholesale confiscation of native lands by William the Conqueror.[14]

In the report, Davies only mentions, this "en passant", as a point raised by one of the counsels during the hearings. But he does not really refute the point and hardly seems aware of the implications of conquest for the historical and comparative argumentation which he advances in favour of the Common Law. He cursorily dismisses the opinion to the two French authorities, by saying that they were misinformed and by making a brief reference to the Doomsday Book.

If Davies appears not concerned by the fact that his argumentation in the report could be read as justifying usurpation it is probably because both *A Discovery* and *Le Primer Report* were addressed primarily at the English audience of the day. It is not incidental that *Le Primer Report* is dedicated to no less a personage than the Lord Chancelor, Thomas Egerton Lord Ellesmere. Davies's main purpose in publishing his reports was surely to persuade his English audience that despite previous failures, the Common Law could be used with success as a political instrument for establishing law and order in Ireland..

On the other hand, here is no doubt that Davies was aware that the argument about the unreasonable origins of Irish customs could be turned around against the Common Law by those in England, who wanted to challenge its alleged supremacy of and concerned. In the *Case of Tanistry* he did not attempt to resolve the ideological quandary in which he found himself as regards the origins of the Common Law. But to forestall the impact that this might have on his English audience, Davies turned the dedicatory *Preface* that he wrote to *Le Primer Report*, from the conventional hymn to a patron which such texts usually are, to a fulsome argument in praise of the Common Law. A detailed analysis of this long preface of thirty-two pages lies outside the scope of this paper. But three main points are advanced by Davies in it and deserve to be highlighted. As regards conquest Davies stated that the Norman "found the ancient laws of England so honourable and so profitable...that the change that was made was but in formilis juris (sic)..." (*Preface*, p. 7). As regards the origins of the Common Law he stated that that they were immemorial and were to be found in

---

[14] The reference is to Jean Bodin's *Six Livres de la République* (Ist edition, Lyon, 1559), Bk 6, ch. 2, where Bodin discusses royal domains and alienation, and to Rene Choppin's *De Domanio Franciæ Libri III* (Paris, 1574) Bk I, tit.3, where Choppin writes (p. 21) "Quanto iniqius Willelmus ille Britannicus, lata lege Agraria qua se omnium possessionum dominum jactavit...".

a jus non scriptum "recorded and registered nowhere but in the memory of the people" (*Preface*, p. 3). This enabled Davies to define the laws of the Common Law as expressing the strength of wit and reason of the English people. The Common Law was born "out of their wisdom and experience, (like a silk-worm that formeth all her web out of herself onely)" (Preface, p. 6).

The bulk of Davies's *Preface* is devoted to developing these points. The *Preface* shows that Davies had grasped the constitutional implications of his discussion of tanistry. In it, the historical argumentation which was developed in *Case of Tanistry* becomes entirely subsumed under an essentialist analysis of the Common Law. Out of his historical quandary therefore, Davies produced the premises of an ideological view of the Common Law as co-extensive to and the expression of the identity of the English nation. On the other hand nowhere in the *Preface* did Davies use this as an argument in favour of the anglicisation of land custom in Ireland. All considered, one comes to the conclusion that Davies wrote and published his reports as a means of self-promotion and self-justification as Crown lawyer rather in order to provide a blueprint or a theoretical justification for the conquest of Ireland. However this does not mean that his view of the Common Law did not contain in it the notion of its inherent superiority, a notion later to be developed into a powerful argument in favour of England's imperial projects.

The King's Great Matter: Shakespeare, Patriarchy and the Question of Succession

Ian Ward

University of Newcastle

In many ways the related issues of patriarchy and patrimonial law finds their symbolic, and indeed material, apogee in the matter of royal succession. Nothing was more important to any reigning English king than his death, and what happened after it. The king's first duty, and the queen's, was to produce a fit and healthy heir; preferably a whole gamut of them. This matter was even more sensitive for dynasties of dubious provenance. It was for this reason that Henry VIII, a king whose marital difficulties have passed into historical folklore, was peculiarly concerned by the succession. The Tudor dynasty was far from settled, memories of the Wars of the Roses merely a generation or two away, still very fresh in the collective consciousness of the English nation. Nearly a century later, moreover, when William Shakespeare revisited the issue in his final, and unjustly neglected, play, *Henry VIII*, the question of succession, both Tudor and Stuart, was again very fresh. Shakespeare's England was obsessed by Henry's daughter, Elizabeth, Gloriana herself; just as obsessed after her death, indeed, as it was before. When Shakespeare considered the question of Elizabeth's succession in *Henry VIII*, he engaged in a fascinating, and still tendentious, debate surrounding the legitimacy of the Tudor dynasty itself, the English reformation and the constitutional propriety of the English crown.

1. A Great Matter

In 1527, Sir Thomas More was walking in the gallery of Hampton Court with his 'master', Henry VIII, when 'sodaynly' the King expressed the urgency of 'his great mater'. Henry, it seemed, was disturbed by the possibility that his marriage to Queen Catherine was contrary to divine law. The absence of a male heir, Henry had convinced himself, was an expression of divine judgement. More particularly, Henry was troubled by a passage in Leviticus 20:21, 'If a man should take his brother's wife, it is an impurity: he hath uncovered his brother's nakedness; they shall be childless'. Henry had married Catherine only after marriage to his brother Arthur had ended in the latter's death.[1]

---

[1] For an account of More's discussion with the King, see Peter Ackroyd, *The Life of Thomas More* (London: Chatto & Windus, 1998) 262-3.

The issue of whether Catherine and Arthur had consummated their marriage became critical, for if they had then the Levitical injunction was material. Pope Julius II had granted a dispensation for Henry to marry his brother's wife precisely on the condition of non-consummation. The idea that such a dispensation might be erroneous was not novel. Archbishop Warham had expressed doubts at the time of the grant in 1509, but then Catherine was young, pretty and likely to produce sons, and so Henry was rather less troubled. By 1527, she was old, considerably less pretty, and Henry had stopped sleeping with her. He had also begun to fancy the young and vivacious, and teasing, Ann Boleyn.

Behind the raw concern regarding Henry's fancy and Catherine's fertility were a multitude of other factors. First, Henry was obsessed by the problem of succession. All kings were. But Henry, conscious of the dubious legitimacy of the Tudor dynasty, assured only by military force on the battlefield of Bosworth, was peculiarly so. Moreover, so much stake was placed by the King's apparent virility, the fact that he could not produce a son was incongruous to say the least. It had to be somebody else's fault. Secondly, and relatedly, if Henry was to leave no male heir, history suggested that the succession would be all the more precarious; and, once again, the Tudor dynasty was anyway something less than settled. Third, there was the cultural, and indeed legal, tradition regarding the nature of patriarchy. All families, and all commonwealths, were supposed to be governed by men. We shall revisit this issue in greater depth in the next section.

And fourthly, there lurked the far larger issue of constitutional jurisdiction. It was this that led to the English reformation, and the break with Rome in1530. Henry needed the Pope's dispensation in order to divorce Catherine and marry a second wife. This, of course, required the Pope to first dispense with a former dispensation, and to rule that Henry's marriage to Catherine was indeed contrary to Biblical injunction. Politics militated against this eventuality, with Catherine's nephew, the Holy Roman Emperor Charles V, posting his army at the Vatican gates. As Henry's patience began to wane, he caustically reminded Pope Clement that the Old Testament was stuffed full of kings who had married dozens of women, and they did not need papal dispensation. Clement, however, was rather more worried by the Emperor's troops than he was by distant Old Testament monarchs and was not persuaded.

In the end, Henry had to break with Rome if he was to secure his divorce, and satiate his sexual appetites. The men to whom he turned for assistance were the common lawyers. Unsurprisingly, they relished the opportunity to assure the King that his authority was bolstered, not by Rome, but by the English common law. The sovereign body in England was the King-in-Parliament, not the Pope. In this, of course, Henry had ventured into deep, and murky, constitutional waters. The issue of the Crown's relation to the common law was a vexed one, and would remain so for another century or more. The common law position

The King's Great Matter

was that the king, although he enjoyed certain prerogative exemptions from the ordinary course of the law, still owed his prerogatives to the force of the common law. In other words, the common law defined the public office of the king. This view was famously expressed in Shakespeare's *Henry IV part 2*, with Prince Hal's symbolic supplication before the Lord Chief Justice.

Such an idea of kingship may not have chimed with Henry's personal view of monarchy. Commenting on *Hunne's Case*, and the question of applying writs of *preamunire* against canon courts, Henry observed, 'for the kings of England in time past have never had any superior but God alone'.[2] But for now the common law was a necessary ally, and no one felt the urge to press the deeper constitutional questions of jurisprudential competence; this issue would come to the fore with a vengeance during the first part of the seventeenth century. Instead, encouraged by Thomas Cromwell, soon to be Henry's new Lord Chancellor, common lawyers such as Christopher St.German obligingly turned out treatises such as a *Little Treatise Called the New Additions*, which could confirm, with suitable ambiguity, that a king of England was 'the high sovereign over the people, which hath not only charge on their bodies, but also on the souls of his subjects', as, of course, the common law pronounced.[3]

The idea of a break with Rome had begun to take on a life of its own. First, however, Henry had to be rid of Catherine. In May 1529, a legatine court assembled at Blackfriars to assess the meaning of Leviticus 20:21, the validity of the first papal dispensation and the legality of the King's marriage. It resolved nothing. Clement was, by now, a gibbering wreck, anxiously peering over Vatican ramparts at the Emperor's troops. And so, four years later, buttressed by a succession of Parliamentary statutes, including an Act in Restraint of Appeals, which prevented any matter being referred to the assumed jurisprudential competence of Rome, a rather different court, devoid of papal legates, gave judgement for Henry. Indeed, it demanded that he should be divorced. Henry happily obliged his court, and its head, his new Archbishop of Canterbury, Thomas Cranmer.[4] Not only was Henry King of England, and Emperor as the Act in Restraint grandly declared, but so too was he Governor of a new Church of England, and, perhaps most importantly, at least to him, single.

But not for long. A couple of weeks later, Henry married an already pregnant Ann Boleyn. In the end, Henry broke with Rome because he and Catherine had failed to produce a male heir, and the constitutional and cultural consequences of this failure were too dreadful for the King to countenance. The

---

[2] See Jack Scarisbrick, *Henry VIII* (New Haven: Yale University Press, 1997) 233-7, and John Alexander Guy, "Henry VIII and the Praemunire Manoeuvres of 1530-1531", *English Historical Review* 97 (1982): 481 and 497.

[3] See Guy, *Henry VIII* 1982.

[4] For Cranmer's willing participation in the trial and surrounding events, see Diarmaid MacCulloch, *Thomas Cranmer* (New Haven: Yale University Press, 1996), 88-9, 93-4.

enormity of Henry's actions cannot be overestimated. England was cut adrift from the theological, political and cultural mainstream. The flipside of this process, of course, was the forging of a distinctive English, and in time British, political and constitutional identity. It was for this reason that Frederick Maitland could suggest that the Act in Restraint of Appeals was the 'momentous' event in English constitutional history. In simple terms, it set the foundation for modern Britain, and its constitution.[5]

As we shall in due course, there is a particular irony here. For whilst Henry broke with Rome in his desperate desire for a male heir, it was his female heir, Elizabeth, who reaped all the dividends of an emergent English political identity. In time, Elizabeth would immerse herself in the mythology of a 'New Jerusalem' and a 'chosen people', and it would be this imagery that would enable her to deflect attention from the otherwise vexed matter of her gender.

In the meantime, Henry was free to marry Elizabeth's mother, Anne Boleyn. Their marriage lasted barely a thousand days. Anne, unfortunately, appeared to be as incapable of producing a son as Catherine had been. And Henry was again bored with his young wife, and, more importantly still, smitten with someone else. The time had come for another trial, this time for Anne's alleged adultery with her brother and a couple of other handsome, if unfortunate, courtiers.[6] Rather oddly perhaps, committing adultery with the king's wife was not itself an offence at common law. Instead, Ann was accused of conspiracy against the king's person. The conviction was not in doubt. Cromwell had promised it by 3 o'clock on the final scheduled day of the trial, and so Henry had given the same undertaking to Jane Seymour with whom he was intending to spend the afternoon hunting.

The weeks leading up to the trial were of interest not least because of Henry's repeated attempts to get Anne to admit that their marriage was against religious injunction, and that their daughter, Elizabeth, was thus illegitimate. There was, of course, an obvious and indeed brazen irony in this. The question of the legitimacy of Anne's marriage to Henry is of considerable importance; for the legitimacy of her daughter Elizabeth's succession rested on it. Henry was determined that Elizabeth must be declared illegitimate, like her half-sister Mary before her, so that there could be no impediment to the succession of any future, and much hoped-for, son. Shortly before Anne's execution, her marriage to Henry was duly declared null and void, and Elizabeth was bastardised. Anne herself never agreed to the process. It was a last act of defiance, and one which, as we shall see in due course, provided Shakespeare with his final dramatic

---

[5] Fedrick William Maitland, *Roman Canon Law in the Church of England* (London: Methuen, 1898) 92.
[6] See Eric William Ives, *Anne Boleyn* (Oxford: Blackwell, 1986) 358-82, for a discussion of the charges laid against Anne and her alleged consorts.

flourish.[7]

In time, four more wives would come and go. Jane Seymour, who had followed Ann, would even produce a son, and immediate successor, Edward VI. Acts of Parliament of 1536 and 1543 gave Henry the power to determine the succession; and he duly lined up Edward, Mary, and Elizabeth in that order. But the drama of succession would really be focused on the triumvirate whose fates provided the context for the succession crisis of 1529-30 and the ensuing break with Rome. It was they – Henry himself, Catherine of Aragon, and Ann Boleyn – who would take centre-stage in Shakespeare's study of this crisis, and of the problem of Stuart succession, *Henry VIII*.

2. The Politics of Patriarchy

It goes without saying that sixteenth and seventeenth century England was an intensely gendered and patriarchal society. Patriarchy was embedded in its political, and in the case of the crown, constitutional culture. The protestant revolution, which Henry's reformation enhanced, merely exacerbated this cultural reality. The role of families, and of men and women in them, became a matter of pressing concern. The protestant commonwealth was commonly conceived as being a commonwealth of small commonwealths, of families indeed.

Women in general were thought to be a threat to social stability. This was particularly the case amongst those of a puritan disposition. Tyndale's 1526 translation of the Bible made much of 1 Peter 3:7 and the physical and sexual weakness of women. In his *The Obedience of a Christian Man*, Tyndale had further affirmed that only men could constrain this sexual destructiveness. 'God, which created women', he observed, 'knoweth what is in that weak vessel (as Peter called her) and hath therefore put her under the obedience of her husband to rule her lusts and wanton appetite'. Helekiah Crooke duly observed that 'females are more wanton and petulant than males we think happeneth because of the impotence of their minds'.[8] It was for this reason that William Gouge, for example, could assert that a husband's primary duty was to act 'as a Priest unto his wife', for 'he is the highest in the family, and hath both authority over all and the charge of all is committed to his charge'. The patriarch of the family, Gouge added, 'is as a king in his own house'. Fellow puritan William Sanderson agreed. The 'godly' man, he affirmed, was a 'kind of petty monarch'.[9]

---

[7] For a discussion of the political context of the trial, see Ives, *Boleyn* 1986, 383-408.
[8] See Anthony Fletcher, *Gender, Sex and Subordination in England 1500-1800* (New Haven: Yale University Press, 1995) 71-4.
[9] Keith Wrightson, *English Society 1580-1680* (London: Routledge, 1982) 90, and Christopher Hill, *Society and Puritanism in Pre-Revolutionary England*, (Harmondsworth:

By the beginning of the seventeenth century, the feeling that all women were a menace to a good order, and that women who could be found in the court were even more so, was further enhanced by the rapidly deteriorating reputation of James I's court. Not that women appeared to be in a position of power. It was just that sexual impropriety seemed to follow them around. The 'ladies of the court', as the rather poker-faced Lady Anne Clifford noted, with suitable distaste, 'had gotten such ill names that it was grown scandalous'.[10] Of course, there was an obvious paradox here. The more that the likes of Ann Clifford and Sir James Harrington bemoaned the collapse in morals at the Jacobean court, the more they dreamed wistfully of the age of Gloriana. But, for reasons that we will shortly consider, the glory of Gloriana was never seriously tarnished by the prosaic fact that Elizabeth was a woman. Gloriana represented an almost gender-free monarchical ideal.

All in all, it was generally supposed that women would not make for good monarchs. In case there was any lingering doubt, the inquisitive seventeenth century constitutionalist need only turn to Sir Robert Filmer's great defence of patriarchal absolutism, *Patriarcha*. Famously, Filmer grounded his theory of patriarchy in the Old Testament. 'The first kings', he opened, 'were fathers of families', and it remained the ideal model for good governance. His convoluted Adamic succession, by which he traced the legitimacy of the present Stuart kings from these very 'first kings' in the scriptures followed a purely masculine line. 'There is, and always shall be to the end of the world', he further confirmed, 'a natural right of a supreme father over every multitude'. It was given by the 'secret will of God', and was even applicable, he rather more tendentiously added, if the crown had been unjustly usurped.[11] In another essay, *The Anarchy of a Limited or Mixed Monarchy*, Filmer repeated that 'Every man by nature is a king, or a subject', whilst the 'obedience which all subjects yield to kings is but the paying of that duty which is due to supreme fatherhood'.[12] The sense that patriarchy cut across all aspects of public and private politics in early modern England gained its most explicit, and uncompromising, advocate in Sir Robert Filmer.

And yet, despite this deeply embedded suspicion of women and their place in both public and private life, attitudes towards women in general were slowly beginning to change by the end of the sixteenth century. And this change may go some way to understanding Elizabeth I's position as Queen of England. Whilst there was no question that women could supercede men as the heads of

---

Penguin, 1991), 443-6.
[10] See Lawrence Stone, *The Crisis of the Aristocracy* (Oxford: Oxford University Press, 1967) 188, 299.
[11] In Robert Filmer, *Patriarcha and Other Writings* (Cambridge: Cambridge University Press, 1991) 1-2, 11.
[12] In Filmer, *Patriarcha* 1991, 144.

households, or nations, humanist literature, as Lisa Jardine has recently emphasised, had begun to suggest that educated women could play a supportive role in familial governance. Both Leonardo Bruni and Plutarch had hazarded this thought; amongst those who were clearly influenced by Plutarch, of course, was William Shakespeare.[13] The important criterion here is that such women must be educated. And no one championed her education more loudly than Elizabeth.

According to Thomas Overbury a good wife was:

> A man's best movable, a scion incorporate with the stock, bringing sweet fruit; one that to her husband is more than a friend, less than trouble;
> an equal with him in the yoke. Calamities and troubles she shares alike, nothing pleaseth her that doth not him. She is relative to all, and he without her but half himself. She is absent hands, eyes, ears and mouth; his present and absent all.[14]

The statement is interesting not least because Elizabeth made much of the idea of herself married to her nation. And whilst the relation remained famously opaque, it was clearly implied that she could, thus, undertake the responsibilities of the model educated wife.

In a critical speech to a wary House of Commons in the first year of her reign, 1559, Elizabeth notified her Parliament that 'in the end, this shall be for me sufficient, that a marble stone shall declare that a Queen, having reigned such a time, lived and died a virgin'. It quickly became apparent that virginity would become a central image of Elizabethan monarchy. But virginity did not preclude the idea of marriage; at least metaphorical marriage. For throughout her reign, Elizabeth also toyed with the metaphor of marriage to her kingdom. As she reminded her Parliament on a series of further occasions, 'I am already bound unto a husband, which is the kingdom of England'.[15]

It is certainly no coincidence that Elizabeth's crown seemed less settled at moments when she considered marriage to some foreign potentate. Besotted courtiers such as Sir Philip Sidney invariably greeted such news with the sullen petulance of jolted suitors. In the context of the Queen's apparent dalliance with the Duke of Anjou in 1581, Sidney even took the risk of penning a scarcely veiled rebuke in his *Letter* on the prospective marriage. The 'new Jerusalem', he suggested, should not be despoiled by minor French royalty.

Historically, the monarchy of England was described in terms of corporeal body. The theory of the king's 'two bodies', of a 'public' and a 'private' body, was,

---

[13] Lisa Jardine, *Reading Shakespeare Historically* (London: Routledge, 1996) 49.
[14] In Jardine, *Reading* 1996, 114.
[15] See John E. Neale, *Queen Elizabeth I* (London: Pimlico, 1998) 152-3, and Wallace MacCaffrey, *Elizabeth I*, (London: Arnold, 1993) 94-7.

of course, not solely English.[16] But it was quintessentially English. And in the case of Elizabeth, the idea of distinctive 'public' and 'private' body took on especial importance; for whilst there might still be certain doubts regarding her 'private' body, which was undoubtedly female', the Elizabethan aesthetic concentrated intently on impressing the idea that the 'public' body of any English monarch was irreducibly masculine. The idea found approval in Edmund Spenser's observation that the Queen of 'Albion' 'beareth two persons, the one of the most royall Queene or Empresse, the other of a most virtuous and beautifull Lady'.[17] His epic *Faerie Queene* was written as a defence of precisely this image of monarchy, of a virginal and virtuous 'private' women who is also a 'public' monarch. The assumed masculinity of the 'public' body of the monarchy was famously articulated in Elizabeth's Tilbury speech before the pending arrival of the Spanish Armada in 1588. She had, she advised her troops, the 'heart and stomach of a king, and of a king of England too'.[18]

The metaphorical alliance between Elizabeth and England reassured those who would otherwise have felt uneasy with the presence of a female monarch. It also chimed with the emergence of a collateral myth which we encountered earlier, that of a 'chosen people'. Court literature made much of the particular privilege of divine authority invested in a virgin queen. If God had chosen to make something of an exception to the patriarchal norm, as he clearly had with Elizabeth, then it could only represent a particular mark of justification. The coincidence of her own birthdate with that of the Virgin Mary was one of utmost convenience. Her death on the same date, as Thomas Dekker observed, elevated divine coincidence into the realm of miracle. The two virgins were recruited to the protestant, and English, cause. Elizabeth was the bride, not only of her people, but of Christ too. The imagery abounded. The potential disadvantage of a female monarch was transformed into a positive quasi-divine image of the perfect virginal matriarch. In 1563, she assured the Commons once again, that they would 'never have a more natural mother than I mean to be unto you'. Elizabeth was, in short, both patriarch and matriarch, husband and bride, father and mother. And, above all else, in case anyone still harboured any doubts, she was chosen by God. As the MP Thomas Norton informed his son, 'I have no dealing with the queen, but as with the image of God'.[19]

---

[16] See generally, Hermann Kantorowicz, *The King's Two Bodies: A Study in Medieval Political Theology*, (Princeton : Princeton University Press, 1957), particularly chapter 2.

[17] In Gary F. Waller, *Edmund Spenser: A Literary Life* (Basingstoke: Macmillan, 1994) 101.

[18] Christopher Pye, *The Regal Phantasm: Shakespeare and the Politics of Spectacle* (London: Routledge, 1990) 33, and also Fletcher, *Gender* 1995, 79-80.

[19] For discussion of the Elizabethan aesthetic of monarchy, and its gender subversion, see Stephen J. Greenblatt, *Renaissance Self-Fashioning* (Chicago: Chicago University Press, 1980) 168, Patrick Collinson, 'The Monarchical Republic of Queen Elizabeth I', *Bulletin of the John Rylands Library* 69 (1987): 409, and Claire McEachern, *The Poetics of English Nationhood 1590-1612*, (Cambridge: Cambridge University Press, 1996) 36-7.

Away from the poet courtiers such as Sidney and Spenser who consciously sought to blur the reality and fantasy of Elizabethan monarchy, more stolid constitutional authorities such as Richard Hooker could be found saying pretty much the same thing. Hooker's *Laws of Ecclesiastical Polity* founded the English monarchy in the classical image of the two 'bodies', making much of the fact that the public body was anointed by God. Monarchs like Elizabeth, regardless of the sex of the 'private' body, were selected by Him as their 'natural agents'. This was even more the case, as Hooker affirmed, because Elizabeth had acquired a third 'body', that of the Governor of the established Church of England, the 'subordinate Head of Christ's people'. The implication of the *Laws* was clear. Regardless of the conventions of succession, the common law of England, as perfected by the reformation settlement and the various statutes which legitimated it, vests supreme authority in the 'public' office of the God's chosen 'lieutenant'.[20] The sex of the recipient of God's beneficence was incidental.

Elizabeth, then, bucked the trend in the most spectacular of fashions. She was not the first Queen of England in her own right. Her elder sister could lay claim to that privilege, whilst medieval historians continue to argue the case for Queen Matilda in the twelve century as the rightful sovereign rather than King Stephen. But Elizabeth was the first to impress her authority, and to enjoy it virtually unchallenged. She was certainly the first to be widely revered, even loved. Indeed, there are few monarchs since who have attracted quite such reverence. And she did this despite being a women and despite the overarching suspicion of her gender in public, and private, life. The sheer scale of this achievement cannot be overstated, not least because it asked considerable questions of received ideas of patriarchal succession. It also left William Shakespeare with much to ponder as he contemplated his final composition.

3. Shakespeare's Royal Patriarchs

Shakespeare's attitude to the myth of a Fairy Queen governing her fairyland was famously ambiguous. This ambiguity is nowhere better evidenced than in *A Midsummer Night's Dream*, a play in which allusions to Elizabeth, the 'imperial votress' are overt, but in which the mirror worlds of Athens and fairyland are worryingly fragile ones. Similar ambiguities, meanwhile, can be found in *The Tempest*, a play which, being his most recently completed, would have been prominent in Shakespeare's mind as he wrote, or at least contributed to, *Henry VIII*. Prospero's 'rough magic' is not itself sufficient for the good governance of real political communities.

---

[20] Richard Hooker, *Of the Laws of Ecclesiastical Polity*, (Cambridge: Cambridge University Press, 1989), particularly 140-2, 146-7, 167.

Shakespeare's treatment of the question of succession, and by implication, patriarchy and the crown, are equally ambivalent. This ambiguity is clearly evidenced in the succession of Henry V. First there is the problem associated with his father's apparent usurpation of the crown from Richard II. Shakespeare's Bolingbroke is never, famously, comfortable with the crown. The scene in which Prince Hal precipitately seizes the crown from his dying, but not yet dead, father speaks volumes for the transient, and fragile, reality of monarchical succession. There is little dignity here, as the dying Henry bemoans, 'Is he so hasty that he doth suppose/ My sleep my death?'[21] The legitimacy of their succession to the crown haunts the final exchange between father and son. Henry admits:

> God knows, my son,
> By what by-paths and indirect crook'd ways
> I met this crown, and I myself know well
> How troublesome it lay upon my head.[22]

Hal does his best to make amends, saying that he placed it upon his head 'To try with it, as with an enemy/ That had before my face murder'd my father,/ The quarrel of a true inheritor'.[23] The Bolingbroke usurpation haunts *Henry V*, only seeming to be purged by God's blessing at Agincourt.

Usurpations in general pose awkward questions, none more so, of course, that the potential usurpation of Henry Tudor. Shakespeare approached this vexed issue in *Richard III*, where the only possible legitimacy for Henry's rebellion was to be found in the unremitting evil of Richard, and, of course, in God's providence; a providence that dictates events on Bosworth field. Henry's speech at the end of the play is designed to affirm a retrospective legitimacy that is cast in terms of divine approbation:

> O now let Richmond and Elizabeth,
> The true successors of each royal House,
> By God's fair ordinance conjoin together,
> And let their heirs, God, if Thy will be so,
> Enrich the time to come with smooth-fac'd peace,
> With smiling plenty, and fair prosperous days.[24]

The related question of illegitimacy also occurs elsewhere in Shakespeare. There is very obviously the thoroughly ambiguous figure of the Bastard in *King John*;

---

[21] *Henry IV part 2*, 4.5.60-1.
[22] *Henry IV part 2*, 4.5.183-6.
[23] *Henry IV part 2*, 4.5,166-8,
[24] *Richard III*, 5.5.29-34.

a figure, as Tillyard observed, who is clearly 'more kingly than the king'.[25] In the same play there is also the famous exchange between John and Queen Eleanor on the subject of succession. When John claims his throne in terms of 'Our strong possession and our right for us', Eleanor replies 'Your strong succession much more than your right'.[26] The Hobbesian inference is unmistakable; succession depends on lineage rather less than it does on political power.[27]

In sum, the question of succession reveals a series of ambiguities in Shakespeare; from the uncertainty surrounding the crown of Henry IV, to the divine intervention in support of Henry Tudor, to the more prosaic Hobbesian invocation in *King John*. There is, of course, one clear conclusion. Shakespeare was more than aware that royal succession was a vexed issue. Different kings succeed to thrones in different ways, seeking to establish their legitimacy in a variety of different forms.

And then, of course, there is the question of gender and patriarchy. And, once again, Shakespeare is ambiguous. The more particular issue of female magistracy and female succession is repeatedly treated in Shakespeare. It haunts *King John*, not least in Queen Eleanor's acerbic dismissal of the king's pretended authority.[28] Eleanor takes pleasure in describing herself as a 'soldier', and throughout the play women seem eager, over-eager indeed, to get their hands dirty in the vexed world of politics. It is a play where 'ladies and pale-visag'd maids,/ Like Amazons come tripping after drums', changing 'their thimbles into armed gauntlets' and 'their needl's to lances, and their gentle hearts/ To fierce and bloody inclination'.[29]

It also finds a notable expression in Henry's claim to the throne of France, in *Henry V*. The strength of his claim, traced back to Edward III, depends upon arguments surrounding the Salic law which appeared to bar succession through the female line.[30] Shakespeare is dutiful in presenting the Salic 'case', as he received it from Holinshed, in Act I Scene 2 of the play, where the Archbishop staggers through the ancient precedents in order to suggest that Henry's claim is not barred. The argument here, however, is notably stronger in terms of historical practice, than constitutional right; lots of kings of France have inherited through the female line, and so Henry's claim is no weaker than that of the current king.[31]

---

[25] Edmund W. Tillyard, *Shakespeare's History Plays* (Harmondsworth: Penguin, 1962) 226.
[26] *King John*, 1.1.39-40.
[27] See Paola Pugliatti, *Shakespeare the Historian* (Basingstoke: Macmillan, 1996) 84-7.
[28] Phyllis Rackin, *Stages of History: Shakespeare's English Chronicles* (London: Routledge, 1990) 148, 179-91.
[29] *King John*, 5.2.154-8.
[30] For a modern commentary, see Dominique Goy-Blanquet, 'Two Kingdoms for Half-a-Crown', *Shakespeare Survey* 44 (1991): 55-63.
[31] *Henry V*, 1.2.33-95.

There is not a whole lot of principle here. God's beneficence at Agincourt seems to add a varnish of legitimacy, and the theological argument is reinforced by the Archbishop's observation, at the end of his speech, that Numbers 27:8 provides 'When the man dies, let the inheritance/ Descend unto the daughter'.[32] This might be so, but Shakespeare's audience would also have known that Henry died young, before he could assume the succession which was negotiated in the wake of Agincourt. They would also know that his son would prove to be incapable of seizing his 'right', and the England would be entrapped in a bloody century of struggle with the French, and still emerge with nothing to show for it.

Aside from the histories, there are various allusions to female magistracy to be found in many of Shakespeare's comedies and tragedies. Amongst the former, there are, of course, the serial ambiguities to be found in *The Merchant of Venice*, most obviously those surrounding the figure of Portia, a wealthy landowner, and by implication of figure of some magisterial authority in the peaceful, if 'aweary' and stagnant, Belmont. The ambiguities are written largest of all in Portia's defence of Bassanio before the Duke in Act 4 Scene 1. Here Portia disguises herself as a man in order to give a legal argument before the court in the name of a fictitious lawyer. It is in this guise, as a 'fine bragging youth' that Portia can resuscitate the ailing patriarchalism of Venetian law.[33]

The same essential ambivalence can be found elsewhere amongst Shakespeare's comedies, for example in *All's Well That Ends Well*, *Measure for Measure*, and, of course, *A Midsummer Night's Dream*. The presence of an overtly carnival, even feminine, patriarch in the figure of Oberon in the *Dream* is peculiarly disturbing.[34] As in *The Merchant of Venice*, it becomes ever more difficult to align any clear patriarchal qualities with any unambiguously patriarchal figure. Moreover, although it is never clearly stated, the sense that the 'female' characters might make for rather better magistrates than the male always lurks.

Amongst the tragedies, one play very obviously dwells on the question of succession. Of course, it is present in a brutal, murderous, sense in both *Macbeth* and *Hamlet*. The question of monarchical succession underpins the plots of both plays. But the gender implications come to the fore in *King Lear*. The context

---

[32] *Henry V*, 1.2.99-100.
[33] *The Merchant of Venice*, 1.2.1-2, 3.4.69. I have discussed the gender ambiguities in Portia's pretended magistracy in Ian Ward, *Shakespeare and the Legal Imagination* (London: Butterworths, 1999) 129-33. For further commentary, see also C.Leventon, 'Patrimony and Patriarchy in *The Merchant of Venice*', in *The Matter of Difference: Materialist Feminist Criticism of Shakespeare*, ed. Valerie Wayne (Hemel Hempstead: Harvester Wheatsheaf, 1991) 68-70.
[34] Leonard Tennenhouse, 'Strategies of State and political plays: *A Midsummer Night's Dream, Henry IV, Henry V, Henry VIII*', in *Political Shakespeare: New Essays in Cultural Materialism*, eds. Jonathan Dollimore & Alan Sinfield (Manchester University Press, 1985) 111-13.

within which *Lear* was composed was, of course, dominated by the Stuart succession. The new King James was acutely sensitive to the argument that the idea of a united British 'isles' was both legitimate in terms of principle, and right in terms of practical governance.[35] Shakespeare's *Lear*, with its graphic portrayal of what can happen when a kingdom is unwisely divided, hit all the right notes. Moreover, the fact that Lear is burdened with daughters, rather than with sons, is obviously material. If Lear had produced a son, he need never have ventured into the convoluted process of trying to ascertain some other rationale for the succession.

Ultimately, however, all these questions – of usurpation, of illegitimacy, of female magistracy and succession, of life in fairyland – come together in *Henry VIII*. The play carries a very particular critical baggage, not least with regard to its provenance. Classical Shakespearean commentary remained chary of the play, suggesting that part, perhaps all of it, was written by John Fletcher. There is, for example, no reference to *Henry VIII* in Tillyard's *Shakespeare's History Plays*. More recently it fails to make a showing in Wolfgang Iser's *Staging Politics: The Lasting Impact of Shakespeare's Histories*.[36] The question of authorship remains controversial.[37] So too does the question of conceptual fit, for *Henry VIII* is quite unlike the earlier chronicle histories. It could be easily, if not very helpfully, described as another of the 'problem' plays. But there again, to the extent that this latter set of plays have a unifying feature in their problematic, *Henry VIII* does not really fit. There is, as such, no obviously, or at least obviously comparable, 'problem' in *Henry VIII*. In the light of this oddity, some critics have dismissed the play as mere 'pageantry'.[38]

The criticism is not entirely fair. There is much in *Henry VIII* of interest, not least that which relates to the question of succession.[39] It is commonly suggested that the play was written in anticipation of the marriage of Princess Elizabeth to Frederick of the Palatine, thus placing it within a time frame of 1612-13. If so, then the question of familial integrity, and royal succession, would have

---

[35] For a discussion of this particular context, see Richard Dutton, '*King Lear*, *The Triumphs of Reunited Britannia* and the Matter of Britain', *Literature and History* 12 (1986): 139-51.
[36] Tillyard, *History Plays* 1962, and Wolfgang Iser, *Staging Politics: The Lasting Impact of Shakespeare's Histories* (New York: Columbia University Press, 1993).
[37] For a discussion of this issue, see Robert Fraser, *Shakespeare: The Later Years* (New York: Columbia University Press, 1992) 256-7, and Jonathan Bate, *The Genius of Shakespeare* (London: Picador, 1997) 79-81.
[38] See, for example, Gareth and Barbara Lloyd Evans *The Upstart Crow: An Introduction to Shakespeare's Plays* (London: Dent, 1982) 389-90, and for an earlier commentary H.Richmond, 'Shakespeare's *Henry VIII*: Romance Redeemed by History', *Shakespeare Studies* 4 (1968): 334-5.
[39] For a more upbeat commentary see, Peter L. Rudnytsky, '*Henry VIII* and the Deconstruction of History', *Shakespeare Survey* 43 (1990): 43-57.

provided a very immediate context.[40] Indeed, as Leonard Tennenhouse has suggested, it is in the treatment of this question of succession that Shakespeare's final and 'belated' history play becomes truly interesting. More particularly, more than in any previous history, *Henry VIII* aligns, indeed elides, the genealogical and providential arguments for legitimate succession.[41] The former is rooted in the assumed legitimacy of Henry's father, itself lionised in *Richard III*, whilst the latter is reaffirmed in Henry's own appeal to his 'integrity in heaven'.[42] It is as if Shakespeare is more determined than ever to assert the unimpeachable legitimacy of the Tudor line. And he does so, quite simply, because the legitimacy of the Stuart succession is dependent upon it. This duality of context is central. *Henry VIII* is about the politics of successive successions.[43]

This politics finds its ultimate statement in Cranmer's great set-piece in Act 5 Scene 4 which accompanies the christening of the baby Elizabeth. Here the king's 'matter', in reality more of muddle and mess, finally emerges as England's greatest triumph.[44] Of course, Elizabeth's presence has hovered over the entire play, her qualities vicariously described in the sympathetic portrayal of Ann Bullen. Not the least of these endearing qualities is Ann's pity for Queen Katherine, something which the Lord Chancellor describes in terms of 'a gentle business, and becoming/ The action of good women'.[45] Such a sympathetic capacity, as we have already noted, was commonly seen to be one of the peculiar benefits of a female patriarch. The Lord Chancellor is not alone in making the inevitable allusion to the future, adding:

> I have perus'd her well;
> Beauty and honour in her are so mingled
> That they have caught the king: and who knows yet
> But from this lady may proceed a gem
> To lighten all this isle.[46]

But Elizabeth's physical presence sees the rhetoric of sublimation reach new heights. Cranmer opens by prophesying a future which had, of course, already passed:

---

[40] See Leeds J. Barroll, *Politics, Plague and Shakespeare's Theatre: The Stuart Years* (Ithaca: Cornell University Press, 1991) 205-7.
[41] Tennenhouse, *Strategies* 1985, 123-5.
[42] *Henry VIII*, 3.2.453.
[43] For a discussion of these duality, see William M. Baillie, '*Henry VIII*: A Jacobean History', *Shakespeare Studies* 12 (1979): 247-66 and Stuart M. Kurland, '*Henry VIII* and James I: Shakespeare and Jacobean Politics', *Shakespeare Studies* 19 (1987): 203-17.
[44] See Alexander Leggatt, *Shakespeare's Political Drama* (London: Routledge, 1988) 220.
[45] *Henry VIII*, 2.3.54-6.
[46] *Henry VIII*, 2.3.75-9.

The King's Great Matter

> This royal infant (heaven still move about her)
> Though in her cradle, yet now promises
> Upon this land a thousand thousand blessings,
> Which time shall bring to ripeness: she shall be...
> A pattern to all princes living with her,
> And all that succeed.[47]

The reference to succession is pointed. Elizabeth's presence, and by implication that of her father, pervades the Stuart succession. Cranmer then goes on to describe the virtues of the Queen to come: 'Truth shall nurse her, /Holy and heavenly thoughts still counsel her'.[48] Moreover, 'In her days every man shall eat in safety/ Under his own vine what he plants, and sing/ The merry songs of peace to all his neighbours'; something that would have had a particular resonance in an England which, by 1613, had suffered a series of recent harvest failures.[49] As Alexander Leggatt emphasises, with every sentence that Cranmer utters it just becomes ever more obvious that the England he his projecting is already 'past, lost and idealized'.[50]

Cranmer's prophesy with regard to the Stuart succession, no matter how laudatory, cannot evade this necessary ambiguity:

> but when
> The bird of wonder dies, the maiden phoenix
> Her ashes new create another heir
> As great in admiration as herself,
> So shall she leave her blessedness to one...
> Who from the sacred ashes of her honour
> Shall star-like rise, as great in fame as she was,
> And so stand fix'd.[51]

Inevitably Cranmer is then drawn back to the reflected glory of Elizabeth: 'Peace, plenty, love, truth, terror, /That were servants to this chosen infant, /Shall then be his, and like a vine grow to him'.[52] It is, very pointedly, to Elizabeth that Cranmer closes, to the memory that 'most unspotted lily' who will be mourned by 'all the world'.[53]

---

[47] *Henry VIII*, 5.4.17-23.
[48] *Henry VIII*, 5.4.28-9.
[49] *Henry VIII*, 5.4.33-5.
[50] Leggatt, *Political Drama* 1988, 233.
[51] *Henry VIII*, 5.4.39-46.
[52] *Henry VIII*, 5.4.47-9.
[53] *Henry VIII*, 5.4.61-2.

Despite, then, the unsurprisingly laudatory manner in which Shakespeare plays with prospective history, the ambiguities then remain. Aside from those attaching to the Stuart succession, there are a number of residual ambiguities that attach more immediately to the king's 'great matter'. There is, for example, the ambiguity regarding Henry's real motive for divorcing Katherine and marrying Ann. When the Chamberlain suggests that 'It seems the marriage with his brother's wife/ Has crept too near his conscience', Suffolk acidly observes 'No, his conscience/ Has crept too near another lady'.[54] Shakespeare also emphasises the King's own contradictory attitude to the law, desirous of appearing to clothe his divorce in legal nicety, but repeatedly revealing his own almost contemptuous attitude to the 'dilatory sloth' of the legal proceedings; proceedings which he sees as being 'tricks of Rome'.[55]

Ultimately, however, a Kate Chedgzoy has argued, the most irreducible of these ambiguities are those that relate to questions of gender and patriarchy, and to the related challenges posed by female magistracy. Time and again, the very idea of patriarchy is both guaranteed and subverted in Shakespeare.[56] And nowhere is this ambiguity more obviously displayed than in the question of succession, and in Shakespeare's description of the king's 'great matter' in *Henry VIII*.

---

[54] *Henry VIII*, 2.2.16-18.
[55] *Henry VIII*, 2.4.234-5.
[56] Kate Chedgzoy, *Shakespeare's Queer Children: Sexual Politics and Contemporary Culture* (Manchester: Manchester University Press, 1995) 7-9.

To Have and Have Not in Shakespeare: Patrimonial Questions in "As You Like It"

Giuseppina Restivo

University of Trieste

It is in the comedies that Shakespeare allows more space to money and property questions: in *The Merchant of Venice* and *As You Like It*, in particular, different patrimonial problems are highlighted.

In *The Merchant of Venice* the distance between the impoverished gentleman Bassanio and the fabulously rich heiress Portia, whom he plans to marry, is central to the plot. It sets off all events, leading to Antonio's debt for Bassanio's sake, Shylock's money lending and pound of flesh bond, the ensuing trial and Portia's role in it. Patrimonial and matrimonial issues are here fused together, but the central ideological confrontation is between the spendthrift (or rather prodigal renter) Bassanio, with his generous friend, the merchant Antonio on the one hand, and Shylock, the Jewish money lender on the other. Shylock tries in vain to impart both to Antonio and to Bassanio lessons in economics, insisting on a "thrifty" or "breeding" use of money and property, well aware of a need for banking, risk evaluation and money rates in business. He is despised and discriminated against, and finally embittered and driven to revenge by his daughter's betrayal and elopement; which does not however prevent him from denouncing slavery as a property problem based on the bodily exploitation of menials. He even brings up the salary problem with his servant Lancelot, whom he actually helps to find a higher salary with Bassanio.

All events occur in a social ambience which is basically that of the rising wealthy bourgeoisie: although aristocrats appear in numbers as Portia's unsuccessful suitors (her patrimony being adequate to them), all the genteel protagonists belong to a well-to-do gentry class, with no titles attached to them. Portia, the heiress of Belmont, is connected with the professional class: she plays the part of a young lawyer, first consulting and then imitating her uncle, a well-known Paduan lawyer, while the "royal merchant" Antonio lives on commerce but behaves like a perfect gentleman, as do the originally well-to-do scholar Bassanio (who has squandered his money out of excessive generosity or prodigality) and his friends Lorenzo and Gratiano.[1]

In *As You Like It* economic problems come back, insistently disseminated

---

[1] To the juridical and economic issues crucial in the play, I have devoted an essay, "Law and Individual Rights in Shakespeare's *The Merchant of Venice*", *XLIVe Colloque International d'Études Humanistes : Droit et Justice dans l'Europe de la Renaissance*, 2-7 July 2001, Centre d'Études Supérieures de la Renaissance, Tours.

throughout, more impending and decisive than is initially apparent: they mark the transfer of the new outlook which had surfaced in *The Merchant of Venice*, from the gentry level to that of an ideal new aristocracy, "converted" or ideologically merged with the new gentry, after transformation by a "ritual passage" in the forest. Apparentlty a pastoral drama, often belittled as such in criticism, *As You Like It* is, rather, a forum on socio-cultural problems and patrimonial issues, ranging from male primogeniture inheritance rights to younger brothers' rights and education, from daughters' patrimonial/matrimonial rights, to state succession or master-servant relationships. But before analyzing these specific aspects, an antecedent should briefly be pointed out.

The opening patrimonial/matrimonial case discussion in Shakespeare had appeared in *A Midsummer Night's Dream,* in a sense preparatory to both *The Merchant of Venice* and *As You Like It.* In *A Midsummer Night's Dream* the plot is set out by two marriage issues. In his first words, Theseus, Duke of Athens, announces his marriage with Hyppolita, the Amazon queen he has vanquished in battle, and voices his impatience for the expiration, in four days, of the old moon separating him from his solemn nuptials, which in his words "lingers my desires like to a stepdame or a dowager/Long withering out a young man's revenue". Through these words, evoking typical contemporary forms of delayed primogeniture inheritance, Theseus' dynastic marriage is described and desired as a due patrimony, while Hyppolita never expresses her personal inclinations. Just after the Duke's announcement, before him comes Egeus, who feels outraged by his daughter's rebellion to the marriage he has decided for her. While Hermia is in love with Lysander, Egeus has rather chosen Demetrius for her: though the two young men are socially equivalent, Egeus has sanctioned his alliance with Demetrius and insists on disposing of his daughter as of a patrimonial asset he is not prepared to relinquish. He asks Theseus to grant the observance of an ancient Athenian privilege : "as she is mine, I may dispose of her;/ Which shall be either to this gentleman/Or to her death, according to our law/Immediately provided in that case". Theseus confirms that the law is extant, although it allows one more choice for the daughter: besides complying with her father's will or dying, she may become a nun and relinquish the world. The father's absolute patrimonial powers are evident: the daughter is to obey or else be condemned to patrimonial and social non-existence, be it through death or a nunnery. Taking time for her decision, Hermia actually elopes with Lysander to reach a shelter through the forest, where strange magical adventures occurr, involving the couple, but also the pursuing Demetrius and his former love Helena, Hermia's best friend. Though caused by supernatural agents like Oberon and Puck, the magically-induced love shiftings in the forest expose the uncertainties of the elective or preferential couple, which appears unstable, though claiming its rights against the imperative patrimonial laws Egeus evokes.

In fact, throughout the play, not one couple appears steady and free from infidelities, even when free from magic manipulations: both Theseus and Hyppolita have a past of sexual experiences and betrayals, while Demetrius had already changed his inclinations before he and Lysander suddenly exchange their sexual drives in the forest. Ironically, if patrimonial violence appears heinous, natural or supernatural love instability mines individual choices. The same magic means which produce grotesque dissonance, in the end impose Demetrius' love for Helena and restore Lysander's original inclinations, but questions and doubts remain, though the two couples are happily reunited, after Demetrius renounces his claims on Hermia, leaving her free to marry Lysander. As Egeus' patrimonial demands are, thus, evaded, the parallel love pretences of Theseus also acquire a grotesque resonance. For his marriage celebrations, the Duke chooses a Pyramus and Thisbe play performed by artisans, who actually turn its famous story of love faithful to the point of death into comic parody: an ironic comment on aristocratic pretences of ceremony and display of symbolic absolute values. But in *As You Like It* this same love-to-death tradition is also evoked, to be ridiculed as preposterous by Rosalind, who works out with Orlando a far safer and more promising psychological basis for a couple.

The patrimonial aspects which start the plot of *A Midsummer Night's Dream* and mark throughout *The Merchant of Venice* and *As You like It*, are all closely connected with the deep and vast social change taking place in Shakespeare's England, as is well described by a Princeton scholar, Lawrence Stone, in different studies.[2] Curiously enough, though, these studies, which give proper background and meaning to a vast number of situations and details in Shakespeare's plays (both made more meaningful by and confirming such studies), have not so far been taken into consideration in main stream Shakespeare criticism.

By the end of the sixteenth and the beginning of the seventeenth century the economic and patrimonial problems, connected with a number of attendant questions, stand out prominent in English society, characterized by the decline of the aristocracy, which had lost its military function, and the parallel rise of a new gentry. The very first scene of *As You like It* opens indeed directly on a patrimonial rights quarrel, typical of what was happening in many aristocratic families, whose means were diminishing, the more so as Elizabeth had been most parsimonious in distributing privileges or gifts to the nobility. Young Orlando, the third son of Sir Rowland de Boys, complains with his faithful servant Adam about the insufficient allowance his father has bequeathed him in his will, amounting to "poor a thousand crowns", while charging his brother Oliver to breed him well. But Oliver, the male primogeniture heir, has chosen to

---

[2] Ranging from Lawrence Stone, *The Crisis of the Aristocracy 1558-1641* (Oxford: Clarendon Press, 1965), to Stone, *The Causes of the English Revolution 1529-1642* (London: Routledge, 1972), Stone, *Social Change and Revolution in England 1540-1640* (London: Longman, 1970) and Stone, *An Open Elite? England 1540-1880* (Oxford: Clarendon Press, 1984).

keep his second brother Jaques at school, while keeping Orlando, as he says, "rustically at home", denying him what he considers the proper education for a gentleman of his birth. This "mines my gentility with my education" Orlando later points out in revolt with his brother, claiming his personal rights. "The courtesy of nations allows you my better, in that you are the first-born" he protests, "but the same tradition takes not away my blood, were there twenty brothers betwixt us. I have as much of my father in me as you, albeit I confess your coming before me is nearer to his reverence". Orlando ends up exhacerbated, as he puts a wrestler's grip on Oliver, who decides soon after to get rid of him through a wrestler, daringly challenged by Orlando, or, failing this, to attempt with fire upon his life.

The double problem in Shakespeare's play – the younger brother's allowance and his education – testifies to what Lawrence Stone points out as a major patrimonial aspect in the contemporary dealings of the English landed elite:

> There was little to prevent most of the male children sliding out of it. [the landed élite] Generation after generation, younger sons were left to trickle downwards through the social system, with only some education, some money, and influential patronage to give them a head start in life. This situation is in striking contrast to that in most European countries, where economic primogeniture was not so rigidly practised, where younger sons retained titles of nobility and the legal privileges that went with them, and where status-enhancing offices in government service, and especially in the army, were more numerous and more easy to come by. (*An Open Elite?*, 5-6)

The problem was the outcome of the primogeniture and patrilineal descent laws and practices discussed by J.P. Cooper[3] and described by A.W.B. Simpson in *An Introduction to the History of the Land Law*.[4] These laws expressed

> the prime preoccupation of a wealthy English landed squire to contrive to preserve his family inheritance intact and to pass it to the next generation according to the principle of primogeniture in tail male. (*An Open Elite?*, 69-70)

It was, of course, desirable for the English squire to raise capital to provide for marriage portions for daughters and cash or land for younger sons in order to

---

[3] In "Patterns of Inheritance and Settlement by Great Landowners from the Fifteenth to the Eighteenth Centuries", in *Family and Inheritance*, eds. Jack Goody, Joan Thirsk, Edward Palmer Thompson (Cambridge: Cambridge University Press, 1976).
[4] Alfred W. Brian Simpson, *An Introduction to the History of the Land Law* (Oxford: Clarendon Press, 1961) 54-59.

give them a gentlemanly start in life. But preserving the patrimony and providing for the younger sons and daughters were to some extent in conflict with one another. A juridical remedy was sought for:

> The solution, which is technically known as "preferential partibility", was first to keep the seat and the bulk of the estates tied up more or less in perpetuity for transmission by male primogeniture; but second to leave some small properties, or new properties recently acquired, at the free disposal of the current owner; and also, if only once in a lifetime, to allow him to raise mortgages, cut down woods or convey property to trustees for a term of years, in order to pay off debts or provide cash money for daughters and younger sons. (*An Open Elite?*, 70)

But of course in periods of crisis, when means were being reduced, it became even more difficult to find an equitable solution for inheritance problems, and individuals were sacrified to the interests of the "house" or lineage:

> Since the continuity of the "house" – meaning the patrilinear family line – was the fundamental organizing principle [...] the prime object was to keep together the five component elements which made it up. The first was the seat, the family residence itself; the second was the land, which provided the income without which a seat could not even be lived in, much less maintained, repaired and embellished. If at all possible the main estates and the seat had therefore somehow to be kept together, The third was the family heirlooms which the seat contained [...], relics such as the family archives, portraits of ancestors, family plate and jewels [...]. The fourth was the family name [...] The fifth and last element which it was desirable but not essential, to keep attached to the seat, was the hereditary title, if the owner happened to have one. This might be difficult to achieve, since titles did not pass exactly like property. According to their letters patent, they normally descended in tail male from the first creation, while the seats might pass by will or settlement to a different male relative whose claims predated the title, or in tail general through a daughter or to another family altogether. (*An Open Elite?*, 72)

In Shakespeare's *As You Like It*, as we shall see, the distinction of these different elements becomes important as Orlando's and Oliver's story develops, while it appears most likely, though it is not stated, that the case of the three sons of Sir Rowland de Boys and of Orlando's disparagement must have been originated by their father's lack of means to provide for his third son, as he seems to have been anxious about him rather than wishing to discriminate against him. Indeed, Sir

Rowland had sided with the Duke Senior, whose usurper, Duke Frederick, certainly did not favour his house. This may explain the small allowance he had left Orlando, while recommending to Oliver Orlando's education at his last blessing before dying, as mentioned in the play, and a specific order of precedence seems to have been established, probably reflecting the father's will. Up to a point Oliver might not have been left much of a choice, as his final decisions too seem to suggest, when he confers upon Orlando some of his rights, not by dividing either the estate or the revenue, but by separating revenues and family seat (left to Orlando) from property and political status, wich he retains for himself and his prospective descendance. In fact, he seems to be, at the same time, tied by tradition or testamentary conditions, and free to decide upon the sharing out of the different components of his inheritage. As pointed out by Stone

> If the basic principle of inheritance was strongly preferential partibility with a bias towards primogeniture, the basic mechanism to enforce it was the entail, a deed which settled the succession of an estate inalienably upon the descendants of an individual owner, in a specifically described order of precedence. The legal instruments for implementing this arrangement varied over time, but in some way or another all turned the current owner into a tenant for life, a trustee for the transmission of the patrimony to ensuing generations. [...] For just over a hundred years, from 1540 to the 1650's current owners among the English landed elite enjoyed exceptional discretion in the disposal of their property. (*An Open Elite?*, 6-7).

This exceptional discretion, in the sense of no costriction to provide for all members of the family, is what both Oliver and his father seem to have used, the father leaving to his heir's discretion responsibility for his brothers, and Oliver spending more on Jaques than on Orlando, no legal tie restraining him from excluding a detested brother, whose outstanding qualities had roused his envy.[5]

The problem Shakespeare stages in *As You Like It* was in fact proving a serious one at the time. In the trial scene of *The Merchant of Venice*, as Mark

---

[5] Oliver has indeed enjoyed his rights of primogeniture according to common law and its "rules" or canons of descent, the third of which in particular provided that "where there are two or more males in equal degree, the eldest only shall inherit", as reported by Paul Clarkson and Clyde T. Warren, *The Law of Property in Shakespeare and the Elizabethan Drama* (New York: Gordian Press, 1968) 207. Yet, as Clarkson and Warren point out discussing *As You Like It* (Clarkson and Warren, *Law of Property* 1968, 282), Oliver should have given Orlando his education not only under the command of their father's will, but also "under the general principles of common law", while Orlando could claim the thousand crowns he is entitled to by his father's will only after reaching his majority of 21 years. Clarkson and Warren, though, do not discuss the two brothers' patrimonial issues beyond these last two observations: they consider only formal legal expressions and not patrimonial or legal problems.

Edwin Andrewes pointed out in his *Law versus Equity in "The Merchant of Venice"*, Shakespeare had already presented "a profound study of the greatest judicial problem of English jurisprudence which was at its controversial height", namely the common law versus equity issue, in raising which, as Daniel Kornstein allowed in his *Kill All the Lawyers? Shakespeare's Legal Appeal*, Shakespeare "may have influenced contemporary judges and changed the course of English legal history". Similarly in *As You Like It*, often considered by criticism a "light" pastoral drama, Shakespeare seems to show full awareness of another contemporary socio-juridical problem, which by the mid-seventeenth century would find a solution in a new juridical device called "the strict settlement". This

> enabled a landowner to tie the hands of his heir and turn him into a tenant for life. This was achieved by settling property upon trustees for contingent remainders, including those for children as yet unborn. The terms of the settlement preserved the patrimony for the eldest son of the marriage, or failing a son for the next or closest male relative; safeguarded the bride's jointure or pension if she became a widow; and garanteed adequate financial provision for any daughters or younger sons. [...] Younger sons were also given a garanteed share, at first outlying parts of the estate (usually only for the lives of themselves and their wives), in seventeenth century life annuities, or by the eighteenth century the same cash money as their sisters. [...] If renewed regularly, generation after generation, the strict settlement offered fair protection for the practice of primogeniture [...] By endowing younger sons with assured cash sums, it in theory made it rather easier for more of them to marry, although in practice this advantage was more than offset by the rising cost of education and launching on a career. (*An Open Elite?*, 73-74)

Whatever the degree of protection the strict settlement could provide for property held in primogeniture,[6] it was meant to solve the patrimonial question staged in the Orlando/Oliver quarrell, confirming both its existence and Shakespeare's denunciation. The education problem raised by Orlando was more crucial for the younger son than for the heir, as the former needed it more to get a start in life, while, as he needed a degree, he cost more than the elder son, who often dropped into a university or the Inns of Court only for a year or two.

As Oliver's hate forces Orlando to leave his family seat, followed by his faithful old servant Adam, the desperate situation of the cadet appears most evident. Orlando finds himself an outcast and can but accept Adam's offer of his

---

[6] Llyod Bonfield has actually questioned its effects in his study "Marriage Settlements and the Rise of Great Estates: the Demographic Aspect", *Economic History Review* XXXII (1979).

500 crowns, the savings of his long life (Adam is eighty), in order to survive. Though young and strong, Orlando has no prospect of an occupation or marriage, and could only become a highway man. No legal protection against arrest by creditors defended the younger sons of the nobility:

> there was almost no bottom to the pit of indigence into which a younger son of an English peer could fall. It is hardly surprising that in the eighteenth century it was widely believed – rightly or wrongly – that many highwaymen were younger sons with no alternative employment for their martial skills, and no aptitude or taste for more arduous occupations (*An Open Elite?*, 229)

The "highwayman solution" was certainly not an unknown practice by Shakespeare's times as well, if we think of Falstaff, the succesful character Queen Elizabeth appreciated so much, and of Orlando's own reaction in *As You Like It*, when Adam first proposes to him to flee from his brother's seat:

> What, wouldst thou have me go and beg my food,
> Or with a base and boist'rous sword enforce
> A thievish living on the common road?
> This I must do, or know not what to do;
> Yet this I will not do, do how I can. (II,3,31-35)

It also appears allusive that later Orlando, desperately in need of food, should try to assault the Duke Senior and his men in the forest, where they have taken refuge, just as a bandit would do, although the episode soon turns into a display of gentlemanly behaviour. On the one hand, the Duke Senior is ready to offer hospitality in spite of the villainous assault, on the other hand, Orlando, immediately repenting, happily receives badly needed help for both his starving old servant Adam and himself. Adam's case confirms the crisis of the old feudal order: after a long service at the de Boys seat, from the age of seventeen to that of eighty, he ends up with Oliver's malevolent appellation to him as "old dog", after which he prefers to offer poor Orlando both his life savings and his service, based on a sense of duty rather than on wages, as Orlando stresses in accepting both.

Orlando's patrimonial issue is finally solved as it is interwined with a second patrimonial rights question, denounced in the second scene of the play immediately following the initial Orlando/Oliver quarrel scene. This second issue involves the woman Orlando falls in love with, the female protagonist and actually the protagonist of the play, Rosalind, whom the well-known critic Harold Bloom has considered the most accomplished and attractive heroine in the Shakespearean canon.[7]

The Duke Senior's daughter, Rosalind, has remained at the usurper's court as the beloved friend and companion of Duke Frederick's daughter. She appears at once well aware of having been deprived of an estate, while her friend Celia tries to console her by offering her full equality out of reciprocal love. But, soon after, two important events change Rosalind's condition: as she meets Orlando, they fall in love, while Duke Frederick is soon driven by events to consider Rosalind, now of a marriageable age, a dangerous presence at court, and decides to banish her to prevent her from impinging on his own daughter's prestige and dynastic interests. But Celia chooses to share her destiny with Rosalind and organizes their joint flight into the forest, where Rosalind's father has found refuge with his best friends. Better to face the difficulties of their adventure, the two young women assume a different identity: Rosalind, dressed in male clothes, becomes Ganymede, while Celia changes her name into Aliena and pretends to be Ganymede's sister.

At the same time, Celia provides for their financial needs: while defiantly declaring "Let my father seek another heir" (I,3,95), she actually devises not only to be followed and helped by Touchstone, the court fool, but to get jewels and an amount of "wealth" (gold or cash money) along with her as a common share. More interestingly, as soon as the two girls in disguise have reached the forest, they find a good chance to buy a cottage, surrounded by pleasant olive trees, with pasture and a flock, and take on a shepherd, Corin, "mending his wages", as Celia/Aliena says, for running the pasture and flock. As she appreciates "the soil, the profit and this kind of life" (II,4,96), Celia/Aliena settles down in the cottage with Ganymede, but this never turns her or Rosalind into shepherds, nor the play into a real pastoral drama.

In fact, what we see is not pastoral activities, but a social transformation, which often took place with the younger children of the élite classes. Shakespeare is here facing another aspect of the contemporary socio-financial problems rather than imitating a minor literary tradition: under cover of a country setting, such as pastoral drama usually staged, he is actually dealing with a number of deep social changes, often connected with the younger children's inheritance restrictions already mentioned. Settling down as they do, the two disguised friends in *As You Like It,* though actually confined to the outskirts of the forest and not in a village, seem to allude to that so-called *parish gentry,* of which children of the landed elite could become part, as still retaining a gentry status, as they lived by rent in a country house, and maintained the primary original model of gentry life. But they were certainly in a position different from that of boh the titled aristocracy and the so-called *county gentry*:

---

[7] See Harold Bloom , *Shakespeare, the Invention of the Human* (London: Fourth Estate, 1999).

By the 1580's the gentry were drawing apart into two groups, definable in terms of economic resources, life-style, occupation and range of cultural interests and activities. The first, known to modern historians as the "parish gentry", were men whose interest and powers were limited to the boundaries of one or at most two villages, most of whom had had no education beyond that of the local grammar school, and who were rarely eligible for any administrative post above that of JP. [...] The second are known as the "county gentry", men of greater wealth, power and sophistication, who automatically laid claim to local political leadership, including membership in parliament, who enjoyed the benefits of higher education [...] These two groups lived in houses of different size and function, since they necessarily pursued different styles of life. The parish gentry entertained on a small scale, for short periods of time. (*An Open Elite?*, 6-7)

These Weberian models of ideal types are, of course, only indicative of different social scales and do not perfectly fit the situation described in the play, but they do well suggest one of the possible outcomes of the patrimonial changes we are discussing: Orlando's story and the Rosalind/Celia story so far illustrate two social outcomes of the patrimonial laws in the English social landscape we are considering.

The Rosalind-Orlando love story and the parallel formation of three other couples (a rustic one, Sylvius and Phebe, a mixed one, Touchstone and Audrey, and a second high class couple, formed by Celia and a "converted" Oliver), remain secondary from the point of view of the aspects here discussed, although central to the play. Yet they are partly brought to bear on the present main issue of patrimonial rights.

It is first of all noticeable that the two higher class couples are both formed on what could be called a "patrimonial equality" basis. Before Duke Frederick decides to renounce the Dukedom he has usurped and retire to a convent, both Orlando and Rosalind are deprived of personal means and depend respectively on the exiled Duke Senior and on Celia. This helps to explain why Orlando refrains from looking for Rosalind, although he has fallen in love with her, and ironically insists, like Ariosto's homonymous character, on disseminating the forest with love poems attached to tree trunks. It is only thanks to Rosalind's enterprising disguise and conduct that their acquaintance is carried on, providing a better basis for their ensuing union, which is then made possible by a double social recognition and consequently improved social prospects for both. While Rosalind, abandoning her disguise, is acknowledged as the daughter of the newly restored Duke Senior, and resumes her social and patrimonial status, Orlando as well is suddenly turned into an heir.

Choosing to marry Celia/Aliena, Oliver in fact decides to stay and live with her in the forest cottage she has bought, accepting the country life ideal it represents, and in so doing, as already anticipated, he bestows on Orlando certain rights: "My father's house and all the revenue that was old Sir Rowland's will I estate upon you and here live and die a shepherd" (V,2,10-12). "Shepherd" here means indeed "country gentleman", as Oliver will actually keep his "land and great allies" as later specified in V,4,188. This seems to imply a clear patrimonial partition between the two brothers: while Oliver will keep the property ("land"), the title and political status as signalled by the "great allies", honouring his role as male heir of his house, Orlando will enjoy the revenue of his brother's land and the family seat. The different elements of the landed elite's patrimony previously mentioned have been separated and arranged in order suitably to provide for the two marriages, without compromising the survival of the house, the estate and the rights of the future descendants. This way, up to a point, "patrimonial equality" in marriage has also been ensured, as Orlando will not depend on Rosalind, who on her own part is now a prospective heiress; while Oliver can share his title with Celia, but both share renunciation of inheritance, whether direct (Oliver's) or indirect (Celia's), through Duke Frederick's retirement. Here Shakespeare's plot confirms that

> It was normal to try to marry an heiress not to an impoverished younger son [...] but to an heir with equivalent or near equivalent property of hers. [...] The chances were consequently quite high that the man who inherited the seat and property would be a wealthy property owner in his own right. The fact that this could endanger the continuity of the ties of family to ancestral seat was something of which contemporaries became increasingly aware during the demographic crisis, but this consideration still weighed less than the overriding need to follow the rules and contract of wealthy marriage alliances.(*An Open Elite?*, 111)

Meanwhile, a degree of revolution in matrimonial rules has also taken place in *As You Like It*, as in Shakespeare's play no fathers but the children themselves dispose of their marriages, emphasizing the elective rather than the dynastic couple. Rosalind decides for herself, without consulting her father, in spite of the fact that she has found him, and her mock marriage with Orlando, officiated by Celia in IV,1,117-134, emphasizes her independence, as does her role in the forming of the other three couples in the play. Her father's consent, which she asks just at the start of the actual celebration, in V,4,6-7, seems only to stress the patrimonial implications. The Duke Senior's answer to the question "your Rosalind, will you bestow her on Orlando here?" is meaningful: "That would I, had I kingdoms to give with her"; and, analogously, Orlando's words confirm he is ready to marry Rosalind not unaware of possible patrimonial consequences:

"That would I, were I of all kingdoms king". Even when destitute of real status, these characters never lose sight of possible patrimonial questions, and, indeed, soon after the ceremony, both the Duke Senior and Orlando recover full social status and the marriages their attendant state and dynastic implications.

Hermia's revolt in *A Midsummer Night's Dream* has here been completed. Rosalind has asserted herself as the actual agent and, implicitly, juridical agent of her own marriage, although she then owns, with both her father and husband, that she is "yours" (V,4,115-6), thus recognizing a daughter's and a wife's dependence (Shakespeare could not overtly oppose contemporary legislation), but only after she has made her personal choices. In this sense, she fulfils Hermia's protest and improves on Portia's marriage. In *The Merchant of Venice* Portia's marriage with Bassanio is a love match, but it is made to coincide with the results of the test devised by Portia's father and his testamentary dispositions, and it is only through Bassanio's psychological attitude and specific words, after he has passed the test which entitles him to both Portia and her riches, that upon Portia is, in his words, conferred the right to choose about her own marriage. According to the will of Portia's father, Bassanio does not need to consult Portia, but he insists on doing so by resorting to juridical terms: "I come by note, to give and to receive [...] So stand I [...] as doubtful whether what I see be true/ Until confirmed, signed, ratified by you" (III,2,140 e 146-148). If the first two verbs, "to give" and "to receive", indicate reciprocity and equality within the couple, the close – emphasizing three verbs, "confirm, sign and ratify", as Portia's form of consent – suggests an implicit revolution in matrimonial transactions. This is not so much a play on words, as the posing of a juridical problem: Bassanio has received the woman from her father's will, the conditions of which he has fulfilled, but ignoring his right, he shifts the source of the contract from the father to the daughter. In fact he asks her – who will be the lawyer in the trial scene – to become the agent of her own marriage, and confers on her the right personally to decide what was usually left to men – father and future husband – to determine.

In *As You Like It* the "matrimonial revolution" suggested in *The Merchant of Venice* has emerged more evidently in the presence of the living father, and not unaware of the vast patrimonial responsibilities entailed: with the new elective or preferential couple, new individual rights, as opposed to mere dynastic rights, are being suggested or affirmed, new individual ownership rights are winning over the collective interests of the "house" and its descent. A new historical trend spreading from the gentry to aristocracy is here both announced and favoured. This is actually part of a vaster ideological change.

In the play a parallel contraposition between a corrupt court life and a better countrylife is established, although, at the same time, criticism of facile utopias is not spared by the melancholic commentary of one of the lords attending the Duke exiled in the forest. The renovation process which had started in *The*

Merchant of Venice is taken further in *As You Like It* along with a wider range of connected problems, and the later play could well be read as a manifesto of what Lawrence Stone calls "Country ideology".[8] This aspect, which cannot be dealt with here, would indeed confirm from another point of view the ideological debate and social change which have been evidenced through the patrimonial issues.

---

[8] See both Stone, *Crisis Aristocracy* 1965 and Stone, *Causes English Revolution* 1972.

Macbeth, or the Acquisition of Dominion[1]

Maurizio Pedrazza Gorlero

University of Verona

> ... but, for certain,
> He cannot buckle his distempered cause
> Within the belt of rule.
> Shakespeare, *Macbeth*, V, ii, 15-17

1. Introduction

In the context of this topic "Property Law in Renaissance Literature" "*Macbeth*, or the acquisition of dominion" demands, first of all, to outline its own boundaries. This paper presupposes, in fact, that political power assumes the status of property law, or at least that its acquisition and practice were also realised in accordance with modalities proper to such a juridical paradigm. This is closer to the truth in the feudal period in which the story of Macbeth is set more than it is at the time in which Shakespeare writes and, even more so, than the period of a contemporary constitutionalist. It is therefore necessary to ascertain what the juridical property is expressive of in relation to political power in the long span of time under consideration, in particular during the lifetime of the Shakespearean text, between the Renaissance and modernity.

We approach history with the same gaze as Benjamin's on Klee's *Angelus Novus*, "an angel that seems to be withdrawing from what is seized by our gaze". We also adopt this method according to which categories maintain their name while changing their content through time. These categories are observed in those elements according to which the phenomenon they describe endures as it renews itself, rather than by those elements capable of highlighting the characteristics of the period.

The text is analysed from the perspective of a constitutionalist, that is to say, of a modern scholar of the juridical forms of political power, specifically a scholar of positive law, a science that was born after the text under consideration, but, since its object is a form of power which is obeyed, therefore, "objectively consented" power, it is perhaps capable of extending before its birth, offering conceptual instruments useful for the understanding of phenomena that, once formalised in historical constitutions, will later give rise to constitutional law.

Among these phenomena is the constitution as the nature of the constitutive pact of the political group, which, like any rule superior to all others, concretises

---

[1] All quotations are from William Shakespeare, *Macbeth* (Milano: Garzanti, 1992), translated and edited by Nemi D'Agostino.

the diachronicity of the social bond, that is, the logical hypostasis to which its theoretical foundation might be traced back. Furthermore, there is the assumption in the constitution of juridical rationality as the founding element of the legitimisation of power: it is an alternation, in order to guarantee communal living, between being both exclusive and consensual. Therefore, much more than legitimisation as an "economy of dominion" to which it might lead, however, we should bear in mind that, following this theoretical model, it is different from the rationality of power aiming at its own result, in which the relationship between dominating and dominated is self-erasing, and is different from legitimisation aiming at dominion and the subordination of subjects, in particular the dominated subject, in such relationships.

The various methods of acquiring power in *Macbeth* will be considered in this study: from those more immediately connected to subjectivity and juridical property to those in which subjectivity and juridical property are converted into constitutive elements of modern States. The way in which property comes to be conceptually detached from power and the nation will be noted, although while not renouncing the fact of its influence on them through its metamorphosis in the "real value" of dominion and in its enduring economic dimension. The rationality of a juridically legitimised power, which constitutes the "embryonic matter" of a modern concept of constitution, will succeed the "unnatural" nature of absolute power devoid of legitimisation which constitutes the core of the tragedy. In conclusion, this paper will offer an insight into the actual separation between legitimisation and consensus and into those powers devoid of legitimisation that, in the organisation of "neo-feudal" political pluralism of and between nations, make the concept of power expressed in Macbeth actual and enduring.

2. Macbeth ... Thane of Glamis ... Thane of Cawdor

The heath is the place where Macbeth comes to know his fate as a man of power, where the three witches (...chorus, oracle, metaphysical artificers of a plan of dominion...) announce to him, the Thane of Glamis, that he will also be Thane of Cawdor and the future King. To Banquo, who enquires about himself, they say that he will not be a king, but the father of a king. Macbeth, in his incredulous repetition of the witches' prophesy to himself, says he is the Thane of Glamis because of the death of Sinel. In the previous scene, Duncan, king of Scotland, to the tale told by the noble Ross about the betrayal of Macdonald, Thane of Cawdor, exclaims: "No more that Thane of Cawdor shall deceive/ Our bosom interest. Go pronounce his present death/ And with his former title greet Macbeth"(I, ii, 66-68).

These are two methods of acquiring power that are typical of the feudal system of *Macbeth*. The first of these is that of hereditary succession from Sinel, who in the *Chronicle of England and Scotland* by Raphael Holinshed (1577), from which Shakespeare derived the historical data for his tragedy, also turns out to be Macbeth's father. The second method is that of a title bestowed directly by the sovereign, following the revocation of the title established as the sanction for the betrayal of the *fidelitas* of the previous Thane of Cawdor, and decreed even before his death-sentence. However, the definition of the first method as hereditary succession of the feud and of the title and the second method as assignment of a title and of a feud, that is the acquisition of power bound to dignity and goodness according to property law, could be lenient and perhaps incorrectly concise.

In reality we cannot venture into the feudal system using juridical and patrimonial categories from the Renaissance and modernity. What will later be called the feudal society is, in fact, a constellation of relationships between the king and his *fideles* which change in time and in space, a constellation that converges in the "trading" bond between royal *fidelitas* and the *beneficium* of the *vassi*. Such a *beneficium* is first granted in a compulsory form and then in a regal form, and after the change of exigencies of organisation of royal power, it becomes more and more absorbent not only of the *fidelitas* but also of the *officium*, according to which the central and local functions of the government are divided. This will lead to the point at which, as in the *Capitolare Carisiacum* (877), the substantial transmission to the heirs of great feudal benefits, whose *fidelitas* is to be taken either for granted or imposed by the sovereign, will be permitted.

It is impossible to say, in conclusion, that feudal – and more widely patrimonial – power is a political power in the sense in which we understand it in modern times. The instrumentality of territorial power aiming at the total care of the interests of the human group contained therein is absent from the "association between feuds" which constitutes the feudal regime, as it is absent, after all, in any feud. The power acquired by royal decree through the bestowal of goods ((*cessio bonorum*)) or of royal rights on these goods, which are the feud and the feudatories' prerogatives, serves only for the defence of these rights and goods. It is not by chance that constitutionalist literature does not make use of the concept of the "form of the State" to describe a reality in which the relationships between feudatories and the king are of a contractual nature, whereas the relationships between the feudatory and the feud are of a patrimonial nature. Rather, this literature makes use of the term "juridical organisation with a patrimonial structure", in which, moreover, the negation of the political dimension surfacing there is compensated by the asserted "authority" of the patrimonial bond.

3. Malcolm ... Prince of Cumberland

"We will establish our estate upon/ Our eldest, Malcolm, whom we name hereafter/ The Prince of Cumberland"(I, iv, 38-40). With these words Duncan chooses the moment in which the value and the *fidelitas* of his followers have granted him the victory against Sweno, king of Norway, and the cohesion of the kingdom seems renewed and strengthened so as to be sealed by the designation of the eldest son for succession in regal dignity. This is a method of acquiring royal power conditioned in the future by Malcolm who acquires, as sign of the investiture, the title of Prince of Cumberland. Moreover, this is also a method of assigning royal power that will also be conditioned in the future by Duncan. The fact that it is a son who is invested in the succession to dominion as a king repeats the private institution of inheritance, and therefore the transmission of goods and rights following the scheme of succession by *mortis causa*.

Even at the highest level, the methods of acquiring and exercising power are therefore those typical of patrimonial rights, including primogeniture that, not unlike – *mutatis mutandis* – testamentary succession, has a tendency towards avoiding the fragmentation of the dominion and the bellicose conflicts that might follow in order to reassemble the "limbs" of the kingdom. The designation of Duncan is therefore demanded – if this oxymoron can be granted – by the objective preoccupation to preserve the consistency and the stability of power once it is left devoid of royal guidance. It can be added that such a designation is reinforced by the convergence of two different titles of succession, which Hobbes called hereditary passage by express words, which does not necessarily refer to sons and relatives but whomever a man will declare should succeed them in their State, and transmission by presumption of natural affection, enforced when precise instructions were lacking, such as a will or a custom, since it is believed that men are more inclined to promote their own sons, rather than somebody else's sons. The convergence of these two titles introduces, therefore, a real dynastic succession that in the Middle Ages as well as in the Renaissance seems to better realise, out of the different kinds of succession of political power, the economy of dominion which does not choose – but rather mediates – between loss and appropriation.

This is a form of rationalisation of power that has the function of legitimating the law and which will endure in politico-constitutional history, opening a passage from the succession of sovereigns to the divided sovereign, that is – in the period of contractualism, of popular sovereignty, of political representation, and of interests in the exercise of power – to the reversible and bloodless succession of the political order of government/opposition. The sovereign accepts contradiction of being his own opposite in order to duplicate himself into something other than himself and to invest the "other" with the weight of his own death, giving rise to the two bodies of the king that still characterise the constitutional assets of governmental relationships in Western democracies.

4. Macbeth's 'royal hope'

The "royal hope" prophesised by the witches to the amazed Macbeth and later nourished by excited disbelief in the dialogue with Banquo introduces a period of preparation for Macbeth's enthronement that is characterised by a lucidity of political analysis, by a preoccupation with the "initial legitimisation" in the acquisition of the Crown, and by a perception of the absoluteness of the power aspired to. It is true that the thought of murder infringes such a legitimisation, but it is also true that being the legitimate Thane of Cawdor seems to him, not only in the prophesy of the witches but also in the questions he asks himself, not different from becoming the king of Scotland. If the former is true and good, why is the latter not true and evil? The power is the same, neither good nor evil. Only legitimisation makes it appear either way. Macbeth immediately perceives the threat of Malcolm's designation: "The Prince of Cumberland! That is a step/ On which I must fall down, or else o'erleap, / For in my way it lies"(I, iv, 49-51). He neither hesitates nor opposes himself to Lady Macbeth's announcement that Duncan will not see the sun or to her offer to complete the task. The declaration of his ambition balances the meditation on the double betrayal of Duncan's trust, of whom he is both a relative and a subject. Even Lady Macbeth says that the power Macbeth aspires to is absolute power, the power of Shakespeare's time rather than that of a medieval king: "you shall put/ This night's great business into my dispatch, / Which shall to all our nights and days to come/ Give solely sovereign sway and masterdom" (I, v, 65-68). Macbeth himself is aware of this, and his doubts are nourished by his loyalty to the king and also by the uncertainty of the success of the plot to kill him and, above all, by the sinister presage that absolute power, without the limits of exercise and legitimisation, requires the constant replication of acts of acquisition. "If the assassination/ Could trammel up the consequence, and catch/ With his surcease success – that but this blow/ Might be the be-all and the end-all! – here, / But here, upon this bank and shoal of time, / We'd jump the life to come" (I, vii, 2-7). Macbeth wants absolute power, but he fears such a plan, and the defect of legitimisation for the acquisition of power and the commitment to maintain it with only the strength that it creates, even if he imposes it to everybody. The exercise of power, to his eyes, will be based on the fiction of a legitimate acquisition, but in the end, in order to solve any doubt, it will only be a representation. Duncan will appear to have been murdered by the knives of his own drunken servants, who will perish under the strokes of Macbeth, unable to withhold his frenzy after seeing the noble Duncan beaten to death in his own house.

5. Lady Macbeth

In the *Chronicles*, in which we find all the characters of the historical events, Lady Macbeth, perhaps the central character of the bloody metaphor of power presented by Shakespeare, is dismissed in a few lines as the wife spurring Macbeth to attempt the deed, since she was very ambitious, burnt by an inexhaustible desire to bear the name of Queen.

Various hypotheses and interpretations have been offered about the Lady Macbeth of the play, all insisting on a separation between the characters, roles and actions of the couple in their common ambition. Interpretations drawing from Milton identify Lady Macbeth as a double of the biblical archetype of Eve and Lilith. Lady Macbeth represents irresistible temptation, boundless determination and fundamental unscrupulousness in the acquisition of absolute power, to which Macbeth also aspires, while dreading the lack of legitimisation and, even before this, fearing the failure of the deed.

The fact that it is a woman who triggers the action of the man at a time in which women were above all absent in the exercise of political power, allowed the projection onto Lady Macbeth of the social perception of the instability of power of Elizabeth Tudor, the sexless and heirless queen, whose absolute power, confined within her persona and her lifetime, anticipates a future of anguished uncertainty. This is an uncertainty that, witnessing the various upheavals that we find in the history of the event, will be annulled by the Stuarts, who are the Stewards in the *Chronicles*, and the seed of Fleance, the son of Banquo who fled from the assassins hired by Macbeth. The same circumstance legitimises feminist interpretations which, following the presumption that political power was of masculine concern, identify in the unsexing invoked by Lady Macbeth, no different from that of Elizabeth Tudor, the unnatural sign of the abandonment of femininity to achieve political ambitions. In Lady Macbeth's case, somnambulism and madness will follow, in order to underline the impossibility of surviving a role of power in a society willing to return to the normality of male power.

Lady Macbeth's character suggests to a constitutionalist, that is a scholar of rational forms of power and, therefore, of the phenomenon of power and of its juridical legitimisation, a still different juridical interpretation, which accompanies, without exclusion, those interpretations already mentioned and various others that have been proposed. Lady Macbeth and the king constitute an organic wholeness. Rather than being complementary in the aim they set for themselves, they seem inseparable in the phenomenon they represent. This is a unitary phenomenon since it entails both political power and its juridical legitimisation, that is to say, both the way of acquisition and the initial legitimisation, the methods of exercising power and the "subsequent legitimisation", that could replicate the initial one and/or could derive from a

Macbeth, or the Acquisition of Dominion 111

consented obedience by acts of strength, again repeating the initial one. In this respect, a quick mention of the *Chronicles* and the invocation of Lady Macbeth of the denaturalising of her own sex should be considered as elements of continuity and of mutual identification between the two characters or, it would be better to say, as two different sides of the same character.

6. The King and Lady Macbeth

King Macbeth *solus* understands, as we have seen, and not only represents, absolute power. He experiences the desire for it, the ambition that nourishes it and the burden of the legitimisation of its acquisition and of its preservation. He falters, however, in its direct, "original", and self-legitimating acquisition, which is capable of absolving the very method of the acquisition itself. Macbeth appreciates the dimensions of absolute power, but he fails to perceive the freedom from the bonds of legitimisation at the moment of acquisition. He misunderstands the subsequent legitimisation which cannot depend on the method in which power is attained and even less on the method in which it is exercised. In other words, King Macbeth *solus* is a prisoner of the initial act of legitimisation that refers to the subsequent one and prevents him from understanding that such a legitimisation cannot subsist only in the continuation or in the simulacra of the initial one, but should rely on (autonomous) reasons for spontaneous obedience to his absolute power.

Lady Macbeth *sola* represents absolute power at the moment of its acquisition, both because she enunciates its emancipation from any bond, stating that the ambition to achieve it can be fed on disloyalty, evil and cruelty, and because she frees the acquisition from any initial legitimisation. Thus, it is not difficult for her to highlight the contradiction of Macbeth who legitimately wants a power that does not belong to him: "wouldst not play false, / And yet wouldst wrongly win" (I, v, 19-20). What Lady Macbeth seems not to be worrying about is that the subsequent legitimisation of the power could be realised by the same means of the initial self-legitimisation, that is, by disloyalty, evil and the cruelty by which it was originally acquired. Lady Macbeth is convinced that dominion can be maintained in the same way as it was acquired; while King Macbeth fears to acquire a power that demands to be maintained in the same way that it was obtained. When Lady Macbeth asks him: "Why do you keep alone... Using those thoughts which should indeed have died/ With them they think on? Things without all remedy/ Should be without regard; what's done is done", King Macbeth answers: "We have scorched the snake, not killed it; / She'll close and be herself, whilst our poor malice/ Remains in danger of her former tooth"(III, ii, 8-15). It is not a coincidence that the provisional integration of the concept of power that the Macbeths agree upon has no restraint on the means of acquisition provided that it is acquired, apparently, legitimately. "Will it not be received, / When we have marked with blood those sleepy two/ Of his own chamber, and used their very daggers, / That they have done't"(I, vii, 74-77). In this way, Macbeth becomes the legitimate King of Scotland by parental succession of Duncan, following the assassination, by having Malcolm fled to England, and with the subsequent assignment of the title of Scone.

7. King Macbeth, the tyrant

From now on a difficult balance between subsequent legitimisation by continuation of the initial one and legitimisation by imposition of obedience through acts of command begins. The tragedy will in fact be marked by the progressive unveiling of simulation, and by the necessity of killing those who come to know the truth. The killing of the murderous servants raises questions that put Macbeth in an awkward position. Banquo proposes an enquiry, and Duncan's sons, feeling under threat, shelter in England and in Ireland. Their flight, in Macbeth's words to Banquo, suggests parricide and Banquo begins to look like the real enemy, since it was him that the prophesy of the witches had foretold as the father of a line of kings: "For them the gracious Duncan have I murdered... To make them kings, the seeds of Banquo kings! / Rather than so, come fate into the list/ And champion me to the utterance!"(III, i, 65, 69-71). Fate pushes the sword into Banquo's throat but spares Fleance, the son. Macbeth's "visible madness" begins here. In the same way in which murder and simulation sustained him, a ghost legitimises him, sitting on his own throne. The king who restores sanity seems insane. In the presence of a reassuring and forgiving Lady Macbeth the first crisis of the subsequent legitimisation emerges. Macbeth cannot complete the acts validating the initial legitimisation and perceives the burden of a legitimisation founded entirely upon the use of strength. Macbeth does not fear the living Fleance, but the dead Banquo. "But now they rise again/ With twenty mortal murders on their crowns, / And push us from our stools. This is more strange / Than such a murder is."(III, iv, 79-82). The final collapse of the initial legitimisation coincides with the final unmasking by Lennox who, at the end of the exposition of the real story of Macbeth's accession to the throne, calls him a tyrant.

In fact, Macbeth's behaviour corresponds to the behaviour of those that, in juridical doctrine, from Bartolo to Bodin, qualify the king as tyrant *ex defectu tituli*, that is, for having usurped power. In this regard, the issue is not how he governs, even if he governs well, but that he is a usurper. If the king governed badly, against the law and the subjects, although with a legitimate title, he would be tyrant *ex parte esercitii*. Macbeth is both these kinds since the defect in the initial legitimisation causes him to fall into a series of murders that make a tyrant of him, in addition to the way in which he exercises his absolute power.

The end of the tragedy displays an exchange of "conceptual roles" between King and Lady Macbeth in the definition of absolute power. Lady Macbeth, who represents self-legitimising power which perpetuates itself in the very same way that it was originally conquered, ["What need we fear/ who knows it, when none can call our power to ac-/compt?" (V, i, 36-38)], slips into madness and commits suicide, proving that power cannot subsist without legitimisation. It is as if this category has collapsed from within, failing before it is even applied. King Macbeth, on the contrary, as a disciple of legitimisation until the moment in which his betrayal is revealed, begins to experiment on Lady Macbeth's concept of power. As if he did not want to obtain a different form of legitimisation, he maintains power through acts of strength that repeat the initial usurpation. "Those he commands move only in command, / Nothing in love. Now does he feel his title/ Hang loose about him like a giant's robe/ Upon a dwarfish thief"(V, ii, 19-22).

Power devoid of legitimisation, both in its concept and in its application, collapses even before being halted by the armies of Malcolm, the legitimate king. This power is unnatural, like an act perpetrated by a man who was not born from a woman and like Birnam wood descending on the castle of Dunsinane.

8. Macbeth and the moderns

Macbeth represents the tragedy of absolute power devoid of legitimisation on the verge of a period that, in the history of juridical and political thought, will be marked by the birth of contractualism. Contractualism is a doctrine that explains the origin of society through a contract according to which any individual surrenders his strength on condition of reciprocity, authorising the king to apply such strength to the preservation of the right to life for everyone and to the preservation of the welfare of the political body. Power subsists and is realised in its juridical legitimisation, and its legitimisation, conversely, is realised in consensus as the rational measure of the latter. At the root of these phenomena lies a paradigm, the contractual one, in which the exchange of obligations has a structurally consensual foundation.

The modern nation develops with such a constitutional armour – or, if you prefer, with the "material" constitution of a power which is legitimately held and exercised since it is freely obeyed and consented to. Property, which, as we have seen, characterises the methods of acquiring dominion in feudal times, becomes the territoriality of a political power that, in its turn, loses its personal dimension in favour of sovereignty as a national element. Even if there are people like

Laband who believe that a nation has a patrimonial right to its territory, a preferable and prevailing opinion is that proposed by Romano, according to which the nation's right is a right to the constitutive elements of its own person. Once property is removed from a concept of political power, it still bears witness to its connection with dominion, and thus property represents the economic measure and the "real value" of dominion. These relationships, therefore, are not interrupted; they are only placed in a different environment represented by the pressure exercised by private interests on public power. Such pressure is made possible and insidious by an inner organisation that, in a constitutional view and in the respect of the rights of private individuals, moves almost without any restraint of legitimisation. Power, juridical legitimisation, and consensus will maintain their causal relationship until the most recent stage of constitutional nations in the 18th and 19th centuries, in which the juridical concept of constitution, which became "formal constitution", improves even further as the supreme juridical rule of political power, a juridical rule which is consecrated by a solemn pact and which animates popular sovereignty through its political representation, through its interests, and through the principle connected to majority; a rule that guarantees the fundamental rights of the citizens by means of equality and of the division of power. At the stage of development into a bourgeois nation the constitution does not need any juridical defences since the constituent is the same legislator: the "flexible" constitution, that is, modifiable by ordinary laws, is thus guaranteed by the very same use of the procedure by subjects themselves. In the following historical stage of multi-class nations, the constitution will become "rigid", thus, it will be juridically guaranteed by the aggravations of the process of amendment and, above all, by the control of the constitutional legitimacy of laws, which diminishes the effectiveness of those anti-constitutional laws that the legislator, who is no longer the constituent, might introduce into the legal system.

However, the fact that we have reached a concept in which political power is legally legitimised and in which consensus represents the rational measure of such a legitimisation, does not mean that this is an identification without residues of power in sovereignty. A circular reasoning, in which power is not fully realised in the law and in its norms and, therefore, can change only according to its prescriptions, does not seem persuasive. This is both because power upheavals are almost always realised against the norms of power itself and because a "revolutionary fact" is normative not only in the same way as the instituted system, but, through a repealing or invalidating efficacy of this system, even of the one it replaced, within which, even if it is neither contemplated nor abstractedly considered as illegitimate, it assumes the juridical qualification of the condition capable of invalidating it.

This happens, after all, even without the breaking up of the system, when, in the case of rigid constitution, the power of revision is "legally" exercised in forms that are different from those normally prescribed. In fact, the normative decision of the majority, which introduces a derogation of the constitutional revision, is nothing but a manifestation of "constituent power". Therefore, a portion of sovereignty remains impossible to legitimate juridically and is anchored to a modern concept of sovereignty in the minimum amount represented by consensus. The sequence of legitimisation-consensus is turned upside-down and consensus becomes the decisional factor of legitimisation.

9. The seed of Macbeth

Consensus can be an element of legitimisation since in the convention of the birth of political obligation it has a contractual nature, and, therefore, it can be said that juridical legitimisation implies consensus and that consensus presumes the juridical legitimisation of dominion. We have already testified to a disparity in the ambit of such a correspondence, but this disparity can increase greatly when consensus is granted unwillingly. It is not necessary to think of the techniques of propaganda of totalitarian or authoritarian regimes: it would be enough to bear in mind the diffusion of politico-oligarchical practices of appropriation of mass communication media, the limitations of freedom to which professional categories of information are subjected because of editorial ownership, and the coincidence between the informative and political roles of the owners of information society, to ascertain how much the disparity between consensus and legitimisation is increasing and how it is difficult to contain such a shifting of consensus when the informative power that generates it is exercised freely in an area that is not that of public power, but that of civil society.

Moreover, within economic enterprise it is difficult – or perhaps impossible – to apply the isomorphic matrix of democracy (equality, freedom, representation, majority) that is capable of contrasting the diminishing of the guarantee for the citizen in respect to sovereign power, when the latter, in virtue of political, institutional, and territorial pluralism is left to the use of collective subjects (territorial organisations, association, etc.). Let us imagine that those who represent one of these modern "collective principles", within which the rules of inner democracy do not apply, were attributed the guidance of politico-institutional power, so that in this way a form of authoritarian democracy is realised. This would be a democracy that subordinates to consensus the very same separation of powers that, to begin with article XVIII of the Declaration of Human Rights and of the Rights of the Citizens in 1789, characterises, in accordance with the welfare of fundamental rights, the concept of constitution. Those who apply the law, and should be subject only to this law, are submitted to the consensus that brings representation to life. The same consensus supports and restrains the legislator and the judge in a constitutional horizon in which the principle of consensus comes to absorb the principle of legality.

Alongside situations of consensus devoid of legitimisation, in other words the contrary of Macbeth's usurpation, situations of power devoid of legitimisation can subsist both outside and inside the national assemblage. "Global" economic and financial powers belong to the first group: for example, the power intrinsic in capital power that is constantly moving in search of better marketing conditions and which influences the economic and value politics of nations, as well as the living conditions of their citizens, without being dominated politically. However, these powers, to which interests not susceptible to representation correspond, are governed through their "entrustment" to representatives. Political representation in this way satisfies unrepresentable interests on the grounds of an irrational extension of the consensus beyond a representative relation which structurally is a relationship between representatives of representable interests. We seem to hear once again a far echo of La Boèthie's "voluntary servitude".

The phenomena of self-representation of interests belong to the second type. In these, the interests that are representable *per se* are self-represented through the representatives who subordinate proceedings and wilful acts to a corporate interest that has become their own and that is valued as a general interest: for example, laws that receive the negotiation of social parts. Thus, the interest and the rule of a group become the interest and the rule of a community.

There are, moreover, from a different perspective, partial entrustments of sovereign power to super-national associations in virtue of which, although in the presence of constitutional clauses of self-limitation of sovereignty, citizens are subject to powers not directly consented to. This is, for example, the case of the democratic *deficit* of the European Community. Finally, there are economic and military powers which rely on those powers that employ them even if legal rights do not have any value in legitimising and disciplining their relationships. This echoes Hobbes who places the relationship between nations as lying beyond the nation itself, in the *bellum omnium contra omnes*,.

How could we not see the seed of Macbeth, which was believed to be sterile, in such manifestations of the modern tyranny of consensus devoid of legitimisation, of power devoid of consensus, and of power devoid of juridical legitimisation? The words of Caithness about Macbeth come to mind: "but, for certain/ He cannot buckle his distempered cause/ Within the belt of rule"(V, ii, 14-16).

Patrilineal Law and the Plays of Ben Jonson

Richard Allen Cave

University of London, Royal Holloway College

A focus on patrilineal law allows one to take a look at the plays of Ben Jonson from a new perspective, opening up completely fresh insights respecting their artistry. What astonishes is the extent to which his major comedies turn on issues relating to patrilineal law, lineage, primogeniture and inheritance. At a first glance these might appear to be deployed as little more than useful plot devices to develop or resolve the narrative. The new perspective, however, endows them with a weight of importance, which would doubtless have registered profoundly with many of his first spectators or readers, for whom patrilines were crucial matters, often of pressing urgency.

It is worthwhile momentarily looking again at aspects of Jonson's own life in this context. Nothing is known of his birth father, who died in Jonson's infancy; his mother remarried beneath her social status (or so Jonson would have us believe from his comments on the subject) to a bricklayer who apprenticed the young Jonson to the trade to his later mortification. He quickly began to gather surrogate fathers such as Camden, his master at Westminster School, and later the many learned, usually aristocratic patrons who fostered his career, such as Lord Pembroke, who gave Jonson a regular New Year gift of some £20 to spend on books thus furnishing the poet-dramatist with one of the finest private libraries at the time in England. These were men for whom a patrimony was to be seen not simply as material effects but as the garnering, sustaining and handing on of cultural and intellectual habits. Throughout Jonson's middle years, he suffered the deaths of his various children, starting with the infant Benjamin, who died of plague aged seven in 1603 and was the subject of one of Jonson's most haunting epigrams (XLV); numerous fine elegies were called forth his imagination by the deaths of children, such as Salomon Pavey, the boy actor. Jonson was to die without an heir; his only remaining legitimate son predeceased him by some twenty months. As earlier he had gathered honorary fathers, so now he collected honorary sons, the famous Tribe of Ben, younger poets and playwrights who were his *literary* heirs. If lineage is to be deemed a celebration of sons as mirror images of the father, then here were eminent reflections of Jonson's intellect and artistry. (Sir Lucius Cary addressed a verse epistle to Jonson, which named him as his "noble father".) Circumstance required Jonson to devise his own patriline. Dramatists are not lawyers and can therefore indulge such flights of rhetorical fancy, but noticeably the eminent with their own private concerns for inherited patrimony and lineage were more than content to play his game.

Playwrights, unlike legal practitioners, theorists and philosophers, do not write treatises, so we do not get from Jonson extended statements outlining his thoughts on patrilineal issues. Instead dramatists reflect the impact of such issues as they affect the quality of everyday living. This is the case with Jonson's comedies. Dramatists tend to work between theoretical lines: within the gaps, the silences, the omissions, the exceptions, out of which in the real world, of course, legal cases are created. The focus in the plays is on the human consequences of legal theory: the anxieties involved in safeguarding the patrimony to pass on to one's heirs; the worry of protecting the patriline from the risks attendant on poor marriages or adultery (on the wife's part); the problems where there is no direct line (where the sole heir is female, where the heir has not yet reached his or her majority so requires a fit guardian to protect the patrimony); the vexed matter of cultural and often legal prejudice directed against minors, bastards and women; and the difficulty of determining a precise relation between a dowry and the patrimony. All these issues feature as the motor for Jonson's plotting and as stimulus to his characterisation. Let us turn to some examples.

Unlike Shakespeare, Jonson was not interested in romance, courtship and marriage, but in pragmatic, material conditions of living. Anxiety became a thematic focus from his first play that owned a distinctive personal voice, *Every Man In His Humour* (1598), where the majority of the male characters are anxious about their masculinity and what precisely constitutes a *gentleman*. The play opens with Old Kno'well worrying about his son Edward because he delights in practising poetry "that fruitless and unprofitable art". Stephen, his nephew, appears hoping to borrow a book on hawking and hunting:

> I have bought me a hawk, and a hood, and bells and all; I lack nothing but a book to keep it by. [...] Nay, look you now, you are angry, uncle: why you know, an' a man have not skill in the hawking, and hunting-languages nowadays, I'll not give a rush for him. [...] 'Slid a gentleman mun show himself like a gentleman.[1]

---

[1] Ben Jonson, *Every Man In His Humour*, ed. Martin Seymour-Smith, The New Mermaids (London: A. & C. Black, 1988): 9-10 (I.i.34-6, 38-40, 48). It is a major problem for all Jonsonian scholars that there is still no major critical edition in modernised spelling of his collected plays to which all references may be made. The edition of the *Works* edited by Herford and the Simpsons for the Clarendon Press at Oxford is not readily accessible; moreover, the texts reproduce early modern spelling and punctuation. The editions used for this and subsequent references are single volumes within larger series of edited renaissance playtexts. Wherever possible, I have used the text contained within the New Mermaids series.

Old Kno'well is terse in his disgust: "You are a prodigal, absurd coxcomb" and he justifies the choice of the word 'prodigal' by advising Stephen not to waste his little means afforded by his modest income by casting away money on a buzzard! He admonishes him to have some respect for himself:

> But moderate your expenses now, at first,
> As you may keep the same proportion still.
> Nor, stand so much on your gentility,
> Which is an airy, and mere borrowed thing,
> From dead men's dust, and bones: and none of yours
> Except you make, or hold it.[2]

He is here appealing to Stephen's sense of lineage, stressing the importance of respecting the patriline as his only in *trust*. If Old Kno'well's tone is harsh and extreme, the reason for that is revealed within seconds when they are interrupted by a servant who is suitably deferential: "Save you, gentlemen". This provokes a surprising outburst from Stephen:

> Nay, we do' not stand much on our gentility, friend; yet, you are welcome, and I assure you, mine uncle here is a man of a thousand a year, Middlesex land: he has but one son in all the world, I am his next heir, at the common law, Master Stephen, as simple as I stand here, if my cousin die – as there's hope he will – I have a pretty living o' my own too, beside, hard by here.[3]

Characteristically, Jonson offers us here some sound financial facts, but links them too to legal possibilities and all in the context of inheritance. Patrilineal procedures upheld by law might, were Edward to die, invest all Kno'well's carefully husbanded wealth in the hands of the nephew he dismisses as a peremptory ass. This short sequence informs spectators of the reason for Old Kno'well's scrupulous watching over his son's habits: what initially appeared as absurd behaviour has been given credible motivation with the arrival of Stephen. Old Kno'well's fear is for the future of the patriline and the proper use of the patrimony.

In case we miss the point, Jonson a short while later in this opening act introduces the character of Cob, a water-seller of the lowliest status. 'Cob' in Jacobean parlance carries a punning reference to herrings, the king of fish.

---

[2] Jonson, *Every Man*, 11 (I.i.81-86).
[3] Jonson, *Every Man*, 11 (I.i.88-94).

Asked about his home by a passer-by, he replies: "I and my lineage ha' kept a poor house, here, in our days".[4] When his reference to his lineage gets a hearty laugh, Cob is hurt to the quick and stoutly defends his position:

> The first red herring, that was broiled in Adam and Eve's kitchen, do I fetch my pedigree from, by the Harrots' [heralds'] books. His Cob, was my great-great-mighty-great grandfather.[5]

Even so common a man as Cob has respect for his patriline as source of his personal dignity, taking offence when that lineage is called into question. The joke here is typically ambiguous: it establishes the absurdity of Cob's fixation, but it also looks teasingly at the equally absurd details of a family's former history on which aristocratic heraldry often draws for its emblems. Much of comedy in the ensuing play springs from Jonson's depiction of the ways in which upwardly mobile, would-be gentlemen fall short of the mark, proving themselves *not* the real thing. Jonson teaches his audience how to read the organising thematic principle of his play by two sequences which relate directly to patrilines: the genuine gentleman who fears for the dilution of his line and the dispersal of his patrimony in the hands of a fool; and the upstart clown who vaunts a bogus lineage of his own quaint devising.

The satire here is gentle compared with that of the later comedies, which is altogether darker. The play, which effected a transition in tone, was Jonson's first extant tragedy, *Sejanus* (1603). The date of the work carries some significance: it was the year when Queen Elizabeth died leaving no natural heir to the throne; for many months negotiations had been pursued to establish James, the Scottish king, as the next English monarch. But James was not a universally popular choice and from the turn of the century the Privy Council, Parliament, the court and much of the country had experienced a deep anxiety on political grounds. As if responding to that anxiety Jonson took as his subject Tiberius' reign in ancient Rome and the wish of the emperor's favourite, Sejanus, to influence the succession.[6] Drusus, Tiberius' son, is seen early in the action to be a particular source of envy and hatred in Sejanus, particularly after Drusus insults and shames the favourite in public. Plotting revenge, Sejanus suborns a court lackey, Eudemus, to cajole Drusus' wife, Livia, to join him in poisoning her husband. The murder is accomplished and we as audience have had a fine

---

[4] Jonson, *Every Man*, 22 (I.iii.6-7).
[5] Jonson, *Every Man*, 23 (I.iii.13-16).
[6] Just how acute the anxiety was at the time may be gleaned from the fact that Jonson was apparently summoned before the Privy Council respecting the play on suspicion of seditious intent. This may have occurred because, according to Jonson, the audience, growing restive, attacked the theatre and the actors with the same violence that (within the play) the mob finally metes out to Sejanus in his fall.

demonstration of how Sejanus achieves his objectives through the manipulation of others, whom he deploys and despises as his tools. The irony is that he (unlike the audience) never realises the extent to which he is similarly being used by Tiberius to further his ends. (The play is an incisive and penetrating essay in Machiavellian politics.) Tiberius knows who is the instigator of the event but allows it to go unpunished and unexamined, since Drusus was highly popular and Tiberius wishes for no rival to his eminence. The whole play turns on a central scene, a kind of seduction, in which Sejanus endeavours to manipulate Tiberius into granting him permission to marry the widow, Livia. Were Tiberius to agree to the match, it would virtually establish Sejanus as heir apparent. Tiberius' response to the request is intricate and subtly designed to both flatter and confuse Sejanus' hopes:

> Canst thou believe that Livia, first the wife
> To Caius Caesar, then my Drusus, now
> Will be contented to grow old with thee,
> Born but a private gentleman of Rome,
> And raise thee with her loss, if not her shame?
> Or say that I should wish it, canst thou think
> The senate, or the people (who have seen
> Her brother, father, and our ancestors,
> In highest place of empire) will endure it?
> The state thou hold'st already, is in talk;
> Men murmur at thy greatness; and the nobles
> Stick not, in public, to upbraid thy climbing
> Above our father's favours, or thy scale:
> And dare accuse me, from their hate to thee.
> Be wise, dear friend. We would not hide these things,
> For friendship's dear respect: Nor will we stand
> Adverse to thine, or Livia's designments.
> What we have purposed to thee, in our thought,
> And with what near degrees of love to bind thee,
> And make thee equal to us; for the present,
> We will forbear to speak. Only thus much
> Believe, our loved Sejanus, we not know
> That height in blood or honour, which thy virtue
> And mind to us, may not aspire with merit.
> And this we'll publish on all watch'd occasion
> The senate or the people shall present.[7]

---

[7] Ben Jonson, *Sejanus his Fall*, ed. Whitney French Bolton, The New Mermaids (London: Ernest Benn, 1966) III.ii.551-576.

Sejanus replies with gratitude that this advice has restored him to his senses and yet Tiberius is playing with his favourite, intimating vague promises but proffering nothing beyond the stern insistence that he should know and keep to his place in the social hierarchy. The moment Sejanus leaves him, Tiberius begins to plot to invite Macro, Sejanus' great enemy, to come to Rome the better to keep Sejanus under control. Tiberius leaves for Capri; he abandons the nest of vipers to watch while they destroy each other; he is seemingly indifferent and yet he is absolute architect and controller of everyone's fate in Rome. Sejanus is valued as a useful tool to conserve Tiberius' power until he aspires to establish himself through marriage within the dominant patriline; then he is ruthlessly ousted for his presumption. Tiberius will himself decide his own heir, since the choice will be a demonstration of his absolute rule. Though the play rigorously examines political process, the continual focus of that process is the imperial succession, furthering and protecting the line that derives from Augustus.

In *Volpone* (1606), Jonson's next comedy, a far blacker satire deriving from aspects of patrilineal law is to be found than was evident in *Every Man In His Humour*. The titular hero is a fabulously wealthy Venetian patrician, but there is a thorn in his content:

> I have no wife, no parent, child, ally,
> To give my substance to; but whom I make
> Must be my heir.[8]

He has hit on a scheme to aggrandise his wealth: with the help of his parasite, Mosca, he gives out that he is dying and is contemplating a suitable heir to his fortune. Suitors bring wealth as gifts in hope of attracting wealth by being named Volpone's heir; they compete to outdo each other's generosity. The main force of the comedy focuses on the lengths to which people will go for material gain when spurred on by greed; the circumstantial detail through which this theme is defined and sustained is worth close attention.

Volpone and Mosca's ruse has been in operation for some time before the action commences and the competition between the suitors is now fierce: just how far can they go to win Volpone's favour? Corbaccio, an elderly man in his dotage, prompted by Mosca, agrees to name Volpone his own heir, thereby disinheriting his son and true heir, Bonario (though his hope is to outlive Volpone and thereby eventually to multiply the benefits to his son's patrimony). But the interim means to this end involves declaring Bonario a "stranger to his blood"[9] or, in plain words, a bastard. Corvino meanwhile, an exceedingly jealous husband, is persuaded that the only means of bringing an almost defunct

---

[8] Ben Jonson, *Volpone*, ed. Philip Brockbank, The New Mermaids (London: Ernest Benn, 1968)17 (I.i.73-75).
[9] Jonson, *Volpone*, 70 (III.ii.45).

Volpone back from the grave is to let him sleep with Corvino's warmly nubile wife, Celia. When Celia protests, Corvino instructs her: "Go to! Show yourself /Obedient and a wife".[10] Corbaccio and Corvino in time are even prepared to justify their actions publicly with no sense of shame. Their attempts at unmanning themselves are fortunately thwarted because Volpone overplays his hand and becomes hoist with his own petard. He decides to gloat over the horror his suitors would experience, were none of them to be named his heir, despite all their efforts. He possesses a number of blank wills and inscribes Mosca's name on one, dresses him in robes appropriate to a clarissimo, disguises himself as a servant and watches the discomfiture of the dispossessed. The upshot of all this is that he in turn ironically finds himself dispossessed: dressed as a patrician, armed with the will and in full possession of the keys to Volpone's palazzo (which Volpone has all too eagerly quit to continue mocking his foolish gulls around the streets of the city), Mosca is in absolute control of the situation and the patrimony, which the Venetian court upholds as indubitably his in accordance with patrilineal law. His name is enshrined in the will:

> So now I have the keys and am possess'd.
> Since he will needs be dead before his time,
> I'll bury him or gain by him. I am his heir,
> And so will keep me, till he share at least.[11]

Volpone has nothing now beyond the assumed clothes he stands up in. Refusing to let a servant get the better of him, Volpone reveals all in court, preferring to suffer punishment rather than the humiliation of Mosca's triumph. The tricksters and their gulls are assigned sentences: Corbaccio is declared senile and incapable and the Avocatori agree to "possess /Thy son of all thy state";[12] Corvino is to be displayed along the canals in a fool's garb, then is ordered to make a proper restitution to Celia:

> ...to expiate
> Thy wrongs done to thy wife, thou art to send her
> Home, to her father, with her dowry trebled.[13]

So Bonario comes into his patrimony and Celia is divorced and rendered a tempting prospect for a second husband. Attempts within the comedy to play games with patrilineal law are mercilessly punished and the status quo is firmly restored; but the play has demonstrated the ease with which greed might

---

[10] Jonson, *Volpone*, 81 (III.vii.30-31).
[11] Jonson, *Volpone*, 138 (V.v.12-15).
[12] Jonson, *Volpone*, 154 (V.xii.129-130).
[13] Jonson, *Volpone*, 155 (V.xii. 142-144).

undermine the principles shaping that law. *Volpone* is a dark fantasy and an admonitory warning about the need to respect the seriousness of patrilines and the defined status of father, wife and son within the proper operation of the laws of lineage and inheritance.

That the whole intricate plotting of *Epicoene* (1609) is motivated by a contested lineage is not revealed until the last minutes of playing time. This surprisingly late revelation is not bad craftsmanship on Jonson's part but his way of stressing the seriousness of the issue and the devious lengths to which an heir (Dauphine) may go to safeguard what he sees as his rights. Dauphine's uncle, the elderly Morose decides despite his age and years of bachelordom to take a wife but a woman who must be a silent, dutiful model of femininity. She is to be a presence in his life and his household but one that he firmly marginalizes by robbing her of her voice. But once she is wed, Epicoene, the chosen bride, proves to be loud, vigorous and aggressively controlling. She fills the house with feasting, dancing and carousing till Morose is prepared to do anything to go back to his simple, quiet and above all *single* life. He is even prepared to declare himself impotent in public, if that will serve to gain his freedom from what he deems the plague of matrimony ("...this is worst of all worst worsts that hell could have devised! Marry a whore and so much noise!").[14] At this point Dauphine reveals his hand, promising to free his uncle of his misery. Before he will agree to show him how he will accomplish this, he reminds Morose of a particular aspect of their past relations:

> You know I have long been a suitor to you, uncle, that out of your estate, which is fifteen hundred a year, you would allow me but five hundred during life, and assure the rest upon me after; to which I have often, by myself and friends, tendered you a writing to sign, which you would never consent or incline to.[15]

Dauphine has been heir *in potentia* but has sought a modicum of security in the quality of his living and assurance of a will in his favour. Marriage to Epicoene might result in a child in the direct line, which would disinherit him entirely. Morose agrees to comply with his nephew's wishes and so be rid of Epicoene; and the sheer extent of his desperation is evident in the legal precision of his response:

> My whole estate is thine; manage it, I will become thy ward. [...] Where is the writing? I will seal to it, that, or to a blank, and write thine own conditions. [...] Come nephew, give me the pen; I will

---

[14] Ben Jonson, *Epicoene,* ed. Edward Partridge (New Haven & London: Yale University Press, 1971) 167 (V.iv.132-134).
[15] Jonson, *Epicoene*, 168 (V.iv.158-162).

subscribe to anything, and seal to what thou wilt, for my deliverance. Thou art my restorer. Here, I deliver it thee as my deed. If there be a word in it lacking, or writ with false orthography, I protest before God I will not take the advantage.[16]

Dauphine effects Morose's release by stripping Epicoene virtually naked to reveal that "she" is in fact a boy dressed in women's clothes and a wig. The moment is shocking, but it is a brilliant intellectual conceit to hoodwink his uncle and win him his future security. He needed to preserve an absolute secrecy to succeed in the trick (from the other characters in the play and from the audience).

Jonson is drawing on two popular tropes here: the man who marries a seemingly submissive woman only to discover she is a termagant or a shrew; and the man who is tricked into marrying a boy who has been dressed up as a girl. Traditionally in treatments of the second plot, which goes back at least as far as Plautus in *Casina*, the audience is let in on the hoax from the start. Jonson, however, manipulates both these plots, artfully leading his audience to suppose until this climax that they are watching a variation of the first trope, when in fact they are being shown a cunningly disguised version of the second. Dauphine has needed to exploit levels of Machiavellian duplicity if he, being of the collateral line, is to come into possession of the patrimony and the ease and social status that accompany its acquisition. Patrimony will afford him the means to be a gentleman. But one is left questioning: is it *gentlemanly* to behave as Dauphine does? His dismissal of Morose from the stage and from the action is chilling:

> Now you may go in and rest; be as private as you will, sir. I'll not trouble you till you trouble me with your funeral, which I care not how soon it come.[17]

If patrimony is in part to be understood as including the culture that accompanies wealth, has Dauphine's ruthlessness not devalued both him and his inheritance? His heartlessness has opened up an unbridgeable gap between wealth and worth. 'Dauphine' may denote in its French connotations a princely title, but in common Elizabethan and Jacobean usage it was a term for a hawk, a bird of prey.

The early years of the Stuart regime had seen Jonson create a whole new genre of theatre: the Court Masque. Staging these had introduced him to numerous aristocratic young women who were the performers in many of these events. Perhaps as a consequence of this, the female roles in his comedies steadily grew in size and importance; and a new awareness of women's

---

[16] Jonson, *Epicoene*, 168-169 (V.iv.155, 168-169, 176-180).
[17] Jonson, *Epicoene*, 169 (V.iv.191-193).

predicaments within the complex structures of patrilineal law seems to have provoked a developing focus on such subject matter in his later plays. He had observed the dangers of enforced dynastic marriages where a couple were often affianced long before they were capable of amatory or sexual feelings, as in the case of Frances Howard, or where the spouses were not intellectually and culturally compatible, as was the case of Elizabeth Cary or Mary, Lady Wroth. The two plays with which I wish to conclude take traditional expectations of the woman's part fiercely to task.

The Devil Is An Ass (1616) poses a real challenge for audiences. We initially watch a boorish husband, Fitzdotterel, accept the gift of an ostentatiously expensive cloak (we are twice informed it cost fifty pounds) from a total stranger, Wittipol, in return for allowing the latter an hour's passionate conversation with his wife, Frances Fitzdotterel. This comes uneasily close, as we watch the scene, to a kind of prostitution; Frances tries to object, but Fitzdotterel insists she be obedient to his decision. Wittipol's ardour and charm are utterly seductive. As the play develops, a spectator is torn between wanting Frances and Wittipol to form the alliance that is conventionally the goal of romantic comedy and the uncomfortable perception that for such an ending to come about either adultery or Fitzdotterel's death has to occur. One's sympathies desire the romantic solution but intellectually one knows that such an outcome in this context is ethically questionable. Frances and Wittipol spend much of the early acts of the play trying in vain to be alone together. When finally they manage such an intimate moment, Frances stops dead in its tracks Wittipol's flow of passionate speech with an urgent request:

> 'Tis counsel that I want, and honest aids:
> And in this name I need you for a friend!
> Never in any other; for his ill
> Must not make me, sir, worse.[18]

Wittipol like the audience knows that Fitzdotterel is being gulled by a bevy of sharks, projectors and lawyers, who are devising absurd inventions which they claim Fitzdotterel may patent and make a mint of money. Meantime they are relieving him of more and more of his income in recompense for their financial advice and are trying to get him to name one of them as feoffee of his estate (in modern terms, this would grant the individual power of attorney over Fitzdotterel's financial affairs). Seduced by the chimera of their promises of unparalleled wealth, he has virtually agreed to this but has still to insert a precise name in the deed. What then motivates Frances to seek out Wittipol is sheer fear:

---

[18] Ben Jonson, *The Devil Is An Ass*, ed. Peter Happe, The Revels Plays (Manchester & New York: Manchester University Press, 1994) p. 187 (IV.vi.25-28).

> ...I am a woman
> That cannot speak more wretchedness of myself
> Than you can read; match'd to a mass of folly,
> That every day makes haste to his own ruin;
> The wealthy portion that I brought him, spent;
> And, through my friends' neglect, no jointure made me.[19]

She indeed stands as she imagines on a precipice. A jointure, usually part of the dowry transactions, would make provision for Frances in the event of divorce or widowhood. Not only is her husband giving away his patrimony, he is rendering her destitute too. Wittipol is being asked to demonstrate the depth of his feelings for Frances by protecting her financial security. His passion must manifest itself as calculated pragmatism; and indeed he uses all his ingenuity to frustrate the sharks and safeguard husband and wife's futures. His thanks from Fitzdotterel is not the expression of gratitude that one might expect, but an outburst of horror at the extent to which the situation and Wittipol's controlling power within it compromises his lineage and the honour due to his patrilines:

> Oh!
> What will the ghost of my wise grandfather,
> My learned father, with my worshipful mother,
> Think of me now, that left me in this world
> In state to be their heir? that am become
> A cuckold, and an ass, and my wife's ward.[20]

Here the patrimony is beset by so much depravity and duplicity that it requires the cunning of a Machiavelli on Wittipol's part to protect virtue. He has to resort to the same devices as the sharks in order to outdo them and so keep control of the situation and the property that is at stake. The patrimony and the dowry in this play are seen as socially necessary but dangerous in the degree to which they render the possessor vulnerable to the unscrupulous. As the devil of the play's title who observes the action opines in shock: "Hell is a grammar school to this!"[21] *The Devil Is An Ass* is a real test of an audience's ethical acumen and powers of discrimination.

A more remarkable document still concerning the anxieties attending patrilineal law is *The Magnetic Lady* (1632). Here the heir is a daughter, Placentia; father and mother died in her infancy; the patrimony will be hers as a dowry if she marries with the consent of her aunt, Lady Lodestone. The money has, however, been under the guardianship of an uncle, Sir Moth Interest, who

---

[19] Jonson, *The Devil*, 187 (IV.vi.18-23).
[20] Jonson, *The Devil*, 193 (IV.vii.73-78).
[21] Jonson, *The Devil*, 179 (IV.iv.170-171).

has diligently augmented the bequest but plans to hand over only the original capital sum while retaining the acquired interest himself. The innovation in this comedy and the characters in whom the greatest dramatic energy is centred are a group of lower class women: the aunt's companion, Polish; a nurse; and a midwife. Whenever she appears in a scene Polish, despite her low-class status, confidently takes centre stage. She provokes uneasiness for her want of decorum; but it is not clear why she should. When a conflict breaks out between the three women, we learn that Polish with the others as accomplices, exchanged her own young daughter for the real Placentia, who is now the waiting woman, Pleasance. Polish's confidence springs from her knowledge that her lowly daughter is soon to be a lady of leisure and great estate. The terms on which the three women eventually make up their quarrel are worth studying:

> Come, come be friends: and keep these women-matters,
> Smock-secrets to our selves, in our own verge.
> We shall mar all, if once we ope the mysteries
> O' the tiring-house and tell what's done within.[22]

The three women embody the worst masculinist fear that underlies so masculinist a creation as patrilineal laws: the power that women have at the moment of childbirth, when men were traditionally marginalised from the delivery. Women at that moment in time have control over the succession, of determining the heir; their power resides in the mysteries of the childbed, their "smock-secrets", but could have longer-term repercussions. One might read the plot in which Pleasance's true identity and status are revealed as another example of the popular romantic trope of the lost child found; but that would not have necessitated the amount of stage time devoted to the female trio from below stairs. Cradle-exchanges along with bastardy and adultery compromised the sustaining of the true patriline and the family honour. The women are, however, overheard and Polish's attempt at achieving greatness is frustrated

One could argue of this discovery, that the trio of unruly women has been contained by the play's masculinist conclusion, that they are known and judged and their energies defused. But endings are rarely in Jonson's dramas simple resolutions: they are often deliberately problematised. The conclusions to *The Devil Is An Ass* and to *Epicoene*, discussed above, are characteristic. Volpone may be assigned prison and a dire physical punishment but at the moment that the character is to be led from the stage, the actor bursts out of the action, his energy renewed, to speak a short epilogue requesting the audience's applause:

> The seasoning of a play, is the applause.

---

[22] Ben Jonson, *The Magnetick Lady* in *Works*, ed. C.H.Herford, Percy & Evelyn Simpson, Volume VI (Oxford: Clarendon Press, 1938) 574 (IV.vii.40-43). I have modernised the spelling but retained the editors' punctuation.

> Now, though the Fox be punished by the laws,
> He yet doth hope, there is no suffering due,
> For any fact, which he hath done 'gainst you;
> If there be, censure him; here he, doubtful, stands:
> If not, fare jovially, and clap your hands.[23]

Earlier in the scene to recover his power over Mosca, Volpone has "uncased": that is, he has shed his servant's disguise to reveal himself as the patrician he rightly is. Now the performer is required to "uncase" a second time to reveal the actor who is impersonating the role. But what exactly are we being asked to applaud: Volpone's deviousness or the actor's artistry? Spectators generally laugh at this test of how alert they are to the devices of trickery, which the play has explored. Yet to applaud the acting, as spectators are like to do, is to recognise somewhat uncomfortably that acting has been Volpone's consummate device to win wealth. Acting, the very stuff of theatre, is here being seriously and severely problematised, since this means of staging the epilogue makes us forcefully aware how readily a medium of entertainment may be appropriated by capitalist energies and directed at ends for which that medium was not designed. And what of that word, "jovially"? The surface meaning is intended as "genially", but there are overtones to the usage that clearly invite the interpretation, "god-like" (Jove being king of the classical pantheon of deities). Indeed the audience have, like the gods, overseen all, heard all; and that Olympian insight carries with it the burden of judgement. Which of the two potential meanings of the word, "jovially", will we choose to apply? Equally perplexing is the figure of Face in *The Alchemist*. One can deploy only a term like "figure" to describe him, since throughout the action he is continually reappearing in new disguises (as Lungs, the alchemical assistant; a fairy pageboy; a wide-boy with the skill to outdo a couple of seasoned criminal types; and finally as Jeremy, the butler of the household in which the play is situated). He is an endless shape-shifter and, though he is seen to be the brains behind the elaborate con-tricks, which occupy the action of the play, he contrives to go wholly unpunished at the close. His brilliance may be disarming but it is also deeply disturbing: does he possess a "self", an identity, and where might it reside? None of the conclusions to these earlier plays is "easy".

The unruly women in *The Magnetic Lady* may be frustrated but that moment has to be set within the larger dramatic context of the ending, where the real heiress falls into the hands of a character, Compass, who, though he is designated a professional mathematician, is in reality a superb strategist. Compass can read people's characters astutely and has manipulated situations throughout the play in which the various suitors to the heiress's hand are shown to be preposterously inadequate as potential husbands. Ultimately it is he who

---

[23] Jonson, *Volpone*, 155 (V.xii.152-157).

weds the heiress as the one who has publicly restored to her her proper identity and status. But his artful contriving to expose the weaknesses of others is merciless and leaves spectators ultimately with the impression that Compass is less the ideal spouse than a shrewd opportunist. Inheritance in this play is a bane, since it provokes nearly everyone to evil. Masculine modes of wrongdoing and folly are all the stuff of earlier forms of city comedy as practised by Jonson, Middleton and their peers; feminine modes of malpractice are unusual and attract attention in this play because they have not hitherto been subjects for dramatic treatment. Both sexes within the action are condemned for their appetite for fortune-hunting; both put the patriline in jeopardy.

The birthing process was a point of vulnerability in being a locus of feminine power and agency in the otherwise carefully (one might write, tightly) contained and policed patriarchal construct, which is patrilineal law. Characteristically Jonson's eager intelligence detected it and made that vulnerability a source of dramatic enquiry. Was Jonson trying in this play to exorcise a female demon from the patriarchal homestead; or, after subjecting the concept of patrilines to repeated and rigorous analysis, had he begun to find such elaborate provisions surrounding birthright comic, even absurd? His own career had demonstrated how one could transcend the limitations of one's origins and a tragically high incidence of child mortality respecting his direct heirs. Jonson had his surrogate fathers and his honourable tribe of sons; neither brought him the risks and unceasing anxieties involved in promoting and safeguarding a patriline.

Person and Property in Thomas Middleton's *A Chaste Maid in Cheapside*

Daniela Carpi

University of Verona

1. Person and personhood

According to Margaret Jane Radin's[1] "personality theory of property", property is strictly linked to development of self and to a person's growth, to conceptions of freedom and of individualism. This idea upholds the interrelationship between the law and the cultural implications of property. Indeed, the relationship between property and personhood has always been taken for granted by the law. Nonetheless, the existence of laws regulating property relates to our judgement and evaluation of the justice or injustice of property itself. According to Grozio, all things were originally *res nullius*; it was men in society who, through an agreement, brought about the division of things. As such, things came under the power of men. A total power of disposition was drawn from this, which in turn provided the basis for derivative acquisition from persons whose title was directly or indirectly based on the natural foundation of the original division by agreement.

In a civil society, protection of individual property interests lies at the base of its economic organization. Property and contracts, the security of acquisitions and of business are the field dealt most extensively with by the philosophy of law[2].

If someone is particularly linked to a specific property, this does not however mean that it must be judged as belonging to that person, if that would be immoral. Indeed, theories of natural law are intertwined with economic and metaphysical theories. The latter took shape from the conceptions of Kant relative to the inviolability of man's individual personality, and were strengthened by Hegel's theories stating that property makes individual personal will objective. All this then converges in the theory of *res extra commercium*.

An immediate literary example could by the "pound of flesh" "purchased" by Shylock as a bond for the monetary loan. Shylock considers the pound as personal property since Antonio is no longer solvent. However, such property is

---

[1] Margaret Jane Radin, *Reinterpreting Property* (Chicago and London: The University of Chicago Press, 1993).
[2] See Roscoe Pound, *An Introduction to the Philosophy of Law* (New Haven: Yale University Press, 1954), chapter "Property".

immoral inasmuch as it would bring about the death of the signee, thus it becomes property "inconsistent with personhood or healthy constitution". Hence, where in *Dr. Faustus* Mephistopheles is particularly linked to the property of the soul, upon which his success depends as emissary of Beelzebub, such property does not arouse "moral consensus" and is thus not legally valid.[3]

Both Hegel and Kant maintained that property is necessary to give individuals fulfillment: man must have control over some number of objects in order to feel "at home" in the world. This element emerges clearly in the figure of Shylock who identifies himself as an individual in society inasmuch as he is the possessor of money and gold coins; so much so, that the definitive means for eliminating him, both as an autonomous individual and as a race, is precisely the expropriation of his money, confiscated by the state of Venice. Liberal property theory indeed states that property is strictly linked to individuality and freedom.

From this perspective, the young men fighting against their elderly relatives, or more generally speaking the younger generations against the older ones, in Thomas Middleton's "city comedies of London life", can be considered, yes, a conflict to acquire riches, but also a quest for becoming individuals plugged into society, a ritual of maturation.

> Things that we see as mostly 'outside' can also, at the same time, be seen as partly 'inside' –can become, to some extent, assimilated to the attributes of the person.[4]

The need therefore arises for a procedure that establishes the good or bad implications in the relationship between people and things. Radin places strong emphasis on the fact that the strict relationship between people and things indicates a desire for stability, just as property highlights a reaching towards "being in the world"; on the contrary, a contract indicates mutability and circulation. Consider, for example, the character the Portia in *The Merchant of Venice*: the choosing of a casket conditions her life in the future, thus development of her person and being in society depends upon her connection to one of her belongings. Ergo, her "personhood" is strictly linked to an object of property.

Changing of the cultural context determines change in the concept of property: if during the Renaissance daughters were considered the property first of their fathers and then of their husbands, this also determined into what hands fell the management of property. As such, crimes of carnal violence against young girls became crimes of property damage for the fathers or husbands who "possessed" them: their property wealth, contextualized as the virginity of their

---

[3] See Daniela Carpi, "Validità/invalidità del contratto in *Doctor Faustus* di Christopher Marlowe", *Variis Linguis* (Verona: Fiorini, 2004).
[4] Radin, *Reinterpreting* 1993, 10.

daughters used as exchange merchandise for movements of class and money within society, was diminished.

Traditional liberal theory placed in property ideology (ownership) the aspect of connectedness, and in contract ideology (exchange) the aspect of separability. But because traditional property ideology makes freedom of alienation through contract an essential characteristic of property, the whole ideological system tends towards commodification.[5]

The term "commodity" recurs in many Shakespearean texts specifically to highlight the idea that the society described in his plays is fundamentally based on relationships of transaction (think of how Greenblatt bases his theoretical/ideological construction precisely on terms such as "circulation", "energy", "self-fashioning", etc.). Marital property enters violently into these economic exchange relations, because through the combination of marriages, property wealth is allowed to circulate within society.

2. "Crimes against persons and crimes against property"

Locke advocates absolute inviolability of private property even more so than inviolability of human life (*Two Treatises of Government*, II, SS18; 19; 182).[6]

Fichte (S 19.I; *The Science of Rights*, 1796-97) doesn't hesitate to refer to Roman law and to the law of the twelve tables which authorized robbery and murder of thieves.

Hegel instead makes an accurate distinction between violence against persons and against property. Nevertheless, property too is an expression of a person's will. All crimes must be judged and punished based on their qualitative and quantitative characteristics.[7] Life and property cannot assimilate each other. *The Philosophy of Right* also refers to Shylock when denouncing the "horrible law" contained in the twelve tables that allows a creditor, after lapse of a fixed term, to kill a debtor or sell him into slavery, or even cut him to pieces.

Hegel   PR: § 98
    In so far as the infringement of the right is only an injury to a possession or to something which exists externally, it is a *malum* or

---

[5] Radin, *Reinterpreting* 1993, 31.
[6] John Locke, *Two Treatises of Government*, ed. Peter Laslett (Cambridge: Cambridge University Press, 1963).
[7] See Georg Wilhelm Friedrich Hegel, *Le filosofie del diritto*, ed. Domenico Losurdo (Milano: Leonardo, 1989) 132.

damage to some kind of property or asset. The annulling of the infringement, so far as the infringement is productive of damage, is the satisfaction given in a civil suit, i.e. compensation for the wrong done, so far as any such compensation can be found...
...Apropos of such satisfaction, the universal character of the damage, i.e. its value, must here again take place of its specific qualitative character in cases where the damage done amounts to destruction and is quite irreparable[8]

These declarations of Hegel's perfectly suit the case of Shylock. Shylock suffered property damage because the money he lent Antonio was lost with destruction of the ships. Hence, the pound of flesh requested as bond corresponds to the "qualitative character" of the thing. Nonetheless, demanding payment of a pound of flesh corresponds with asking for Antonio's life and thus, according to Hegel, the compensation exceeds the damage. However, the compensation asked of Shylock for his infringement in making an attempt on the life of a Venetian citizen once again exceeds the infringement, inasmuch as confiscation of Shylock's property corresponds to his social death: the character's means of support is killed. If he exists socially as a person thanks to his property wealth for which he cares so much (the concept of "personhood"), then Shylock is stripped of his social identity. Added to this is the loss of his daughter, whom he considered his personal property: it is a dual social death. As I have expressed in other settings, the "mercy"[9] so strongly invoked in the text is not applied at all in the case of Shylock.

3. "Violation of will"

Hegel: (§ 95)
The initial act of coercion as an exercise of force by the free agent, an exercise of force which infringes the existence of freedom in its concrete sense, infringes the right as right

The plots in which the youth in Middleton's comedies attempt to take their tutor's assets for themselves become crime in that there is an attempt to force the will of another person. If property as such serves to connote the social person, the "crime" against property, the deception perpetrated against property becomes not just a quantitative infringement (the amount being extorted) but a qualitative

---

[8] Georg Wilhelm Friedrich Hegel, *The Philosophy of Right*, trans. Thomas Malcolm Knox (Chicago - London - Toronto: William Bentos Publisher, Encyclopaedia Britannica Inc., 1952) 37.
[9] Daniela Carpi, "L'atto dell'interpretazione in *The Merchant of Venice*", *The Merchant of Venice, dal testo alla scena*, ed. Mariangela Tempera (Bologna: Clueb, 1994).

Person and Property in Thomas Middleton's A Chaste Maid in Cheapside 135

one (infringing upon the person as such). There is infringement upon "The subjective element of the will, with its particular content –welfare, is reflected into itself and so stands related to the universal element, to the principle of the will" (P.45).

> In fraud, rights are still recognized, and the other is given the impression that no injustice whatsoever will befall him; the principle for which the rights of others must be respected is not denied.
> It is one of the most prominent maxims of our time to enter a plea for the so-called "moral" intention behind wrong actions and to imagine bad men with well-meaning hearts, i.e. hearts willing their own welfare and perhaps that of others also. This doctrine is rooted in the "benevolence" (guten Herzens) of pre-Kantian philosophers. (p.45, &125)

Indeed, the frauds that the youth perpetrate against the elders in Middleton's city comedies appear legal. The youngsters find contorted means of robbing their relatives of their property, but they are seemingly legal means.

In regard to private property, Hegel asks whether or not it is legitimate to fill the gap created between those who have and those who have not: is it legitimate for Middleton's youths, impatient to manage their own economic independence, to force the hand of their "forefathers" in order to satisfy their own needs? "An intention of my own well-being... cannot justify an illegal action" (PR. § 126).

> My particularity, however, like that of others, is only a right at all in so far as I am a free entity. Therefore it may not make claims for itself in contradiction to this its substantive basis, and an intention to secure my welfare or that of others (and it is particularly in this latter case that such an intention is called "moral") cannot justify an action which is wrong. (P.45)

The youths' "moral" intention to act in the name of an elusive "retributive justice", redistributing the wealth accumulated by few who had little need for it given their age, is a "thing of fortuity, arbitrary, of one's own specific decision" (L 1824-5: § 125 AL). There is a collision between well-being and the law.

According to Hegel, crime is any coercion through which the principle of will is attacked and the law is violated inasmuch as it is law. (Hegel, L1817-8; § 45; PR:§§ 95-6)), and if "that which is mine is attacked, denied in such a way that, if I allowed it, I would not lose just my property, the universal element of my existence", then the frauds attempted against the "elders" in Middleton's comedies infringe upon the law as law, the universal element of free will. There is an attempt to infringe upon the will of the subject, forcing him to make monetary concessions he would never want to make. Will is infringed upon in its determination.

The attempt at fraud infringes upon social stability, which is based on the right to property; it infringes upon personal will, which cannot be forced by coercion. The crime of deceiving of a defective mind is triggered off, because the will of another person is forced through construction of false images of goodness, love, loyalty, and disinterestdness. There is moreover a desire to force state laws, which base commercial relations on free exchange.

In that crime, the law itself is denied, as well as the specific will of the other. This is an infinite negative judgement. Though Hegel claims that in fraud there is no infringement on the law of will, I feel that forcing the will of the "elders" means giving a false illusion of free will, in that will itself is unduly influenced and artfully deviated.

4. "Property as separation from nature"

In *Two Treatises of Government and other political writings*, John Locke states:

> From all which it is evident that, though the things of Nature are given in common, yet Man (by being....master of himself, and Proprietor of his own Person, and the actions or Labour of it) had still in himself the great Foundation of Property, and that which made up the great part of what he applied to the support or comfort of his being, when Invention and Arts had improved the conveniencies of life, was perfectly his own, and did not belong in common to others[10]
>
> Thus Labour, in the Beginning, gave a right of Property, where-ever any one was pleased to imploy it, upon what was common" (p.341)

In this way, Locke explains the birth of private property, which basically separates what God gave as a whole, meaning nature and the earth. Hence, private property arises almost as an Edenic sin of loss and separation: man is separated from an indiscriminate common good based on "things really useful to the life of Man" for things such as "...Gold, Silver and Diamonds...things that Fancy or Agreement hath put the value on, more than real use, and the necessary support of life" (p.342).

> This partage of things, in an inequality of private possessions, men have made predictable out of the bounds of Societie, and without compact, only by putting a value on gold and silver and tacitly

---
[10] Locke, *Treatises* 1963, 341.

agreeing in the use of Money. For in Governments the Laws that regulate the right of property, and the possession of land is determinated by positive constitutions." (p.343)

If Locke seems to stigmatize the birth of private property as a distancing from God, his judgment enters nicely into the analysis of Middleton's comedies of London life, filled with a moral corruption barely contained by the author's irony. The world that emerges from these comedies is a dark world of deception and abuse, where cunning opposes cunning, suspicion opposes suspicion, and poverty is not fought with work but with "tricks to catch the old ones". And yet, society at that time was changing rapidly: a society based on land ownership was quickly transforming into a society based on commercial trade and the growth of the merchant class, and thus on work. However, the aristocratic class, was used to living off private income and was uninterested in work. Thus changed economic fortunes turn thousand-year-old privileges into economic and financial troubles, clearly reflected in Middleton's comedies. Such fast flow of money furthermore makes it necessary to get rich quickly, without the pains of the slow process of working and saving. As I have stated elsewhere,[11] this historical phase presents ample foretelling of capitalism, where fortunes can be made and lost instantly.

5. "*A Chaste Maid in Cheapside*"

To better understand the previous statements, between practice and morals, I would like to take into consideration Thomas Middleton's comedy *A Chaste Maid in Cheapside*. The work is particularly emblematic of situations dealing with the concept of property, transmission of wealth, and the distinction between "ownership" and "possession". Theatrically, it is the story of Allwit, whose wife is the concubine of Sir Walter Whorehound. It would therefore seem to be a case of property infringement (where the wife is considered personal property), but it is really a case of exploitation rights. Allwit, the husband, capitalizes on Sir Walter's cupidity towards his wife, obtaining colossal economic benefits and gaining a high standard of living, devoid of any sort of troubles.

> I'm like a man
> Finding a table furnished to his hand,
> As mine is still to me, prays for the founder, -
> Bless the right worshipful the good founder's life!
> I thank him, has maintained my house this ten years;
> Not only keeps my wife, but 'a keeps me

---

[11] Daniela Carpi, "Borghesi e mercanti: la nuova società capitalistica in *The Merchant of Venice*", *Strumenti Critici* 97- XVI (September 2001): 398-429.

And all my family; I'm at his table:
He gets me all my children, and pays the nurse
Monthly or weekly; puts me to nothing, rent,
Nor church-duties, not so much as the scavenger:
The happiest state that ever man was born to!
I walk out in a morning; come to breakfast,
Find excellent cheer; a good fire in winter;
Look in my coal-house about midsummer eve,
That's full, five or six chauldrosn new laid up;
Look in my back-yard, I shall find a steeple
Made up with Kentish faggots, which o'erlooks
The water-house and the windmills: I say nothing,
But smile and pin the door. When she lies in,
And now she's even upon the point of grunting,
A lady lies not in like her; there's her embossings,
Embroiderings, spanglings and I know not what,
As if she lay with all the gaudy-shops
In Gresham's Burse about her; then her restoratives,
Able to set up a young 'pothecary,
And richly stock the foreman of a drug-shop;
Her sugar by whole loaves, her wines by rundlets.
I see these things, but, like a happy man,
I pay for none at all; yet fools think's mine;
I have the name and in his gold I shine:
And where some merchants would in soul kiss hell
To buy a paradise for their wives, and dye
Their conscience in the bloods of prodigal heirs
To deck their night-piece, yet all this being done,
Eaten with jealousy to the inmost bone,-
As what affliction nature more constrains,
Than feed the wife plump for another's veins?-
These torments stand I freed of; I'm as clear
From jealousy of a wife as from the charge:
O, two miraculous blessings! 'tis the knight
Hath took that labour all out my hands:
I may sit still and play; he's jealous for me,
Watches her steps, sets spies; I live at ease,
He hath both the cost and torment[12]

---

[12] Thomas Middleton, *A Chaste Maid in Cheapside,* ed. Havelock Ellis, *Thomas Middleton* (Michigan: Scholarly Press, 1887) republished, act I, scene ii.

The importance of the topics presented in this monologue required me to quote it in its entirety, as it stages some of the main points already covered: a need for property in order to exist socially, the woman as commercial property, the need to appear in society through money, the duty to protect one's property and make it yield, making use of personal property, the paraphrasing of a case of rental or one in which possession is separate from property, usufruct compared to bare ownership, the morality of possessing a good, the social rites entailed by possession, a final balance of costs and return.

In primis, Roman law distinguished between "ownership" (dominium) and "possession": it may happen that someone owns a good but does not possess it. That is precisely the situation between Allwit and his wife: Allwit is the owner of the good, where the wife is considered like a plot of land, almost a *res mancipi* (category which included livestock, land, slaves, and animals used in agriculture, etc.).

In secundis Roman law distinguished between *res mancipi* and *res nec mancipi*, where the former included those things requiring an explicit contract with ample publicity in order to be transferred, while the latter included things that could be transferred informally. In Middleton's text, the contract does not appear openly, but the entire situation occurs before the eyes of society, of the gossips, of the suppliers who see the paying of the bills, and of the servants who witness the concubinage. The woman is treated like real property, managed and made to yield (both financially and in terms of offspring). However the fact that there is no actual stipulated contract could mean that the situation falls under the case of an informally transferable good: and yet, the fact that, for some unknown reason not spoken of in the text, Sir Walter pays all the bills and takes care of the woman in the capacity of an actual substitute husband, makes him the "possessor" of the woman.

In regard to the ambiguity of such terms, consider this point in the text, where the servants speak of Sir Walter as their "master":

> 1st Ser: Is our master come?
> Allwit: Your master! What am I?
> 1st Ser: Do not you know, sir?
> Allwit: Pray, am not I your master?
> 1st Ser: O, you're but
>   Our mistress' husband.
> Allwit: Ergo, knave, your master.
> 1st Ser: Negatur argumentum. ...
>   He's but one peep above a serving-man (I,ii)

This discussion expounds the property issue quite clearly, which the servants intend as linked to the money spent to hold it.

Nevertheless, the concept of property expressed by the interested parties themselves, Allwit and Sir Walter, is quite different: upon birth of the latest daughter, generated by Sir Walter, Allwit states:

> Allwit: Faith, sir, I thank yout worship for this girl
> Ten thousand times and upward.
> Sir Wal: I am glad
> I have her for you, sir. (II,ii)

Thus by tacit consent, the children continue to be considered as property of the husband, who is still legitimate owner.

The distinction between "ownership" and "possession" is important in understanding what kind of responsibility is entailed and upon whom it rests legally: just think of Allwit's statement that Sir Walter sees to paying the midwives and to organizing the home. All financial and moral responsibilities therefore rest with Sir Walter. In this case it can truly be said that it is the possessor who is in charge: it is also he who goes through the suffering typical of a husband, such as jealousy, anxiety over the wife giving birth, putting up with her moods, etc. This is a legal case that can also be defined as "personal servitude": it is part of property law, but it could also fall under the case of usufruct. Mistress Allwit is momentarily ceded to Sir Walter, who makes use of her as if she were a servant, for whom he pays a price (the maintenance of Allwit as well). "Personal servitude" indicates the right to use property for a specified and limited period of time, while usufruct indicates the right to use property belonging to someone else, and to keep the fruits it produces (the children in this case). Sir Walter does pay Allwit a "right to servitude", which also implies that Allwit must abstain from having relations with his wife as long as the contract exists. In this case, Allwit holds the position of a third party to whom interference is prohibited, otherwise he would be subjected to *vindicatio*. Indeed, if the contracting party's use of the property is interrupted before due time, then the party could sue for damages. Payment by Sir Walter is carried out through nature (procreation) and financially; following is a list of the goods produced by it: silks, garments, fine foods, servants. The degree to which all this implies a commercial transaction is made evident by the fact that it is precisely Sir Walter who feels an urgency to defend his property (spies who check on the woman, jealousy, anxiety). Like a true owner, Allwit maintains his name as husband ("I have the name"), thus preventing the possibility of "usucaption" because the property is never entirely abandoned. It could be asserted that Sir Walter is the renter of the property, and that as long as he pays the "rent" he can use it; all relations would cease were he to fall short of his financial obligations.

However, since alienation of the property occurred not through an official written contract, but through a simple transfer of the property to the acquiring party, what sort of legal guarantee does the contractor have? By law, the husband remains the owner of the property in this case. Apparently, Sir Walter has no insurance; the husband could still secretly enjoy the favors of his wife, and Sir Walter could have no *vindicatio*, if not that of receding from the agreement and the fruition, which would behoove neither party.

To these difficulties, yet another must be added: there is a similar separation between legal property and equitable property in the case of goods that constitute part of the dotal property for the establishment of a marriage. The husband becomes the owner of the wife's property for the entire duration of the marriage, but that property returns to her in the case that the husband predeceases her. Nonetheless, in this case the dotal property consists in the actual body of the wife, which is indeed made to bear fruit. At that time, the law established restrictions upon the husband: he was prohibited to alienate the property without the wife's consent, which in this case is given *toto corde*. Otherwise, the wife could have performed a *vindicatio utilis*, just like an emphyteuta, to regain dotal control through an *actio in rem*. What I mean is that, the web of property and possession present in *A Chaste Maid in Cheapside* would create quite a legal problem, were it to be challenged.

The peculiar legal situation that arises in the strange relationship between the Allwits and Sir Walter could also be read as an example of emphyteusis law regarding land possession. In the Middle Ages, land possession held particular importance, and despite changes to the law over time and the different legal values linked to land, land ownership continues to fall under a particular legal system. Roman law commentators saw a resemblance between the position of a renter of the land and that of the Roman emphyteuta. The latter enjoyed a *vindicatio utilis*, while the owner enjoyed a *vindicatio directa* (for example, the possibility to reclaim possession of the land if the renter did not pay the rent). Consequently, the two parties had different rights: there was a *dominum utile* in the case of the renter, and a *dominum directum* in the case of the true owner. Hence, the *dominum* was attributed to the renter, while the owner had a mere *ius in re aliena* (almost like a hypothecation). This entire situation is summarized by the pact that regulates the relations between the Allwits and Sir Walter. Hypothesizing that, in this case, the woman acts as land property (a good which can be "cultivated", "plowed", and made to "bear fruit" by the renter of the woman's body, being Sir Walter), and that the property can be differentiated into direct property and the right to another's property, then this is a case of an emphyteusis contract, as just described. Allwit maintains hypothecation rights on a good in use by someone else; he is, yes, the owner, but he has alienated the use. Hence Roman laws on predial servitudes survive in their essential aspects.

What must be seen here, in terms of moral judgment, is the condemnation of women's lack of freedom at that time: if the right to personal property is excluded, then the right to freedom must be excluded as well. Indeed, since women at that time were unable to manage their own property (which belonged to the father prior to marriage and to the husband afterwards), then it must be deduced that women were not entirely free, because they were never matrimonially autonomous. Consider the property issues underlying the tragedy of *The Duchess of Malfi*, in which part of the brothers' persecution of the widowed Duchess was linked to management of her wealth. At that time, perhaps only widows could enjoy their wealth. Think also of the sad case of Ophelia, who doesn't even possess her words: the social pressure upon her is so great that she is subject to the verbal violence of both Hamlet and her father, who wanted to control even her meeting with Hamlet from the outside. The words she must speak, which are supposed to set a verbal trap to deduce the cause of Hamlet's strange behavior, are put into her mouth by her father: Ophelia is hence stripped even of her words and of the pleasure of speaking with her beloved.

Mistress Allwit's situation in the text instead constitutes an epoch-making change: since the woman does not have control of her own property, as previously mentioned, through her consenting behavior towards the pact with Sir Walter she becomes a participant in management of the property. Her concession to the sexual negotiation is not forced; on the contrary, it becomes a form of legal loyalty, as Mistress Allwit abstains from relations with her husband in compliance with the usage contract. As such, though generally excluded from property management, the woman succeeds both in using the property and in taking advantage of the resultant benefits. The scope of the law consists in realization of the greatest free individual achievement. Any interference with the possession someone has over the fruits of his greatest ingenuity, aimed at creative or acquisitive self-affirmation, would therefore infringe upon the scope of the juridical order, for whom *jus disponendi*, implicit in the very notion of property, is sacred. Thus, aside from the moral judgment, the situation is not legally actionable, because it is not exploitation of prostitution (Mistress Allwit gives in only to the charms of Sir Walter), it is not a crime of "seduction" (it is merely an economic calculation), it is not undue influence of an incompetent (Sir Walter is entirely mentally competent), and it's not a public scandal (everything occurs within the home). The law is not, therefore, violated. What is violated is ethical behavior, both for the situation itself and above all because, during the course of the play, an attempt at redemption on the part of Sir Walter is blocked. Sir Walter would like to legitimately marry, but the Allwits block the attempt immediately so as not to lose their rich income.

> Sir. Wal: I'll marry!...
> Allwit: I'll stop that gap
>   Wher'er I find it open: I have poisoned

His hopes in marriage already with
Some old rich widows, and some landed virgins;
And I'll fall to work still before I'll lose him;
He's yet too sweet to part from. (I,ii)

With this, moral judgment of such a situation is withheld, as is always the case in Middleton's comedies. The author refrains from expressing a personal judgment on the moral corruption in the world he describes, letting it emerge directly from the situations.

Nonetheless, apart from this predominant relationship in the play, upon which the entire scenic action hinges, the text is completely focused on the issue of the children in the marriage, intended as property and whose yield implies poverty or wealth according to the occasions. The Kixs watch their hopes for heirs and increased wealth vanish due to their sterility, while the Touchwoods must abstain from sexual intercourse because they are burdened by too many children and not enough money. Children are constantly alluded to in terms of "price", "fruitfulness", "get", "not get", "goods": they are considered only as yield, economic return, or capital to invest. The mercantile mentality permeates the entire text, stressing the economic-property aspect of marriage. Existence as a person within society is strictly linked to the conception of fruit bearing within marriage: a couple will succeed in holding a specific social position only with the right balance of children and wealth. In other words, children become the means through which to increase one's wealth.

Emerging irrepressibly from this monetization of feelings is a damnation of property as the separation from a harmonic communion between man and nature: mercantile relations falsify the morality of the situations. A healthily fruitful marriage becomes infernal inasmuch as it is tormented by a lack of money; a sterile marriage is demonized for its lack of heirs; work ethics are derided through exploitation of individuals' libido. Thus the family as the base and nucleus for good social progress instead becomes the wellspring for all deviations from the norm: in the text, private property therefore becomes the cause of the moral fall of society.

At all times in history, the relationship between protecting the right to property and protecting human values, in particular the values of life and freedom, has constituted a problem. Norms have hence changed over time with changes in social customs. Moreover, the same logic of protecting human dignity against proprietary abuses governs norms regarding the nullity of contracts and pacts: this because if law, as Dante said, is "hominis ad hominem proportio", then protection of individuals, and not just of their property, must always be pursued in parallel with protections and counter-protections that constitute an unfailing mission for legislators and a constant stimulus for jurists. Because, if society is truly in continual evolution, it is clear that the law must be as well. However, one of the most fascinating aspects of the legal discipline is the perennial "backwardness" of positive law; precisely because, when a new law is made to protect new situations, as soon as it is enacted, it has already been overcome by the social body, which has gone "beyond". Law is truly a sort of social engineering, a job entailing research and measuring of the interests at play in the social relations of a certain time and place.

The literary text thus becomes experimentation of a hypothesis that must be proved. In this case, Middleton's text becomes an experiment in exploitation of a presumed property, conducted in the liminal zone between economics, law, and morality. Expansion of the concept of making property yield thus becomes a project to satisfy those material needs that came into contrast in the field of human relations. The vital nucleus of the utilitarian "morality", which Middleton expresses in this play, centers upon the absolute will of unscrupulous individuals to expand the meaning of the law and of morality in order to acquire socially, and furthermore shows how society moves according to material needs. The result is a field of economic struggles where single interests clash and guide the course of wealth. The life of the law thus results to be an unstoppable debate that puts spirit, law, and nature in opposition. As such, the static and stable nature of the law (which establishes who property goes to in the case of inheritance) clashes with its mobility (individuals' ceaseless adaptation to situations in order to gain coveted profits).

From Law to Literature: Guillaume de La Perrière's Intellectual Path[1]

Géraldine Cazals

University of Toulouse

1.

La Perrière was born in 1499, in Toulouse, in a rather modest but noble family. He studied law in the Universities of Toulouse and Avignon, where he may have met Alciat, and then returned to his native city, where he spent the rest of his life, living off the accumulation of small benefits, and devoting his entire time to literature. His first work, the *Invective satirique*, was published in Toulouse, in 1530. It seemed to reveal his desire to use literature as a way to reform society and to commit himself in a "political" sense. His second work offered him great success: his *Theätre des Bons Engins*, offered in a manuscript form to Marguerite de Navarre in 1535 and published by Denis Janot in 1539, was a very original work and the first French Emblem book. Indeed, the fame La Perrière still has today is largely due to his emblematic works: the *Theatre* but also the *Cent considérations d'amour* (published in 1543), the *Considérations des Quatre Mondes* and the *Morosophie* (published by Macé Bonhomme in 1553). Beside those specific works, he was also involved in the first edition of the *Chronique de Joinville*, in 1546, and above all, he wrote a lot for the local magistrates of Toulouse (the "capitouls"), producing historical chronicles of the local civic life, introducing municipal judicial compendiums, and organizing the political reflections he developed by working for those magistrates in his *Miroir Politicque*, which was published in 1556.[2]

On the whole, those books are moralistic in essence, and indeed all but judicial. Even the *Miroir politique*, in which La Perrière shows and develops a great interest for political questions, does not reveal a very technical judicial culture, although he had followed, in the Universities of Toulouse and Avignon, technical judicial courses and obtained a licence in law. By studying his training, I will thus try to understand how Humanism led the young jurist that he was to embrace wholeheartedly a literary career, and why he avoided all technical

---

[1] English revision by Alice Bendinelli and John Scaggs.
[2] Géraldine Cazals, *Guillaume de La Perrière (1499-1554), Un humaniste à l'étude du politique*, doctoral thesis attended the 17 December 2003, University of Toulouse I, to be published.

knowledge in the *Miroir Politicque*, in the way that he took on judicial issues and especially that of private property.

During the first decades of the sixteenth century, in Toulouse, the teaching of the Arts was more dynamic than in other towns in the South of France, but was not very flourishing. As in Paris, the study of grammarians was still preferred to the direct study of poets and the old handbooks still had authority.[3] Furthermore, the structural weaknesses of the University prevented it from becoming a famous centre of study and teaching. So, during his first years of learning, La Perrière must have known how to talk and write in medieval Latin. And, when the rudiments of grammar were mastered, he turned to the Faculty of Law, which gave access to the most prestigious careers of Church and State.

The Toulouse Law Faculty was also short of money and, if it still went on attracting a great number of students, it found it very difficult to take the path of modernisation which became more urgent and necessary from day to day. The rooms where civil law training was given threatened to fall into ruins and it was only in 1515 that the Parliament reacted, ordering the capitouls to build new classrooms near the "rue des Lois".[4] It is unlikely that La Perrière could take advantage of these new buildings: it is not in fact before 1522 that the first three auditoriums were finished.[5]

In that context, the salaries given to Toulousan regents were not sufficient to attract to the city the prestigious masters to whom the Italian Universities already gave very comfortable wages. Law teaching still remained in the hands of masters whose formation was essentially local, and whose teaching vocation must have sometimes been quite doubtful.[6] It does not seem that those long years in chair were the occasion of a precocious renewal of the science diffused by the University. Etienne Aufrery (1458-1511), professor of canonical law, later counsellor and president of the Toulouse Parliament, was the only person to publish several books at the time;[7] even then, those works testify much more

---

[3] Augustin Renaudet, Préréforme et humanisme à Paris pendant les premières guerres d'Italie (1494-1517) (Genève: Slatkine Reprints, 1981) 466.
[4] Decision of the 17 january 1515, ADHG, B. 16, fol. 316-317 v., quoted by René Gadave, Les Documents sur l'histoire de l'Université de Toulouse et spécialement sa Faculté de droit civil et canonique (1229-1789), thèse pour l'obtention du doctorat en sciences juridiques (Toulouse: E. Privat, 1910) n. 255, 256; Henri Gilles, "Les "Estudes" de l'Université de Toulouse", Université de Toulouse et enseignement du droit XIIIe-XVIe siècle (Toulouse: S.E.D.U.S.S. - Picard Diffusion, 1992) 341-344.
[5] Gadave, *Université de Toulouse* 1910, n. 259, 260, 261, 267; Gilles, "Estudes" 1992, 417.
[6] Cazals, *La Perrière* to be published, 38-40.
[7] Etienne Aufrery, *Decisiones capelle Tholosane* (Lyon: Jacques Sacon, 1503) published several times; *Repetitio Clementine prime Ut clericorum, de officio et potestate judicis ordinarii* in *Opuscula aurea* (Lyon: Jean Moylin and Jacques Sacon, 1512); Stilus Parlamenti, arrestorum, processuum et ordinationum, Lyon, S. Vincent, 1513; De officio et potestate judicis ordinarii. Accessit tractatus de potestate secularium super ecclesiis ac personis et rebus ecclesiasticis, item de potestate ecclesiae super laïcis, Paris, 1514; finally the Decisiones

to his experience as a pratician than to his teaching.[8] Jean d'Ayma, also a canonist, made himself known by his commentary on the Concordat of 1515. By then, he was the only foreign teacher in Toulouse University, which is a remarkable coincidence. But, coming from Bayonne, he only arrived in the city in 1522 or so, and he was only given tenure of the second chair of canonical law in 1528; it is quite impossible for La Perrière to have counted him among his professors.[9]

All those masters probably still taught following the old scholastic and bartolist methods. Did La Perrière appreciate them? He does not quote these titular regents in any of his works. The only teacher he evokes, with praise, was one of those «hallebardiers» who taught at the Faculty under circumstances that remain totally unclear. The personality of the doctor shows anyway what wind of change blew, towards 1510, on the University of Toulouse. Descending from a long lineage of meridional jurists, Nicolas Bertrand had pursued his studies *in utroque jure* in Toulouse, and there he had obtained his "baccalauréat" and his licence (in 1493 and 1499). From that moment on, his judicial talents earned him the recognition of his peers.[10] In 1512, Nicolas Bertrand published a *Repetitio de inquisitione hereticorum*, which has been forgotten if it has not disappeared,[11] and it is his second *opus*, published in 1515, which ensured him a definite fame, even today: it remains one of the rare illustrations of the composition of political treatises by members of the local Faculty in that same period, and clearly showed a great desire to use history, literature and epigraphic knowledge to serve political considerations.[12]

---

curiae archiepiscopis tolosanae, Lyon, 1616.
[8] Jacques Poumarède, "Les arrêtistes toulousains" in *Les Parlements de Province. Pouvoirs, justice et société du XVe au XVIIIe siècle*, eds. Jacques Poumarède and Jacques Thomas (Toulouse: Framespa, 1996) 375-376.
[9] Gilles, "Estudes" 1992, 314-315 and 316 note 10.
[10] About Nicolas Bertrand, see Ernest Roschach, "Etude sur l'historien Nicolas Bertrand, auteur des *Gesta Tholosanorum*", *Bull. Acad. Sci. Insc. Belles-Lettres de Toulouse*, 1897-1898, 25-27; "Nicolas Bertrand, docteur, avocat, historien", *Recueil de l'Académie des Jeux-Floraux*, (Toulouse: Douladoure 1905) 194-201; Jules Villain, *La France moderne. Grand dictionnaire Généalogique, Historique et Biographique* (Montpellier: Haute-Garonne et Ariège, 1911) 806; Andrè Navelle, *Familles et notables du midi toulousain au XVe et XVIe siècle* (Toulouse: Publication des Recherches Historiques du Midi, 1995) 160-161.
[11] Nicolas Bertrand, Habetis hic, romane fidei spectatissimi cultores, insignem ac unionibus comparandam repetitionem ut inquisitionis hereticis [...] in VI luculenter et composite digestam ac Domino Nicholao Bertrand, Impressum Tholose industria magistri Johannis magni Johannis in angulo vie porte Arietis commorantis anno M.D.XII, In-6°, 22 [fol.].
[12] Nicolas Bertrand, *Opus de Tholosanorum gestis ab urbe condita cunctis mortalibus apprime dignum conspectibus*, Impressum Tholose industria magistri Johannis Magni Johannis in angulo vie Porte arietis commorantis, Anno Domini M.V.XV, die XIII julii, Laus Deo. In-2°, goth., [8], 90 fol.

Guillaume de La Perrière knew him quite intimately, as he was friends with François, Nicolas's own son, who was perhaps a student of his. Even if he accepted, many years later, to prepare an edition of the French translation of the *Opus de tholosanorum gestis*, he did not forget to pay tribute to the ancient master:[13] he made in fact an apology for History and recalled the "good exhortations the late good lord [Nicolas] gave me in my first years, while you [François] and I were studying companions".

> bonnes exhortations que ledit feu bon seigneur [Nicolas] me donnoit en mes premiers ans, du temps que vous [François] et moy estions compaignons d'estudes.[14]

But, as La Perrière noted, Nicolas Bertrand was torn between two vocations: his career as an officer serving the king, and his teaching career. Indeed, he could devote himself precisely neither to the former, nor to the latter. At the beginning of the sixteenth century, as in the Middle Ages, most teachers simultaneously had a University career and another professional activity.[15] In the poorest Faculties like that of Toulouse, the "épices" obtained by the parliamentary offices mostly came to complete the ordinary and insufficient wages given to the regents. However, that accumulation was then criticised, and, in 1510, the Parliament of Toulouse forbade the "sénéchaux", "juges-mages" and other judicial officers "de distribuer aucun procès aux régents en droit, pour ne point les distraire des lectures".[16]

Already, Humanism implied a division between the intellectual apprehension of Law and its practice; the ideal of the *jurisconsultus* had changed since the Middle Ages. Were the Toulousan legal professions calling for the coming of the judicial humanism defined by Budé and Alciat, in the decision of 1510? If the members of Parliament, who were all University graduates, had already foreshadowed the importance of such a reform, they did not see its realization very soon. The works of Nicolas Bertrand reveal his continuing respect for medieval authorities and, in Toulouse, everything seems to show that Law teaching was for quite a long time based on a profound respect for traditional authorities and for the *communis opinio*.

---

[13] Navelle, *Familles et notables* 1995, 160-161.
[14] Guillaume de La Perriere, preface to the reviewed edition of Nicolas Bertrand, Les gestes des Tolosains, & d'autres nations de l'environ. Composées premierement en latin par monsieur maistre Nicolas Bertrand tresexcellant personnaige & tresfacond advocat au parlement de Tolose. Et depuys faictes françoises, reueus & aumentées de plusieurs Histoires qui ne feurent oncq imprimées. On les vend à Tolose en la maison de Iacques Colomies, maistre imprimeur dudit Tolose, Avec privilege, 1555, fol. [A III v.].
[15] Jacques Verger, "Peut-on faire une prosopographie des professeurs des universités françaises à la fin du Moyen Age ? ", *Mélanges de l'Ecole Française de Rome* 100 (1988): 58.
[16] Gadave, *Université de Toulouse* 1910, n. 247.

From Law to Literature: Guillaume de La Perrière's Intellectual Path 149

The phenomenon was not specifically local. If a weighty conformism, consecrating in principle a hostility to novelty, confined teaching to the transmission of a judicial technique and to the knowledge of an intangible *corpus* of traditional authorities,[17] the jurists themselves needed a certain time to realize that the humanistic renewal also had great implications in their own discipline.[18] The *mos gallicus* was not to impose itself on all French Universities before the second half of the sixteenth century, and not without difficulties.[19] The dissociation between law teaching and judicial practice was not very efficient in the absence of a financial reform of University structures, and indeed, the Parliament failed in its desire to prevent the regents from exercising other professional activities.

Therefore, even if the first humanist fumblings of the Toulousan masters awakened the curiosity of the students, they could not satisfy it. The University of Avignon was not that far away, and already had the good taste to welcome the new masters coming from Italy. Students were flocking to Avignon, and La Perrière, like a great number of his contemporaries, could not resist.

The University of Avignon was already famous for the science of Law.[20] In 1478, the Town Council authorized foreign doctors to apply for teaching chairs;[21] a few years later, a new statute came to modernise the Faculty[22] and, in 1514, Léon the Tenth allowed the affectation of new incomes to the exclusive use of teachers' wages.[23] Nevertheless, in 1515, regents were all, without exception, trained locally. Had they known before how to adapt themselves to

---

[17] Jacques Verger, "A la naissance de l'individualisme et de la pensée individuelle: la contribution des universités médiévales" in Janet Coleman, *L'individu dans la théorie politique et dans la pratique* (Paris: Puf, 1996) 84; and Jacques Verger, *Histoire des Universités en France* (Toulouse: Privat, 1986) 126.
[18] See the lists of jurists established during the first part of the sixteenth century. Patrick Arabeyre, "Aspects du «nationalisme culturel» dans le domaine du droit au début du XVIe siècle: les grands juristes français selon Barthélemy de Chasseneuz", *Annales de Bourgogne* 74 (2002): especially 173-188.
[19] Jean-Louis Thireau, "L'enseignement du Droit et ses méthodes au XVIe siècle", *Annales d'Histoire des facultés de droit et de la science juridique* 2 (1985): 27-36.
[20] Victorin Laval, *Cartulaire de l'Université d'Avignon (1303-1791)* (Paris: Seguin frères, 1884) xxviii.
[21] The town council of Avignon had deliberated on the 17th of october 1478 to accept the competition of foreign doctors to the access of University chairs. Marcel Fournier, *Les statuts et privilèges des Universités françaises depuis leur fondation jusqu'en 1789* III-1950 (1892): 664-666. Anyway, it does not seem that the decision caused a rapid change: according to J. Verger, the traces of contacts with Italy remain rare before the first third of the sixteenth century. Jacques Verger, "Les rapports entre Universités italiennes et Universités françaises méridionales (XIIe-XVe siècles)", *Università e società nei secoli XII-XVI, Pistoia, 20-25 settembre 1979* (Pistoia: Centro Italiano di studi di storia e d'arte Pistoia, 1982): 163 and 170.
[22] Fournier, *Les statuts* (1892); Reformation of the statutes by Galeot du Roure, the 29th of April 1503, n. 1421.
[23] Laval, *Cartulaire* 1884, 198-206.

the new standards that surrounded the teaching of Law? That year, the number of students registered in the Law Faculty increased greatly, culminating, in 1518, with the recruitment of two founding fathers of judicial humanism, Alciat and Ripa.

Despite his young age, Alciat was already famous.[24] He was the very model of the humanist jurist who refused to lock up his science in his own field but wanted to turn to good use the fields of linguistics, grammar, and philology as well as history, so as to distance himself from medieval authorities and move on to the direct study of sources and to the comprehension of Law. As a practitioner, he still appealed to the *communis opinio* for the interpretation of texts, and as a real supporter of judicial humanism, he still considered Roman Law as a living legislation that the interpreter should explain and expand. Seven thousand pupils came from the whole of Europe to Avignon, crowding his classes.[25]

Francesco Ripa, who had arrived with Alciat in 1518, had for the same reasons become famous in the Italian Universities.[26] No doubt thanks to those two masters, the Law Faculty of Avignon became a propitious centre for the diffusion of judicial humanism in France.[27] Jean Montaigne, who, in his *Tractatus* of 1510, had not proved to be very open to modern authors and historians,[28] had undoubtedly broadened his horizons there. His teachings gained him the friendship of Boniface Amerbach,[29] the respect of Barthélemy de Chasseneuz and that of Jean de Boyssoné.[30]

---

[24] For a treatment of 500 shields for the mere year of 1518 (600 shields starting from 1520), that is to say five or six times more than the ordinary fees, he had signed with the town council a "conduite" of three years. Verger, *Histoire des Universités* 1986, 154.

[25] The jurisconsult was however trying to return to his native country and, in April 1522, as the plague interrupted his teaching and damaged municipal finances, a lesser treatment was proposed to him: Alciat refused and returned to Milan, till 1527.

[26] Ripa arrived in Avignon in 1518 and stayed there probably until 1533, with, according to some authors, an escape to Pavie during the plague of 1522. Having died prematurely in 1535, he does not seem to have left a great number of books and still remains, despite his former fame, quite unknown. See nevertheless Mario Ascheri, *Un maestro del 'mos italicus': Gianfrancesco Sannazari della Ripa (1480 c.-1535)* (Milano: A. Giuffrè Editore, 1970).

[27] Pierre Legendre, "La France et Bartole", *Bartolo da Sassoferrato: Studi e documenti per il VI centenario*, (Milano: A. Giuffrè Editore, 1961) 133-172; Jean-Louis Thireau, L'enseignement du Droit 1985, 30-31.

[28] Patrick Arabeyre, "Aux racines de l'absolutisme: Grand Conseil et Parlement à la fin du Moyen Age d'après le *Tractatus celebris de auctoritate et preeminentia sacri magni concilii et parlamentorum regni Francie* de Jean Montaigne (1512)", *Droits et pouvoirs, Cahiers de la Recherche Médiévale* 7 (2000): 196.

[29] Boniface Amerbach came to Avignon in the spring of 1519. He obtained his doctorate there in 1524. In 1527, he was already back in Basle. Edilbert De Teule, *Chronologie des docteurs en droit de l'Université d'Avignon (1303-1791)* (Paris: Librairie historique des Provinces, Emile Le Chevalier, 1887) 26. See his correspondance to Erasme, Didier Erasme, *La Correspondance d'Erasme, traduite et annotée d'après l'Opus epistolarum de P. S. Allen,*

The presence of Alciat is likely to have attracted the young Guillaume de La Perrière to Avignon. The Toulousan came to follow the teachings of the Milanese master, stayed several years in the city, and therefore also taught there, as he himself relates in a digression in his *Miroir Politicque*, reporting several conversations he had formerly exchanged with the main rabbi of Avignon:

du temps que je lisoys en ladite ville et université.[31]

The mention is brief and lacks eloquence, but nevertheless testifies to the reputation the young humanist already enjoyed. It was common for students to give lectures: titular regents generally shared out between themselves ordinary lectures (which in Avignon dealt with the *Digeste*, the *Infortiat* and the *Code* in civil law, the *Décrétales* and the *Clémentines* in canonical law),[32] but they were rather frequently replaced. Moreover, non-titular graduates often held additional lectures (dealing with other law books, which were commented on by the regents or considered as less important).[33] However those lectures were assigned to the best students, whose capacities and doctrine were formerly checked by a censor, and who had to obtain previous authorization by the "primicier".[34] Guillaume de La Perrière, who had been noticed by his teachers, had begun his university career in that way.[35]

Very soon, however, La Perrière in Avignon knew what preoccupations tormented the humanists. Indeed, Guillaume also mentioned that the town's

---

H. M Allen, et H. W. Garrod, vol. IV (1519-1521), ed. Marcel A. Nauwelaerts (Bruxelles: Presses académiques européennes, Institut pour l'étude de la Renaissance et de l'humanisme, 1970), lettre 1201, May 1521; vol. VII (1527-1528), eds. P. Laurens and F. Desbordes (Bruxelles: Presses académiques européennes, 1978), letters 1914, 1933, 1937.

[30] Jehan de Boyssone, "De la mort de Montaigne, docteur d'Avignon" XXXII, "De l'Université d'Avignon" XLVI, "Première centurie des dizains" XXVIII, éd. Jacoubet (1923) 106-107; Jehan de Boyssone, *Elegiorum liber*, BMT, manuscrit 835, Elégie XX, *Ad cives Avenionenses*, fol. 40.

[31] Guillaume de La Perriere, Le Miroir Politicqve, Œuvre non moins utile que necessaire à tous Monarques, Roys, Princes, Seigneurs, Magistrats, et autres surintendans & gouuerneurs de Republicques, par Guillavme de La Perrière tolosain, [marque 1 de Macé Bonhomme] (Lyon: Macé Bonhomme, 1555), 3.

[32] Fournier, *Les statuts* 1891, n. 1421, § 14 "De libris legendis".

[33] Verger, Histoire des Universités 1986, 54-55.

[34] Since the papal brief of the 18th of June 1488, some qualified bacheliers could been admitted to lecture to replace titular regents, for «*causa legitima subsistente, necessitatis tempore*». Fournier, *Les statuts* 1891, n. 1421, § 12 "*Declaratio precedentis statuti de non legendo per substitutum*".

[35] Like Antoine de Gouvéa, Henri de Mesmes, Paul de Foix ou Jacques Cujas. Gilles, "La Faculté de droit de Toulouse au temps de Jean Bodin", *Université de Toulouse et enseignement du droit XIIIe-XVIe siècle*, (Toulouse: S.E.D.U.S.S. - Picard Diffusion, 1992) 215, note 8.

main rabbi (Servo Deo, Benedicto and Balaam), had asserted the importance of the unwritten nature of some of the Jewish traditions, for:

> les juifz estiment tant les secretz de leur Cabale, qu'ilz ne les mettent jamais en escrit, ains les apprennent et revellent de bouche, de l'un à l'autre, comme par succession hereditaire, reputant que l'ecriture les profaneroit, et qu'en sortant de la bouche du precepteur, et entrant en l'oreille du secret auditeur, ilz sont en plus grande veneration.[36]

However, towards 1520, contacts between Jews and Christians were still rare, so this anecdote patently shows how the time spent in the university meant for La Perrière a sort of intellectual enrichment which largely exceeded the lessons offered by the *Studium*. In Avignon, which was about to rediscover Laure's tomb, Guillaume de La Perrière found out how infinite and inexhaustible humanistic matters were. With a much greater fervour than in Toulouse, he learned that history, philology or even the Kabbhala worked for the renewal of Law sciences, which might open up a brighter future for men. He was also undoubtedly discovering Erasmus's ideas (and particularly the Erasmian desire to moralize law) through Boniface Amerbach's contribution.[37]

Between Toulouse and Avignon, La Perrière got a licence *utriusque juris* at the end of ten or thirteen years of study.[38] If he never obtained a doctorate,[39] he had at least obtained a solid judicial formation and had been ordained priest.

He came back to Toulouse in the spring of 1526. Then, on the seventeenth of September, «*jurium licenciatus, Tholose habitator* », he authorized his friend Ymbert de Sauzet to gather all his books as well as several *medaliarum* (ancient coins) he had left in Avignon, some of which were in the hands of Pons de Ranco, sacristan of Nîmes and abbot of Franquevaux.[40] Those books and that collection of coins point out that, ever since his years of apprenticeship, La Perrière harboured a profound taste for antiquities. Did the company of Alciat

---

[36] La Perriere, *Le Miroir* 1555, 2-3.
[37] Denis Crouzet, *La genèse de la Réforme française 1520-1562* (Paris: SEDES, 1996) 74-75.
[38] Verger, *Histoire des Universités* 1986, 57-58; Fournier, *Les statuts* (1892), «Réformation des statuts par Galeot du Roure», 29 April 1503, § 39; Antonin Deloume, *Aperçu historique de la faculté de droit de l'Université de Toulouse. Maîtres et écoliers de l'an 1228 à 1900* (Toulouse: Privat, 1900) 31, 33. See also the decision of the 13th of September 1470, in Bernard de La Roche-Flavin, *Arrests notables du Parlement de Toulouse, donnez et prononcez sur diverses matieres, civiles, criminelles, beneficiales, et feodales [...]* (Toulouse: Guillaume-Loüis Colomiez et Jerôme Posüel, 1682) 401.
[39] Most of the students registered in the University didn't graduate. Jacques Verger, "Le rôle social de l'université d'Avignon au xve siècle", *Bibl. Humanisme Renaissance* XXXIII (1971): 490.
[40] ADHG, Arch. Not. Rolle, 3 E 6771, "Instrumentum procurationis domini Guillelmus de Pereria", fol. 120 v.-121; and the renewal, 3 E 6772, «Procuratio nobilis dominum Guillelmus de Pereria», fol. 16 v.

also give him the taste for emblematics? Probably so, if we consider that a few years later La Perrière produced the first French Emblem book ever written.[41]

These years in Avignon might have been the only years La Perrière spent far from Toulouse. Indeed, he seems to have spent the rest of his life in his native city, living off the accumulation of small benefits: the annual payments coming from the churches of Saint-Loube d'Amades in the diocese of Lombès (near Toulouse), one canonical prebend in the metropolitan church of Narbonne, the cure of Parazan (all along the left bank of the Aude, in the Minervois), and finally, the position as prior of Saint-Mathurin college in Toulouse.[42]

Torn between Law and Literature, he finally made his choice: enjoying a comfortable financial situation, he dedicated himself to Humanities, avoiding, henceforth, all technical knowledge in the treatment of judicial questions, as we will see in the case of private property.

2.

The question of property was one of the principal preoccupations of all judicial systems of Roman inspiration (from Justinian to Napoleon) and also a central theme in political thought.[43] At the beginning of the Renaissance, it was revived by humanists, due to the return to the Bible, to the credit granted to Cicero or other classical authors such as Caesar.[44]

La Perrière has evoked the question several times, probably in his first work, later on by translating Saint John Chrysostome's famous homily into French, *Du pauvre et du riche*, in order to encourage the rich to have mercy and be charitable (« pour inciter les cueurs des riches aux œuvres de misericorde et de charité »)[45] and lastly, in his *Miroir Politique*.[46]

---

[41] Guillaume de La Perrière, Le Théâtre // des bons en-//gins, auquel sont con- // tenus cent Emble-/mes. // Auec priuilege. // On les vend à Paris en la rue neufue nostre // Dame à L'enseigne sainct Jehan Baptiste, pres // saincte Geneviefue des Ardens: // [A la fin:] Imprimé à Paris par Denis Janot libraire et imprimeur, demourant en la rue neufve nostre Dame à l'enseigne sainct Jehan Baptiste pres saincte Geneviefve des Ardens, [s. d.], In-8°, [108] fol.; édition A, published in facsimile (Bnf, Rés. Z 2556) by Alison Saunders (Menston: The Scholar Press, 1973).
[42] Cazals, *Guillaume de La Perrière*, to be published.
[43] *Histoire de la pensée politique moderne (1450-1700)*, eds. John Horne Burns and Mark Goldie (Paris: Presses Univ. France, 1991) 63.
[44] Cicero (*De officiis*, I, 7, 21), Caesar (*De bello gallico*, VI, 22), quoted by André Castaldo and Jean-Philippe Levy, *Histoire du droit civil* (Dalloz: Dalloz Précis, 2002) 311 and 371.
[45] Guillaume de La Perriere, *Le petit courtisan avec la maison parlante, et le moyen de parvenir de pauvreté à richesse, et comment le riche devient pauvre* (Lyon: Pierre de Tournes, 1551) petit In-16°. The work has disappeared but La Perrière mentioned it in his *Miroir Politicque* 1555, 183 and it was evoked by Du Verdier, t. IV, p. 113 and by Paul Louisy, *Nouvelle Biographie Générale* (Paris: Firmin Didot Frères, 1859, and t. 22, 1967) 518-519.

La Perrière did not return to the question of primitive natural right[47] and his meditations on human nature led him to assert that men needed food, houses, clothes and weapons to feed, protect and defend themselves.[48] He suggested that man's rule over things did not express any natural principles based on a universal order, but a principle based on the consideration of man's very nature: the idea that man's rule over things answered his needs, which was about to be developed by the Second Scholastic, announcing modern jusnaturalism, centred on the problem of human rights.[49]

Avoiding any reference to man's fallen nature, he asserted that God himself had ordained the division of property; ordered that men should earn their living from their labour, should obey the magistrates who approved of private property, and, lastly in the Decalogue, that everybody should be content with his own, and consequently should not steal.[50] By then, he definitely approved of private property,

> car si les biens estoyent tant à l'un qu'à l'autre, il n'y auroit point de larrecin, quand chacun y auroit part, et l'on ne peust desrober ce qui est sien, car larrecin est contractation de chose d'autruy, contre le vouloir d'icelluy auquel la chose appartient.[51]

Finally La Perrière, following the book of Joshua, reminded us that God had ordered the sons of Israel to divide among themselves the promised land, and assigned each tribe a limited portion of land.[52]

3.

That demonstration, although rather seductive, remained superficial. Indeed, if the Holy Scriptures could demonstrate the divine origin of private property, they could on the contrary demonstrate that God preferred communism. Some extracts from the Leviticus expressed the idea that men had only received the use of things; the Gospels enjoined a life of poverty to reach eternal bliss; the logic of Christianity could imply the idea of a communion.[53] Indeed, the Holy

---

[46] La Perrière, *Le Miroir* 1555, In-fol., [6] fol., 199.
[47] While the belief in a communism which had existed before the Fall was by then a real myth. Marie-France Renoux-Zagame, *Origines théologiques du concept moderne de propriété* (Genève and Paris: Librairie Droz, 1986) 255-308, especially 261.
[48] La Perrière, *Le Miroir* 1555, 186, 188.
[49] Renoux-Zagame, *Origines théologiques* 1986, 98-106.
[50] La Perrière, *Le Miroir* 1555, 94-96.
[51] La Perrière, *Le Miroir* 1555, 96.
[52] La Perrière, *Le Miroir* 1555, 96.
[53] See *Leviticus*, XXV: 23; *Psalms*, XXIV, 1; *Numbers*, 33: 53-54.

Scriptures involved the subservience of things to men, but were at least equivocal for what concerned the nature of the precise relationship between men and things. In the end, La Perrière, limiting himself to giving his own opinion on the question, avoided becoming involved in the scholarly quarrels which, for more than a millennium, had vainly tried to solve those contradictions.[54]

From a pragmatic point of view, and agreeing with most of his contemporaries, he asserted that community of rights was against nature,[55] and that it was neither acceptable, nor permissive, since it could only generate evil or popular sedition, as Aristotle had already shown,

> si les biens estoyent communs, s'ensuyvroit grans inconvenientz entre plusieurs autres, c'est qu'une infinie multitude de maraux, oysifz et negligens, nayz en ce monde tant seulement (comme dit Horace) pour devorer et consumer les biens de la terre sans vouloir travailler, se nourriroyent & vestiroyent du bien de ceux qui à grand sueur de leurs corps & vexation de leurs espritz gaignent journellement leur vie [...].[56]

These arguments, also drawn from the Decree of Gratien (*Ia pars, dist. I,* c. VII), were the most standard ones (see Aquinas, *Summa, IIa IIae, Q. 66, art 2*). Ever since the first part of the sixteenth century, theologians had not considered them as irrefutable arguments, capable of justifying the division of property[57] by natural and divine right, and Thomas More had already shown their superficiality in his *Utopia*.[58] Nevertheless, La Perrière did not take pains either to deepen, or to resolve the contradiction resulting from their confrontation with assertions he had already developed in his *Miroir politicque* and that proved what damaging effects private property could breed.[59] He once more limited himself to roughly summing up his point of view about the question, maintaining that community of goods could only be imaginary and unreal, a pure fantasy, like Plato's *Republic* and Thomas More' *Utopia*,

---

[54] Renoux-Zagame, *Origines théologiques* 1986, 68, 74.
[55] Cfr. Vitoria, De Soto, Medina, Molina, Salon. Renoux-Zagame, *Origines théologiques* 1986, 276.
[56] La Perrière, *Miroir* 1555, 94.
[57] Renoux-Zagame, *Origines théologiques* 1986, 276.
[58] Thomas More, Le traité de la meilleure forme de gouvernement ou l'Utopie, ed. Marie Delcourt (Bruxelles, La Renaissance du Livre, 1966); Martin Fleisher, Radical reform and political persuasion in the life and writings of Thomas More (Genève: Droz, 1973) 37; Quentin Skinner, "More's Utopia and the Language of Renaissance Humanism" in The languages of political Theory in Early-Modern Europe, ed. Anthony Robin Pagden (Cambridge: Cambridge University Press, 1986): 123-157, or Quentin Skinner "Thomas More's Utopia and the virtue of true nobility" in Visions of Politics: Renaissance Virtues (Cambridge: Cambridge University Press, 2002) 216-217.
[59] La Perrière, *Miroir* 1555, 99, 103, 104, 106.

car telle republicque (comme souz le nom de Socrates, Platon en son imagination forgea) ne fut jamais mise en effet, ains est plus imaginaire que Realle, comme par similitude nous pouvons dire de la Republicque sainte, que Thomas Morus descrit en son Utopie.[60]

Plato's *Republic* had just been rediscovered, but was quite misunderstood. The Renaissance was not aware of the theoretical nature of the treatise, and did not seem to know that the philosopher had relinquished those conclusions in his *Laws*. The *Republic* was, indeed, condemned unanimously.[61] Everybody expressed similar critical comments to the ones expressed by La Perrière and blamed the *Republic*, which was considered to be useless. In fact, Marguerite de Navarre for instance thought that it could be written but not experimented (« s'escript et ne s'experimente poinct »).[62]

The judgement passed on *Utopia* was roughly identical. The work had rapidly become talked about, and in France had already been published several times when in 1550 Charles L'Angelier published a new French edition (even before the first English translation). However, by then, apart from Rabelais, most readers were convinced that the English Chancellor had proposed a model to be followed, and his text was taken literally.[63] The L'Angelier edition, prepared by Jean Le Blond and prefaced by an old letter addressed by Budé to Thomas Lupset, was to promote a better perception of the work. Indeed, Budé equated *Utopia* with Hagnopolis (a Holy city mentioned in the *Apocalypse*), and suggested that the island was out of time and of men's world. At the same time

---

[60] La Perrière, *Miroir* 1555, 94.
[61] Indeed, Jean Céard considers that only Marcile Ficin, Jean de Serres and Jean Bodin responded coherently to the problem set up by Plato. Jean Céard, "Le modèle de la *République* de Platon et la pensée politique au XVIe siècle" in *Platon et Aristote à la Renaissance. XVIe colloque international de Tours* (Paris: Librairie Vrin, 1976) 177-178.
[62] Marguerite de Navarre quoted by Jean Céard 1976, 179 and 187; See also the judgement of Barthélemy Aneau in Jean Céard, "La fortune de l'*Utopie* de Thomas More en France au XVIe siècle" in AA.VV. *La Fortuna dell'utopia di Thomas More nel dibattito politico europeo del '500. II giornata Luigi Firpo (2 marzo 1995)* (Firenze: Leo S. Olschki, 1996) 53 and Renoux-Zagame, *Origines théologiques* 1986, 265.
[63] The second edition was published in 1517, in Paris, by Gilles de Gourmont. The work was very soon criticised (see Germain de Brie's *Antimorus*, in 1520 and Thomas Elyot refutation in 1535) but was largely diffused, as many references contained in a pamphlet addressed in 1526 to the Sorbonne's theologians testify (see Geoffroy Tory' *Champ Fleury* in 1529, and Gratien Du Pont's *Controverses* in 1535). Rabelais was one of the first to understand the fictional side of the book (*Pantagruel*, ch. 2, 8, 9, 29 et 31). The first French translation was given by Charles l'Angelier in 1550; another one attributed to Barthelemy Aneau, was made in Lyon, by Jean Saugrain, in 1559; another one by Gabriel Chappuys in 1585. Céard, *La fortuna* 1996, 43-73.

he considered that its story could represent a model for some possible institutions and Budé especially praised the institution of equality of goods.[64]

La Perrière, carried along by the utilitarian principles guiding his *Mi roir Politicque*, and well aware of the utopian character of Thomas More's work, dismissed its communism. In fact he reached the same conclusion as More, but not for the same reasons.

More had finally been forced to conclude that it was impossible to abolish private property because of its incompatibility with the contemporary society's conceptions of nobility or splendour. To him, respect for the *communis opinio* imposed a heavy sacrifice on the whole community of men: giving up the possibility of achieving the best possible commonwealth.[65] La Perrière, anyway, refused on principle to consider that private property could be beneficial to men, and could hardly understand how some people had believed in its value. In his desire to make that demonstration, he left aside any contradictory arguments.

Indeed, he twice censured the Nicolaïtes' error,[66] but did not allude either to the first Christian communities following the logic of poverty professed in the Holy Scriptures, (*Acts of the Apostles*, II, 44 et IV, 32; *Decree of Gratien, Ia pars, dist. VIII et IIa pars, causa XI, 1*),[67] or to more recent texts he had heard about, unable to understand what diabolic inspiration could have inspired them:

> par qu'elle instigation diabolicque (encore de nostre temps) aucuns ont faict leurs effortz de rescusciter l'erreur de Platon sur la communication des biens temporelz, femmes & enfans.[68]

Indeed, this veiled allusion to Munster was at the origin of the development of his conceptions on private property, and the fatal issue that ended the unfortunate Anabaptist experience was, for sure, largely responsible for his sharp and quick-tempered treatment of the question.[69] La Perrière may have seen a potential risk in Plato and More's works (*Utopia* had first been translated into German in 1524[70]). Maybe he believed in the existence of a link between those

---

[64] Franck Lessay, "Le Prince d'Utopie: remarques sur une absence", *Thomas More, Utopia: Nouvelles perspectives critiques*, eds. Jean-Marie Maguin and Charles Whitworth (Montpellier: Centre d'étude et de recherches sur la renaissance anglaise - Université Paul-Valéry, 1999) 64 and 69.
[65] Skinner, More's Utopia 1986, 213-244.
[66] La Perriere, *Miroir I555*, 93 and 96.
[67] Castaldo and Levy, *Histoire* 2002, 402-403.
[68] La Perriere, *Miroir I555*, 93.
[69] See the papers by Catherine Dejeumont and Bernard Roussel at *Anabaptismes. De l'exclusion à la reconnaissance. Journée d'étude du 17 mars 2001 à l'Institut Protestant de Théologie*, Bull. Soc. Hist. Prot. Français, t. 148, janvier-mars 2002.
[70] Ferdinand Seibt, "Tommaso Moro nel dibattito utopico tedesco del cinquecento" in AA.VV. *La Fortuna dell'utopia* 1996, 25-42.

works and the German attempts of the 1520's, and consequently felt it necessary to include in his *Miroir Politicque* their very explicit *Confutation*[71] as the absolute condemnation of those who had tried to follow that error:

> Ces perturbateurs de la tranquillité publicque doivent estre exterminés (comme membres pourris) du corps politicque, car en voulant changer la façon de vivre par tant de siecles observée, ne taschent qu'à esmouvoir seditoin aux cités, et faire revolter les vassaux contre les princes, et le rude et mution populaire contre les magistrats, et n'est autre le but de leur visée.[72]

For, in reality, if La Perrière proved to be entirely convinced by the necessity to recognize the principle of private property, he appeared far from permissive about its practice.

If some Fathers had asserted that private property had been introduced into the world « *per iniquitatem* », and was, hence, an usurpation, La Perrière did not consider wealth an injustice.[73] But, as a priest, he could not help considering it as one of the most dangerous extant institutions, for man's fallen nature led him inexorably to damnable temptations, lust for wealth and miserliness,[74] which could ruin the Republic, as

> c'est convoytise qui commet les sacrileges et larrecins, qui exerce les rapines, qui dresse les batailles, qui perpetre les homicides, qui vend les benefices, qui fait les scismes, qui retarde le concile, qui dissimule

---

[71] "D'autant (lecteur) que la plus pernicieuse peste, que puisse onq survenir à un corps Politicq, est sedition et mutination entre les cytadins (pour eviter lesquelles avons estendu les nerfz de nostre debile et foyble engin à commenter les Arbres précédens) et que la Republicque Platonicque (laquelle Platon attribue à Socratés) donnoit occasion d'esmouvoir sedition pour la communité des biens, femmes et enfans, plus que toute autre, avons icy inséré ce que s'ensuit", La Perriere, *Miroir* 1555, 93.
[72] La Perrière, *Miroir 1555*, 96-97.
[73] "Natura igitur ius commune generavit, usurpatio jus fecit privatum", Saint Ambroise, *Les devoirs*, trans. by Maurice Testard (Paris: Les Belles Lettres, 1984) XXVIII-132, 158-159 and 252-253.
[74] "Car en ceste vie mortelle (en laquelle plus que jamays les voluptez sont courtes, et les douleurs longues), sans ouvrir noz yeulx à regarder nostre misere, et exciter noz cueurs, à contempler nostre calamité, nous ruynons journellement noz Ames, pour ediffier noz corps, et pour trop vouloir heriter en terre, nous faisons hexereder du Ciel. Faisans ung semblable et aussy peu proffitable eschange, que feist jadis Esau, qui pour la gloutonnerie du potaige fraternel, perdist la benediction paternelle. [...]. Les mortelz demandent journellement biens a Dieu, mays ilz ne luy demandent pas, qu'il leur donne grace de bien en user. Ilz desirent incessamment que fortune soit favorable a leurs affections, et ne s'estudient aulcunement que leurs voulentez soyent conformes a rayson. Ilz prennent grand peyne a embellir leurs corps, mayson, et domicille, et ne travaillent pas a decorer leur esperit. Ilz cherchent curieusement et achaptent a gros pris les medecines des maladies corporelles, et des maladies de l'ame n'en font aulcun compte", Guillaume de La Perrière, *Annales de Foix*, 1539, fol. [10-10 v.].

les abuz, qui iniquement demande et deshonnestement reçoit, qui injustement tracasse, qui dissout les pactes, qui viole les juremens, qui corromp tous tesmoignages, qui pervertist les jugemens, et qui finalement confond tous droitz tant divins comme humains. O feu inextinguible? O gouffre qui ne se peut combler? Se trouveroit-il homme en ceste valée de misère, qui fust content à son souhait? Quand nous avons ce que nous souhaitons nous en desirons d'advantage: nous ne constituons iamais la fin en ce que nous avons, ains en ce que nous pretendons avoir, car (comme dit le poëte), tant comme croist la pecune, tant croist l'amour & convoytise d'ycelle.[75]

Indeed, La Perrière is absolutely convinced of the necessity to prevent men from accumulating too much wealth. His first work, *Invective satiricque*, was devoted to the public denunciation of some « monopolies», recently punished by Toulouse Parliament.[76] Today, the work is no longer in fashion but the title is very explicit and seems to point out the practice of some merchants who accumulated grains to raise prices, and sold them at a higher cost in time of shortage, wholly unconcerned either about the poverty of the people who crowded around the city, or about the years of scarcity or even about epidemics. Such practice had already been condemned by the Gospels and was recurrent in the area of Toulouse in the sixteenth century,

> Toulouse Parliament should have dealt severely with these merchants:[77] in his *Miroir Politicque*, La Perrière greatly regretted the inefficiency of those condemnations, stressing the fact that in the past Roman law condemned such criminals to the death penalty.[78]

---

[75] La Perrière, *Miroir 1555*, 79.
[76] Inuective satyricque // nouuellement tyssue & composée par mai-//stre Guillaume de La Perrière, licen-//tié es droicts: citoyen de Tholose. Contre les suspects monopoles de // plusieurs crimineulx satellites: et gens de vie reprouvée: imitateurs // de ceux qui furent naguieres pu-//gnyz et iusticiez audict Tholose par auctorité de la souveraine cour de // Parlement miroir de vertu: et fontaine de iustice. // (A la fin:) Gulielmus a Perriera iurium licen. Tholosae Dicta-//bat anno Reparate Salutis per Iesum Christum. // MDXXX. Idibus Octobris. // In-4°, goth., 16 fol.
[77] Decision of the 29th of April 1530, repeated many times. Bernard La Roche-Flavin, Arrests notables du Parlement de Toulouse, donnez et prononcez sur diverses matieres, civiles, criminelles, beneficiales, et feodales [...] (Toulouse: Guillaume-Loüis Colomiez et Jerôme Posüel, 1682) 40-41; decisions of the 3rd of March 1531, 20th of April and 6th of May, in AMT, AA 5, n. 305 et 210-213, summed up by Ernest Roschach, Inventaire des archives communales antérieures à 1790, t. I, série AA (Toulouse: Privat, 1891) 86 and 95; other decision, especially that of the 1st of February 1545, ADHG, BB 39, 1545-1546, fol. 141 v.-142 v. or that of the 17th of August 1564, B 57, fol 792, quoted by Philippe Wolff, Documents sur l'histoire du Languedoc (Toulouse: Privat, 1969) 180.
[78] La Perrière, *Miroir 1555*, 101.

4.

This last allusion to Roman Law is quite remarkable, because very rarely does La Perrière allude to Roman law in his *Miroir Politicque,* with the exception of references to annona or sumptuary laws. La Perrière seems to have already been aware of the relativism of the law.

More than a lawyer, La Perrière is in fact a moralist. Like his contemporaries, he considers private property as absolutely necessary, and as the very cause of men's ordeal.[79] Dedicating his *Miroir Politicque* to Toulouse magistrates, the "capitouls", he limits himself to practical considerations about the legitimacy or use of private property, without really arriving at the core of those questions. He was influenced by the revival of stoicism, the intention of which, via Cicero and Erasmus, was to release the law from its technical nature to attempt to attain some great moral principles, in character with men's reasonable nature.[80]

---

[79] Céard, *Le modèle* 1976, 184.
[80] Jean-Louis Thireau, "La doctrine civiliste avant le code civil", *La Doctrine juridique* (Paris: Centre l'Histoire du droit et de recherches inter-normatives de Picardie, Centre universitaire de recherches administratives de Picardie, Presses univ. France, 1993) 27 and 30. Michel Villey, "L'humanisme et le droit", *Seize essais de philosophie du droit dont un sur la crise universitaire* (Paris: Dalloz, 1969) 60-72; Thireau, "La nature des choses", *Seize essais* 1969, 42.

«De l'affection des pères aux enfants»: Sentimental Bonds and Juridical Bonds in Montaigne, *Essais*, II, 8

Giovanni Rossi

University of Verona

In late medieval Europe all the way into the first modern age, one of the most common and harassing preoccupations that could torment a *pater familias* was the fate of the family's wealth after his death.[1]

The mission of preventing fragmentation of the family's assets – something that could be disastrous for the family's very survival – became a veritable torment, omnipresent in the last will and testament of any aristocrat and in general of the prosperous classes and capable of triggering the most comprehensive strategies for the management of family property.[2] The exercise of measures deemed economically convenient for the attainment of this end therefore takes on the value of an ethical imperative and becomes common practice in terms of concrete juridical actions, only rarely left unapplied. Indeed, such a transgression would weigh like a stone on the consciousness of any father senseless enough to neglect his duties and thus doing to put at risk the material means necessary for the conservation of his house and for its prosperity.[3]

The historian therefore inherits the image of an entire society engrossed in the spasmodic effort of thinking up any means in general relevant to the rules of

---

[1] For an introduction to the topic from the historical and juridical viewpoint, see Andrea Romano, *Famiglia, successioni e patrimonio familiare nell'Italia medievale e moderna* (Torino: Giappichelli, 1994) especially 1-85; Vincenzo Piano Mortari, *Gli inizi del diritto moderno in Europa* (Napoli: Liguori, 1982) 171-195; see also the 'items' of Manlio Bellomo, *Famiglia (diritto intermedio)*, in the *Enciclopedia del Diritto*, XVI (Milano: Giuffrè, 1967): 744-779 and Gigliola Di Renzo Villata, *Persone e famiglia nel diritto medioevale e moderno*, in *Digesto IV edizione*, sez. Civile, XIII (Torino: Utet, 1996): 457-527, 497-513. Older but still useful is also Nino Tamassia, *La famiglia italiana nei secoli decimoquinto e decimosesto* (Roma: Multigrafica, 1971, first published in 1911), especially 104-149 and 248-265.

[2] In addition to the references indicated above, of a historical/juridical nature, there are also works from non-jurists anyhow attentive to the juridical aspects of family assets; see Gerard Delille, *Famiglia e proprietà nel regno di Napoli. XV-XIX secolo*, trans. Maria Antonietta Visceglia (Torino: Einaudi, 1988); Gerard Delille, *Le maire et le prieur. Pouvoir central et pouvoir local en Méditerranée occidentale (XVe-XVIIIe siècle)* (Rome-Paris: École française de Rome – Éditions de l'École des hautes études en sciences sociales, 2003); Renata Ago, "Ruoli familiari e statuto giuridico", *Quaderni Storici* 88 - XXX (1995): 111-133.

[3] An effective representation of this feeling, predominant in much later times too, that directly and heavily affects life-choices of individuals, is found in Roberto Bizzocchi, *In famiglia. Storie di interessi e affetti nell'Italia moderna* (Roma-Bari: Laterza, 2001).

conduct commonly observed in the field of social discipline and more specifically juridical, capable of preserving the integrity of the family's fortune, safeguarded and handed down by descent following the male line of succession. This was an indispensable tool in the management and development of trade and credit activities as well as the basis and guarantee for the social and political importance of the lineage.[4]

This scenario could be found basically unchanged throughout most of Europe, despite the obviously substantial differences existing in the various states in terms of sources of legislations in force and actual juridical regime. It should be noted, in fact, that all the way into the modern era the law immediately applicable to the topic of proprietary relations within the family everywhere is governed mostly by local customs, that are characterised by being absolutely particularistic sources, based on local dictates and lacking unifying legislative models capable of linking or even of effectively routing the spontaneous evolution of praxes within the various states.

Amongst the most significant documents in revealing the vigil focus of 16th century European society on interpersonal relations within the family are several pieces of Montaigne's *Essais*. This author in fact tackled the issue at length in various places but most extensively in the *Essai* II, 8, *Of the affections of fathers to their children*[5] that contains precious indications of his critical reconsideration of the entire issue about the relationships between a *pater familias* and his wife and children. The result is a comprehensive reflection on the configuration traditionally taken on by the family *societas*, of which he lucidly and shrewdly analyses the various elements: the emotional component and the institutional, economical and more typically political ones, based on the tie existing between the *familia* and the *respublica*. The fertile starting point for Montaigne, that reveals the difference in mentality separating him from the Middle Ages, consists in the admission that such relationships must not be limited to a merely economical vision, nor to their legal formalization, as they fully involve the sphere of individual subjectivity.[6] Indeed, Montaigne's analysis unveils the slow onset within the collective consciousness of modern Europe of the awareness that it is not enough to take into account only the material interests involved. Conversely, any reflection on the family by this time involves focusing first of

---

[4] For a specific highlighting of the match created in both literary and juridical literature between *substantia* and *memoria* of the family, one instrumental to the perpetuation of the other and both ensured using adequate juridical tools for succession issues, see Thomas Kuehn, "Memoria and Family in Law", *Art, Memory, and Family in Renaissance Florence*, ed. Giovanni Ciappelli and Patricia Lee Rubin (Cambridge: Cambridge University Press, 2000): 262-274.

[5] As regards the date in which this essay was written, as demonstrated by Villey, it is later than 1578: Pierre Villey, *Les sources et l'évolution des Essais de Montaigne*, t. I, *Les sources et la chronologie des Essais* (Paris: Hachette, 1908) 360-361.

[6] See James Casey, *La famiglia nella storia* (Roma-Bari: Laterza, 1991) 183-206.

all on private life that only now, in full 16th century, is painstakingly surfacing in literature as being worthy of notice. Thus we see the emergence in the late Renaissance of an authentically subjective dimension that perhaps for the first time consciously underlines the aspect of individual psychology. This gives rise to a widespread dialectic that features the institutional and juridical world on the one side and interpersonal relations on the other.[7] Indeed, while the former proves to be longstanding and relatively stable in time, and actually clearly tends to stiffen in modern times – by providing family structures with a patina of inelasticity based on institutions such as parental authority and its corollary, the father's interference in matrimonial choices, and the will and testament, with the *fidei-commissum* set up to guard over preservation of the estate – the latter instead evolve towards giving greater importance to the emotional element in family relationships and to individual subjectivity, although encased in juridical frameworks functional to the regulation of the roles[8] that increases precisely between the 16th and 18th centuries.

Today all this constitutes commonly accepted historiographic knowledge, although still requiring further and detailed research on the sources and despite the necessary rejection of several historiographic theses of a mechanically evolutionary order that stemmed from a vein of studies on the history of mentality, based on a markedly sociology-oriented standpoint. Indeed, such theories in the past were highly acclaimed but also sparked heated debate, and we deem them highly unsatisfactory as they lack any in-depth research of the sources, are at times naïve and excessively simplify the social and cultural life of the Middle Ages and of the Renaissance, the extreme richness and complexity of which cannot be constrained within the banalising description of a linear progressive motion.[9]

---

[7] On this topic, see also Giovanni Rossi, "La roba e gli affetti: rapporti patrimoniali e legami personali nella famiglia da Leon Battista Alberti a Montaigne e Charron", *Il diritto nella letteratura rinascimentale europea. Percorsi di ricerca interdisciplinari*, ed. Giovanni Rossi (Padova: Cedam, forthcoming).
[8] On the regulation of the society in the modern age see Pierangelo Schiera, "Disciplina / Disciplinamento", *Annali dell'Istituto storico italo-germanico in Trento* XVIII (1992): 315-334; *Origini dello Stato. Processi di formazione statale in Italia fra medioevo ed età moderna*, eds. Giorgio Chittolini, Anthony Molho, Pierangelo Schiera (Bologna: Il Mulino, 1994); *Disciplina dell'anima, disciplina del corpo e disciplina della società tra Medioevo ed età moderna*, ed. Paolo Prodi (Bologna: Il Mulino, 1994); see also Giorgia Alessi, "Discipline. I nuovi orizzonti del disciplinamento sociale", *Storica* II (1996): 7-37.
[9] The mandatory reference is to the research conducted by Philippe Ariès and especially to the many enthusiastic and at times clumsy followers of the French sociologist, whose merit it is to have set under the lens of historiography several very important issues until then unfairly neglected, including relations between generations and the space assigned to youth – and therefore to children – in modern society: cf. firstly Philippe Ariès, *Padri e figli nell'Europa medievale e moderna* (Paris: Plon, 1960), trans. Garin (Bari: Laterza, 1968). A reconsideration of the issue is found in Marzio Barbagli, *Sotto lo stesso tetto. Mutamenti della*

Within the context indicated above, one can quite rightly agree with the widespread definition of Montaigne's "modernity".[10] Proof of this author's vivid participation in the problem concerning the relationship with one's children, found in several pages of moving autobiographical sincerity in his *Essais*, is revealed first of all as a psychological malaise personally experienced by the author and caused by the difficulty in cultivating a relationship capable of bringing him close to them from the human viewpoint, in the attempt to break a constrictive tradition that seems to impose the setting up of family relations in function of the choices regarding the future destination of the family wealth, used with cold calculation as a formidable instrument of power over the potential heirs. Relations between generations should not in fact rely on the heavy conditioning of the children's life applied via cynical recourse to the right to deal as one pleases with one's own assets, both in life and *post mortem*, replacing spontaneity and sincere sentiments with simulated affection stemming solely from filial expectations of the father's inheritance:

> I would endevour by a kinde of civil demeanour and milde conversation to breede and settle in my children a true-harty loving friendship, and unfained good will towards me [...].[11]

To know the inclination of each child, to appreciate their company, to live with them in an atmosphere of relaxed unselfishness, without imposing one's presence and without laying down the law in the family *ménage* with the prerogative of despotically deciding to bequeath family assets to one rather than to another: this is the family model championed by Montaigne, who more in general dedicates many pages of his masterpiece to the in-depth analysis of issues concerning the many facets of the relationship with one's children, starting from the theories developed in the extensive and significant essay *Of the Institution and Education of Children* (I, 26).

---

famiglia in Italia dal XV al XX secolo (Bologna: Il Mulino, 2000) 14-18 and 245-269, where an attempt is made to add to the traditional consideration for the structural elements that tend to be stable over the long-term, those concerning «authority and sentimental relations between persons » (245) that imply greater attention paid to change; it also contains bibliographical references to the actors of the historiographic *querelle*, a starting with the important work by Lawrence Stone, *Famiglia, sesso e matrimonio in Inghilterra fra Cinque e Ottocento* (London: Weidenfeld and Nicolson, 1977), trans.E. Basaglia (Torino: Einaudi, 1983). See now also Jack Goody, *La famiglia in Europa* (Roma-Bari: Laterza, 2000) 89-102.

[10] Even though it seems fitting to circumstantiate the judgement, so as not to fall prey to the indefiniteness of commonplace; cf. the critical position expressed by Peter Burke, *Montaigne. Un profilo* (Oxford: Oxford University Press, 1981), trans. Bianca Lazzaro (Roma: Donzelli, 1998) 9-13.

[11] *Essai* II, 8 (we use the Florio's translation of Montaigne's *Essays*, first published in 1603).

From this viewpoint, the usual and well-proven juridical solutions common to those times[12] – certainly well-known to those who, like Montaigne, for many years wore the gown of a magistrate – lose importance, with their conditioning technicism, when confronted with the attempt to unflinchingly restore the rich and fertile *humus* underneath made of sentimental bonds that it is right and humane to cultivate and to privilege instead of the political and economic interests of lineage and of political faction, even if inextricably intertwined with blood relations and with kinships. There is indeed no lack of juridical rules erected to help prevail at all costs the perpetuation of the group, via the guarantee of an estate's integrity, against that of the individual to freely express his own individuality, exploiting to this end the marked hierarchical structure of the family by which the *pater* is given the task of becoming the indisputable representative of the group and therefore is allowed to impose his sovereign will on wife and children, especially when such will typically takes on the shape of a written testament.

The position of head of the family and house therefore is two-fronted and after all ambiguous: on the one side the law seems to provide extremely effective tools to safeguard his subjectivity, such as the testament and the fideicommissary mechanism,[13] but on the other his prerogatives prove to be the expression of a *munus*, i.e. they take on the meaning of a power/duty exercising

---

[12] For first information on the issue, in the French kingdom, see Pierre Ourliac, Jean De Malafosse, *Histoire du droit privé, III. Le droit familial* (Paris: Presses Universitaires de France, 1968) 58-85 and 515-537; Pierre Ourliac and Jean Luis Gazzaniga, *Histoire du droit privé français de l'An mil au Code civil* (Paris: Michel, 1985) especially 251-284 and 317-356; see also Emmanuel Le Roy Ladurie, "Système de la coutume. Structures familiales et coutume d'héritage en France au XVIᵉ siècle", *Annales ESC* XXVII (1972): 825-846, reprinted in English "Family structures and inheritance customs in sixteenth-century France", *Family and Inheritance: Rural Society in Western Europe, 1200-1800*, eds. Jack Goody, Joan Thirsk, Edward Palmer Thompson (Cambridge: Cambridge University Press, 1976): 37-70.

[13] See Mario Caravale, "Fedecommesso (diritto intermedio)", *Enciclopedia del diritto* XVII (Milano: Giuffrè, 1968): 109-114. Regarding this topic we have an ample but quite inhomogeneous literature in terms of interest and value; in addition to the ever useful Romualdo Trifone, *Il fedecommesso. Storia dell'Istituto in Italia. I. (Dal diritto romano agli inizi del sec. XVI)* (Napoli: Luigi Pierro & figlio, 1914), see, among the more recent historical/juridical works, Antonio Padoa Schioppa, "Sul fedecommesso nella Lombardia teresiana", *Studi in onore di Antonio Amorth* (II, Milano: Giuffrè, 1982): 425-447, and now in Antonio Padoa Schioppa, *Italia ed Europa nella storia del diritto* (Bologna: Il Mulino, 2003) 439-459; Andrea Padovani, *Studi storici sulla dottrina delle sostituzioni* (Milano: Giuffrè, 1983); Maria Carla Zorzoli, *Della famiglia e del suo patrimonio: riflessioni sull'uso del fedecommesso in Lombardia tra Cinque e Seicento*, in *Archivio Storico Lombardo* CXV (1989): 91-148, and in *Marriage, Property and Succession*, ed. Lloyd Bonfield (Berlin: Duncker & Humblot, 1992): 155-213; Romano, *Famiglia* 1994, 60-83 and 139-170; Maura Piccialuti, *L'immortalità dei beni. Fedecommessi e primogeniture a Roma nei secoli XVII e XVIII* (Roma: Viella, 1999).

which the father wrestles with the difficult obligation of pursuing the interests of the family group, as such superior to the *pater* himself.[14]

Montaigne's position innovatively shifts the focus from the objective and therefore unquestionable conditions that rule over the handing down *mortis causa* of the family assets – among which *in primis* the juridical discipline in force – over to the subjective implications of the inheritance mechanism, functional to a predefined family arrangement that in that form can no longer be accepted *a priori*, but only after having concretely verified its compliance with superior criteria of equity and humanity. Children must not be subjected to a harsh destiny that makes them mute extras of a storyboard written by others, according to rules aimed at perpetuating the family through the safeguarding of its estate. The rigid hierarchy that reigns within the family and underpins all of its components to the will of the *pater*[15] confirms and legalises a generational subordination of the children, formally founded on age and sanctioned by law, that actually is concretely based on and coactively embodied for its implementation and perpetuation in the exclusive control of the family wealth firmly placed in the hands of the *pater familias*. Montaigne's corrosive analysis is precisely against such coercion acting as basis of the family structure, stating that it is the origin of deep-rooted social malaise:

> *(a)* As for mee, I deeme it a kind of cruelty and injustice, not to receive them [*i.e.* the children] into the share and society of our goods, and to admit them as Partners in the understanding of our domestical affaires (if they be once capable of it and not to cut off and shut-up our commodities to provide for theirs, since we have engendred them to that purpose. It is meere injustice to see an old, crazed, sinnowshronken, and nigh dead father sitting alone in a Chimny-corner, to enjoy so many goods as would suffice for the preferment and entertainment of many children, and in the meane while, for want of meanes, to suffer them to lose their best dayes and yeares, without

---

[14] The more recent historiography touches upon the powers and duties padding out the legal position of the *pater*, underlining the complexity as well as the partial flexibility of the roles played within the family, in a dialectic that continued into the 19th and 20th centuries: see the works in *Pater familias*, ed. Angiolina Arru (Roma: Biblink, 2002).

[15] One of the privileged environments in which this hierarchical structure is more evident because it directly affects the destiny of the property and becomes part of complex lineage strategies, is that of the choices linked to the marriage of the children, destined to perpetuate the family within the framework of a legitimate conjugal match, or excluded from this possibility and induced to remain unmarried. On the motivations for these decisions and on the dialectic between principle of authority and free determination of one's own destiny, see Renata Ago, "Giovani nobili nell'età dell'assolutismo: autoritarismo paterno e libertà", *Storia dei giovani. I. Dall'antichità all'età moderna*, eds. Giovanni Levi and Jean Claude Schmitt (Roma-Bari: Laterza, 1994): 375-426.

thrusting them into publike service and knowledge of men; whereby they are often cast into dispaire, to seeke, by some way how unlawfull soever to provide for their necessaries. And in my dayes, I have seene divers yong-men, of good houses so given to stealing and filching, that no correction could divert them from it.[16]

The free will of the father, that sometimes takes on arbitrary and even cruel forms, should therefore meet its necessary limitation in the expression of subjectivity of each individual, so as to produce a fair adaptation of the various interests at stake, all worthy of consideration.

All of which also must pass through the radical and healthy relativization of the preoccupation for the perpetuation of lineage, which torments most of the European 16th-17th century aristocracy:[17]

(c) We somewhat over-much take these masculine substitutions to hart, and propose a ridiculous eternity unto our names.[18]

In short, these pages give us a very personal reflection that sometimes breaks into autobiographical introspection and then returns to the lucid tones of an attentive and penetrating interpretation of contemporary society, with an outlook that we may define as essentially sociologic.[19] As often occurs with Montaigne, it is possible to identify various levels in his writing, which once again proves to be a veritable mine of quotations from ancient authors, all in a refined intellectual game that matches echoes of classical knowledge with dazzling annotations of topical customs. This generates a very thickly weaved argumentative fabric, consisting of heterogeneous material remelted without any apparent effort into a meditation as varied in its many arguments as it is unitary in its development around a single object: mankind in general and, as its representative, one man in particular, Montaigne himself, depicted as microcosm and "character" of humanity as a whole.

In detail, the piece dedicated to a father's affection for his children gets its title from *De amore prolis*, one of Plutarch's moral operettas.[20] After all, this

---

[16] *Essai* II, 8.

[17] Giulio Vismara, "L'unità della famiglia nella storia del diritto in Italia", *Studia et Documenta Historiae et Iuris* XXII (1956): 228-265, now in Giulio Vismara, *Scritti di storia giuridica*, 5. *La famiglia* (Milano: Giuffrè, 1988) 1-44, 35; Jack Goody, *Famiglia e matrimonio in Europa. Origini e sviluppi dei modelli familiari dell'Occidente* (Cambridge: Cambridge University Press, 1983), trans. Francesco Maiello (Milano: Mondadori, 1984) 267-287.

[18] *Essai* II, 8.

[19] On the French family see Jean Luis Flandrin, *Familles. Parenté, maison, sexualité dans l'ancienne societé* (Paris: Seuil, 1984), especially 69-90 and 117-142.

[20] For a detailed interpretation of Plutarch's operetta, correctly aimed at contrasting Epicurean

perfectly matches the entirely peculiar importance Plutarch has in Montaigne's thinking, and more in general in French 16th century thought, also thanks to the French translation from Greek of the *Moralia* made in the seventies by Jacques Amyot[21] and highly appreciated by Montaigne.[22] After all, his interest is perfectly in tune with that era's deep love for the classical authors and with the conscious reuse of their works. Indeed, this French moralist meditates at length on an author whom he feels very close to, preferring him even to the beloved Seneca[23] and to the select group of classical authors collected in his library and which provide many starting points for his reflections.[24] No wonder then that the opening of *Essai* II, 8 picks up in an evident manner (and perhaps for this reason not declared, deeming the annotation superfluous) the assumption on which Plutarch's treatise is based, centred around the demonstration in anti-Epicurean style of the natural origin of the parents' love for their children, the presence of which – and therefore its universality – is easily demonstrated even in animals:

> *(a)* If there be any truly-naturall law, that is to say, any instinct, universally and perpetually imprinted, both in beasts and us, (which is not without controversie) I may, according to mine opinion, say, that next to the care which each living creature hath to his preservation, and to flie what doth hurt him, the affection which the engenderer beareth his off-spring holds the second place in this ranke. And forasmuch as nature seemeth to have recommended the same unto us, ayming to extend, encrease, and advance the successive parts or parcels of this her frame; it is no wonder if back againe it is not so great from children unto fathers.[25]

---

utilitarism, cf. Adelmo Barigazzi, *Studi su Plutarco* (Firenze: Università degli Studi di Firenze – Dip. di Scienze dell'Antichità G. Pasquali, 1994) 141-181. As regards the text of the work, see PLUTARQUE, *Oeuvres Morales*, VII.1 (Paris: Les Belles Lettres, 1977) 177-184, and PLUTARCO, *L'amore fraterno. L'amore per i figli*, ed. Anacleto Postiglione (Napoli: D'Auria, 1991) ("Corpus Plutarchi Moralium", 7).

[21] The first edition is dated 1572, then followed by others in 1574, 1575, 1579; the translation of *Parallel lives* dates back to 1559; to this regard see Robert Aulotte, *Amyot et Plutarque: la tradition des moralia au XVIème siècle* (Genève: Droz, 1965); Robert Aulotte, *Plutarque en France au XVIe siècle: trois opuscules moraux traduits par Antoine Du Saix Pierre de Saint-Julien et Jacques Amyot* (Paris: Klincksieck, 1971).

[22] See the explicit statement in this sense at the beginning of Essay II, 4.

[23] See Villey, *Les sources* 1908, 198-200 for Plutarch; 214-217 for Seneca; Hugo Friedrich, *Montaigne* (Bern –München: Francke, 1967, first published in 1949), respectively 71-79 and 62-68.

[24] For a documented summary-description of Montaigne's education, based on the books he owned and actually used, see VILLEY, *Les sources* 1908, 271-280.

[25] *Essai* II, 8.

We have here, therefore, a literary text of purely Humanistic inspiration, that however reveals an unexpected consistency as it blends learned reminiscences with a lucid and original analysis of contemporary family relations and dwells upon common social phenomena that have economic, political and juridical weight. In fact, it contains suggestions of various kinds – in accordance with the unique thick-page stylistic code of the Essays – and the reader can easily find there, either watermarked or explicitly indicated, precise references to the world of law, from which one is obliged to derive the tools concretely usable for achieving the desired objectives.

To this regard, we feel compelled here to make a quick digression in order to point out the problem regarding the technical training in the specific field of law acquired by Montaigne in youth and the juridical knowledge he truly had. Some scholars, in fact, have clearly belittled this component of his cultural baggage, to the point of doubting his law studies in Toulouse[26] that tradition credits him with, whereas others have gone so far as to attempt a comprehensive interpretation of his work based on the recovery of typically juridical literary genres (and thus on the underlying mental schemes) such as the gloss, which according to them Montaigne would have used as peculiar tool of expression for his thought.[27] Apart from the problem of casting light on a specific biographical datum and with the promise of discussing elsewhere the role of law in the *Essais* – a very complex topic with many relevant implications[28] – we feel that it is

---

[26] See the book by Roger Trinquet on Montaigne's youth, that does not hesitate to propose a strongly dubitative reinterpretation of what he defines as the «myth of the Toulouse studies »: Roger Trinquet, *La jeunesse de Montaigne. Ses origines familiales, son enfance et ses etudes* (Paris: Nizet, 1972) 509-535. To be fair, no certain information is available about such studies or in general about his doings around the year 1550. His attendance of law studies at the Toulouse University has been based on clues and reasonable assumptions but never irrefutably proven. Scholars agree on this point: see the considerations developed, for example, in Paul Bonnefon, *Montaigne et ses amis*: *La Boétie – Charron – Mlle de Gournay*, t. I (Genève: Slatkine Reprints, 1969, first edition Paris: Colin, 1898) 47-51; Jean Plattard, *Montaigne et son temps* (Genève: Slatkine Reprints, 1972, first published in 1933); Madeleine Lazard, *Michel de Montaigne* (Paris: Fayard, 1992) 74-76.

[27] We refer here to the theories formulated in André Tournon, *Montaigne. La Glose et l'essai* (Lyon: Presses Universitaires de Lyon, 1983, republished in Paris: Champion, 2001), especially 147-202, concerning Montaigne's knowledge of law and its influence on his work. Regarding the elements present in the *Essais* based on the alleged legal culture of the author, also see André Tournon, "L'essai: un témoignage en suspens", *Carrefour Montaigne* (Pisa-Genève: Ets/Slatkine, 1994) 117-145; Ian MacLean, "The place of interpretation: Montaigne and humanist jurists on words, intention and meaning", *Neo-Latin and the vernacular in Renaissance France*, ed. Grahame Castor and Terence Cave (Oxford: Clarendon Press, 1984): 252-272; André Tournon, "Montaigne et le droit civil romain", *Montaigne et la rhétorique. Actes du Colloque de St. Andrews (28-31 mars 1992)*, eds. John O'Brien, Malcolm Quainton, James J. Supple (Paris: Champion, 1995): 163-176.

[28] The issue, among other things, has two complementary but distinct facets. On the one hand it concerns the Tolouse studies and on the other his activity as magistrat performed from

anyhow difficult to refute Montaigne's precise knowledge of family and succession law as in force in France in those times, based on his rather long period of activity as magistrate in the *Parlement* of Bordeaux. Certain passages in which he recalls his own experience as judge and certain very clear diagnoses on the state of justice and more in general on the conditions of the Kingdom's legal system are in our opinion irrefutable proof of his legal training.[29]

In tackling the topic, Montaigne expresses clear-cut positions that imply precise disapproval of traditional juridical institutions and of mainstream sociopolitical choices that have determined their great success in French and European society in the late 16th century. His refusal of the rich and greatly effective arsenal of compliant solutions thought up by legal praxis and therefore refined by juridical doctrine during the course of the centuries regarding family and succession law appears to be unequivocal. The conscience of people who, like Montaigne, by that time seem to intend the family no longer as a monolithic entity subject to the unquestionable decisions of the *pater* that is its leader and lord, but rather as a *societas* formed by individuals who have feelings worthy of respect and who hold legitimate expectations regarding the inheritance that cannot be disappointed and reject those rules that unjustly coerce the life of each one and deprive the father himself of the absolutely human pleasure of enjoying the company of his dear ones in an atmosphere of unselfish familiarity. From this stems the explicit and *ante litteram* criticism that invests parental authority (because it prevents the children, *vivente patre*, from obtaining their part of the heredity when it would be most useful to them and forces them to remain subjected to the father *sine die*, without reaching the economic independence that would grant them an autonomous life), the testament (as it allows the expression of an arbitrary will in the choice of heir), the fideicommissary clauses (as they bind the heirs to the sovereign decisions of the *de cuius*, theoretically *in infinitum*), the devices of life tenancy in favour of the widow (as they render purely nominal for many years the children's right to inherit the father's wealth):

> *(a)* I have also observed another kinde of indiscretion in some fathers of our times, who during their owne life would never be induced to acquaint or impart unto their children that share or portion which, by the Law of Nature, they were to have in their fortunes: nay, some

---

1554 – when he became counsellor of the *Cour des Aides* of Périgueux, implemented at that time by Henry II – to 1570 – when he abandoned the Parliament of Bordeaux, entered in 1557, following the suppression of the other court and the incorporation of its magistrates into the *Parlement*; see Bonnefon, *Montaigne* 1969, 52-101.

[29] Useful platform for this topic are the rich pages of Luigi Mengoni, "I pensieri di Montaigne sul diritto", *Studi in memoria di D. Pettiti* II (Milano: Giuffrè, 1973): 901-919, and in Luigi Mengoni, *Diritto e valori* (Bologna: Il Mulino, 1985) 103-119.

there are who, after their death, bequeath and commit the same auctoritie over them and their goods, unto their wives, with full power and law to dispose of them at their pleasure. And my selfe have knowen a Gentleman, a chiefe officer of our crowne, that by right and hope of succession (had he lived unto it) was to inherit above fifty thousand crownes a yeere good land, who at the age of more then fifty yeeres, fell into such necessity and want, and was run so farre in debt, that he had nothing left him, and, as it is supposed, died for very need: whilest his mother, in her extreme decrepitude, enjoyed all his lands and possessed all his goods, by vertue of his fathers will and testament, who had lived very neere foure-score years: a thing (in my conceit) no way to be commended, but rather blamed.[30]

This consideration, however, even if it targets juridical institutions typical of the *ius commune*, is made without resorting to the vast repertoire of invectives, insults and ferocious caricatures often utilised liberally by French intellectuals in their zealous criticism of late medieval juridical praxis.[31] In this case, Montaigne places himself on the margin of the Humanist movement that in 16th century France saw one of its major supporters in "learned" jurists while he manages to remain substantially extraneous to the controversy arising from the urge to renovate the methodology of Italian jurisprudence of "Bartolist" extraction.[32]

In *Essai* II, 8 all of this actually remains in the background, almost as if to underline the importance and fragility of an issue that does not tolerate a shift of focus onto false polemical targets.

The problem concerning the proper equilibrium in the interests at stake in view of the opening of succession *mortis causa*, both in the relations with the children and in those with the wife/widow/mother, is solved by Montaigne with the use of a balanced approach that tries to save the position of each party. This does not mean however that the author hides his own preferences and aversions, stemming also from the sharing of ideas and prejudices typical of his age. His reasoning, for example, clearly indicates his persuasion of the psychological and physical inferiority of women compared to men, invoked as the reason for choices that concretely tend to restrict the female sphere of action. The role of the woman, identified *tout court* as the wife, is the important and delicate but

---

[30] *Essai* II, 8.
[31] Emblematic the case of Rabelais and of his unrelenting satire against Judge Bridoye, contained in his *Tiers livre* (published in 1546 and then again in its final version in 1552: François Rabelais, *Le Tiers Livre*, ed. Michael Screech (Genève: Droz, 1974).
[32] The issue is quite complex and of capital importance toward the construction of juridical modernity; see the overview offered in Vincenzo Piano Mortari, *Cinquecento giuridico francese: lineamenti generali* (Napoli: Liguori, 1990), as well as the updated interpretation in Italo Birocchi, *Alla ricerca dell'ordine. Fonti e cultura giuridica nell'età moderna*, (Torino: Giappichelli, 2002) 1-49, with its additional abundant bibliography.

undoubtedly limited and subordinate one of keeper and administrator of the household, under the supervision of the husband whose primary task is to provide the family with resources through his activity in the outside world as well as to constantly guide and supervise the spouse who enjoys only limited autonomy, as resulting from a passage from the essay *Of Vanity*:

> *(b)* The most profitable knowledge and honourablest occupation for a matron or mother of a familie is the occupation and knowledge of huswiferie. I see divers covetous, but few huswifes. It is the mistresse-qualitie that all men should seeke after, and above all other endeavour to finde, as the onely dowry; that serveth either to ruine and overthrow, or to save and enrich our houses. *(c)* Let no man speake to me of it; according as experience hath taught me, I require in a maried woman the Oeconomicall vertue above all others [...].[33]

What we see here therefore is unconditional agreement with the teachings of economics provided by the pseudo-Aristotle and by Xenophon and still fully backed by the best Renaissance thinkers, founded on the functional distribution of tasks between spouses and at the same time on the stiff hierarchy between sexes, once again enhancing the validity of the authority of the *pater familias*.[34] All of this is based on the conviction of woman's incapability to stand the family burden on her own and to profitably manage the wealth inherited, founded on an entire set of *argumenta* and pseudo-scientific medical and naturalistic proof of Aristotelian extraction,[35] still deeply rooted and widespread in 16th century culture:[36]

> *(c)* But to return to my former discourse, *(a)* me thinkes we seldome see that woman borne to whom the superioritie or majestie over men is due, except the motherly and naturall; unlesse it be for the

---

[33] *Essai* III, 9: *Of Vanitie*.

[34] The good fortune of the "economic" in the early modern age has been underlined by Otto Brunner, "La 'casa come complesso' e l'antica 'economica' europea" (1958), now in Otto Brunner, *Per una nuova storia costituzionale e sociale*, ed. Pierangelo Schiera (Milano: Vita e Pensiero, 2000, first editino 1970): 133-164; see also Daniela Frigo, *Il padre di famiglia. Governo della casa e governo civile nella tradizione dell'«economica» tra Cinque e Seicento* (Roma: Bulzoni, 1985).

[35] After all, Aristotle's presence in Montaigne is certainly not secondary or negligible: see Enzo Traverso, *Montaigne e Aristotele* (Firenze: Le Monnier, 1974) who addresses the problem and investigates in particular the direct influence of Aristotle's *Politics* and *Nicomachean Ethics* on the *Essais*.

[36] For these issues, cf. now, also for updated bibliography, Giovanni Rossi, "«Viri uxoribus imperanto. Uxores viris obediunto». I rapporti coniugali tra modelli classici e diritto consuetudinario in André Tiraqueau", *La tradizione politica aristotelica nel Rinascimento: tra «familia» e «civitas»*, ed. Giovanni Rossi (Torino: Giappichelli, forthcoming).

chastisement of such as by some fond-febricitant humour have voluntarily submitted themselves unto them: But that doth nothing concerne old women, of whom we speake here.[37]

In this instance Montaigne questions the idea itself of the natural feeling of maternal love: «*(a)* Moreover, experience doth manifestly shew unto us that the same naturall affection to which we ascribe so much authoritie, hath but a weake foundation [...]».[38]

More in general, Montaigne refutes even the mere suggestion that the wife may be preferred by the *de cuius* over the children in the testament, as already seen above:

> *(a)* Some colour of reason there is, men should leave the administration of their goods and affaires unto mothers whilest their children are not of competent age, or fit according to the lawes to manage the charge of them: And ill hath their father brought them up, if he cannot hope, these comming to yeares of discretion, they shal have no more wit, reason, and sufficiencie, than his wife, considering the weaknesse of their sexe.[39]

It must be said however that he believes even more disdainful the provision that subjects the widow to the will of the children.[40]

The solution proposed by Montaigne at this point is easily imagined: if the sovereign will of the individual, made manifest in the testament, often produces unjust results,[41] placing the mother or the children in an untenable condition of

---

[37] *Essai* II, 8. The passage continues in the same vein, defining the judgement: «*(a)* It is dangerous to leave the dispensation of our succession unto their judgement, according to the choyse they shall make of their children, which is most commonly unjust and fantasticall. For the same unrulie appetite and distasted relish, or strange longings, which they have when they are great with child, the same have they at al times in their minds [...] For, wanting reasonable discourse to chuse, and embrace what they ought, they rather suffer themselves to be directed where nature's impressions are most single as other creatures, which take no longer knowledge of their young ones than they are sucking» (*ibidem*).
[38] *Ibidem*. The example given to corroborate the statement is that of the wet-nurses, who agree to abandon their natural children to the teats of the goats in order to nurse the children of others and who become more sentimentally attached to the latter, of a sentiment as strong as that which grows between the goats and the children they feed.
[39] *Ibidem*.
[40] «*(a)* Yet truly were it as much against nature so to order things that mothers must wholy depend on their childrens discretion. They ought largely and competently to be provided wherewith to maintaine their estate according to the quality of their house and age: because 'need and want is much more unseemely and hard to he indured in women than in men:' And children rather than mothers ought to be charged therewith» (*ibidem*).
[41] In itself the testament can have a quite varied and complex content, and Montaigne proves

subjection; if the law, on the other hand, is the tangible expression of the prince's authority and leaves out justice and reasonableness, let alone that, as interpreted by the doctors, it cannot give proof of itself honourably because *interpretatio* adds a factor of uncertainty that in turn opens the door to the inevitable but pernicious recourse to the unregulated will of the judge, then habit in the end is the most secure haven. Indeed, despite the fact that Montaigne's innate scepticism and relativism prevent him from believing that *coutume* truly embodies natural law, custom appears anyhow suitable for reproducing «the common and legitimate order» since it is not subject to the contingent interests of either the private individual or of the prince and can offer a well-balanced and time-proven discipline for the various situations.

After all, the testator may be suborn and anyhow easy prey to momentary but violent passions and, when close to the final moment, lose much of his reason. The enormous power concentrated in the hands of the *pater* due to his right to make a will and, in this way, to dispose of the family property should be limited and saved from the mood of the moment, finding its guide and containment in «reason» and in «common use », capable of mutual integration in indicating the best solution possible:

> *(c)* I see some towards whom it is but labour lost, carefully to endevour to doe any good offices. A word ill taken defaceth the merit of ten yeeres. Happy he that, at this last passage, is ready to sooth and applaud their will. The next action transporteth him; not the best and most frequent offices, but the freshest and present worke the deede. They are the people that play with their wils and testaments as with apples and rods, to gratify or chastize every action of those who pretend any interest thereunto. It is a matter of over-long pursute, and of exceeding consequence, at every instance to be thus dilated, and wherein the wiser sort establish themselves once for all, chiefly respecting reason and publike observance.[42]

Montaigne in this manner also feeds his professed misoneism, which assuages his scepticism about the things of the world (and especially about human

---

he knows this and considers the preparation of this deed as a very delicate affair, to be carried out only after carefully weighing the consequences of the declarations of last will: cf. *Essai* I, 7: *That our intention judgeth our actions*: «*(c)* I have in my dayes seene many convicted by their owne conscience, for detaining other men's goods, yet by their last will and testament to dispose themselves, after their decease to make satisfaction. This is nothing to the purpose [...] Penitence ought to charge, yet doe they worse, who reserve the revealing of some heinous conceit or affection towards their neighbour, to their last will and affection, having whilest they lived ever kept it secret [...]».

[42] *Essai* II, 8.

«De l'affection des pères aux enfants» 175

society) merged with the embittered disappointment for the changes occurred in the political and religious fields of his century:

> *(c)* In all things, except the wicked, mutation is to be feared; yea, even the alteration of seasons, of winds, of livings, and of humours. And no lawes are in perfect credit but those to which God hath given some ancient continuance: so that no man know their, of-spring, nor that ever they were other than they are.[43]

One must therefore bow to the superior legitimacy and reasonableness of those juridical uses to which the Kingdom's magistrats have turned to for such a long time when seeking to find the true *droit Français*, that is a *species* of that *coutume* of which Montaigne himself has celebrated, almost with a sense of stupefied admiration and reverential fear but not without a necessary amount of aloofness, the enormous and irresistible power, in the famous essay no. 23 of Book 1, that quite appropriately talks about *Of customs, and how a received law should not easily be changed*:

> *(a)* My opinion is that hee conceived aright of the force of custome that first invented this tale; how a country woman having enured herselfe to cherish and beare a young calfe in her armes, which continuing, shee got such a custome, that when he grew to be a great oxe, shee carried him still in her armes. For truly Custome is a violent and deceiving schoole-mistris. She by little and little, and as it were by stealth, establisheth the foot of her authoritie in us; by which mild and gentle beginning, if once by the aid of time it have settled and planted the same in us, it will soone discover a furious and tyrannicall countenance unto us; against which we have no more the libertie to lift so much as our eies; wee may plainly see her upon every occasion to force the rules of Nature.[44]

---

[43] *Essai* I, 43: *Of Sumptuarie Lawes, or Lawes for moderating of Expenses*. A belief that finds its application also in the reflection on the political life and on the institutions of a people: «*(b)* Not to speake by opinion, but consonant to truth, the most excellent and best policie for any nation to observe, is that under which it hath maintained it selfe. Its forme and essentiall commoditie doth much depend of custome [...] Nothing doth so neerely touch and so much overlay an estate as innovation: Onely change doth give forme to injustice and scope to tyranny [...]» (*Essai* III, 9: *Of Vanitie*).
[44] *Essai* I, 23: *Of Custom*. For an attempt (as praiseworthy as it is isolated) of relating and of comparing Montaigne's indications on *coutume* with the coeval and very rich literature of 16th century French jurists, see Françoise Joukovsky, *Montaigne et le problème du temps* (Paris: Nizet, 1972) 143-168.

He's talking here about a tyrannical habit, fruit of conventions arising from historical contingencies and set free from the laws of nature, with a much wider latitude than the juridical notion of *coutume*, but within a same conceptual frame of reference. The recovery of *coutume* as a reliable rule in the delicate moment of family succession obviously gains special importance precisely in the light of the memorable demystifying analysis contained in essay *Of custom*, where the author does not hesitate to unmask the opaque effectual fundament of many *mores*, rooted only in their repeated use in time and lacking whatever superior rational justification:[45]

> *(c)* The laws of conscience, which we say to proceed from nature, rise and proceed of custome; every man holding in special regard and inward veneration the opinions approved, and customes received about him, cannot without remorse leave them, nor without applause applie himselfe unto them.[46]

More specific and to the point – but also partly different and more complex – is the argument relating to the *mores* in the field of law. After revealing the formidable conditioning power of the will of the individual implicit in custom and after outlining its substantial departure from the rules of nature, Montaigne does not fail to point out that, from the juridical viewpoint, the wise must also know how to see its positive features for the praxis, that at least derive from the fact that *coutume* configures, within a given social group and at a specific place and time, the predetermined behaviour to be used in a given situation. It thus offers an antidote to the individual's disorienting and potentially dangerous freedom of judgement and imposes a predefined and shared rule of conduct to which to turn to when trying to overcome the subjectivism and relativism manifested by the political and religious vicissitudes of the late 16th century. Although it has lost the solid medieval anchorage in a superior dimension of objectively recognisable and absolutely valid values – but disguised as uncompromising respect for that natural law that in actual fact it ignores and scorns – it can still play an important role, in any case by binding the associates to a precise conduct that has the merit of being foreseeable and unvarying and of drawing inspiration, according to the parameters of each historical context, from an appreciable rate of reasonableness and common sense. There is instead no

---

[45] Very lucid and convincing pages have been dedicated by Anna Maria Battista to the meaning of this theory, qualified as being a "positivistic approach against the doctrine of natural law" and identified as being the beginning of modern political thought: Anna Maria Battista, *Alle origini del pensiero politico libertino. Montaigne e Charron* (Milano: Giuffrè, 1966), 171-190; Battista, "Nuove riflessioni su «Montaigne politico»", *Studi politici in onore di Luigi Firpo*, ed. Silvia Rota Ghibaudi and Franco Barcia (Milano: Franco Angeli, 1990): 801-848 (quotation on 804, n. 8 end).

[46] *Essai* I, 23.

«De l'affection des pères aux enfants»

guarantee that such qualities are possessed by the royal law, modernly felt as founded uniquely on the authority of a non-resistible force, although not a product of repeated use in time but of contingent political power and thus by definition even more unmotivated, arbitrary and incomprehensible for the subjects:[47]

> *(b)* Lawes are now maintained in credit, not because they are essentially just, but because they are lawes. It is the mysticall foundation of their authority – they have none other – which availes them much: *(c)* they are often made by fooles; more often by men who, in hatred of equality, have want of equity; But ever by men who are vaine and irresolute Authours. There is nothing so grossely and largely offending, nor so ordinarily wronging as the Lawes. *(b)* Whosoever obeyeth them because they are just, obeyes them not justly the way as he ought [...].[48]

At this point, the lesser evil is certainly the habitual tradition born of the general consensus for proven practices and appears better balanced. At least, its artificial character is no longer perceived as such and therefore does not offend the feeling of common justice, as would have been the case of the law of the individual, be it expressed in the *ordonnance* of the king or in the testament of the private citizen:

> *(c)* In generall, my opinion is that the best distribution of goods is, when we die, to distribute them according to the custome of the Country. The lawes have better thought upon them than we: And better is it to let them erre in their election than for us rashly to hazard to faile in ours. They are not properly our owne, since without us, and by a civil prescription, they are appointed to certaine successours. And albeit we have some further liberty, I thinke it should be a great and most apparent cause to induce us to take from one, and barre him from that which Fortune hath allotted him, and the common lawes and Justice hath called him unto: And that against reason we abuse this

---

[47] See the acute interpretational key proposed by Paolo Grossi, who classifies under this aspect Montaigne's meditation in the initial but already perfectly readable moment of emersion of juridical modernity, to be found in the passages dedicated to the characters of the (royal) *loy*, presented by Montaigne as totally unbridled by the limitations placed by medieval tradition and identified with the king's will, not subject to any syndicate when it comes to the ethics of its content: Paolo Grossi, "Modernità politica e ordine giuridico", *Quaderni Fiorentini per la storia del pensiero giuridico moderno* XXVII (1998): 13-39, and in Paolo Grossi, *Assolutismo giuridico e diritto privato* (Milano: Giuffrè, 1998) 443-469 and 458-461. See also the illuminating analysis by Battista, *Nuove riflessioni* 1990, 840-848.
[48] *Essai* III, 13: *Of Experience*.

liberty, by suting the same unto our private humours and frivolous fantasies.[49]

Along this path it is possible to achieve the better result hoped for: «the use of the country» unexpectedly becomes interpreter of «reason» and produces a solution that is not only formally valid and effectively feasible but also a just solution, in the light of that new feeling of enhancement of individuality of anyone who demolishes the power/duty of the *pater familias* of deciding for everyone and acting as the judge of the life of others: the match between «coustume» and nature celebrates an apparently conservationist outcome that is actually steeply bent towards modernity.

Thus, by identifying the source of production of law that, at least in this case, associates the peak of cogence and of effectiveness with the peak of common sense and even of substantial equity, it shall be possible to repeat with Pliny: «*(c)* usus efficacissimus rerum omnium magister».[50]

---

[49] *Essai* II, 8.
[50] *Essai* I, 23. The quotation is found in PLINY, *Naturalis historia*, XXVI, 2.

The Voice of Dominium - Property, Possession and Renaissance Figures in The Cantos of Ezra Pound

Adam Gearey

Birkbeck College, London

1. Introduction

"Real knowledge does NOT fall off the page into one's stomach. Allow, in my case thirty years, thereabout, for a process which I do not yet call finished, the process of gradually comprehending why Dante Alighieri named certain writers. Sordello he might also have touched in spoken tradition. Cunizza, white haired in the house of the Cavalcanti, Dante, small gutter-snipe, or small boy hearing the talk in his father's kitchen, or later, from Guido, of beauty incarnate, or, if the beauty can by any possibility be brought into doubt, at least with utter certainty, charm and imperial bearing, grace that stopped not an instant in sweeping over the most violent authority of her time and, from the known fact, that vigour which is a grace in itself. There was nothing in Crestien de Troyes' narrative, nothing in Rimini or in the tales of the antients (ancients) to surpass the facts of Cunizza, with, in her old age, great kindness, thought for her slaves."[1]

> That freed her slaves on a Wednesday
> Masnatas er servos, witness
> Picus de Farinatis
> And Don Elinus and Don Lipus
>   Sons of Farianato de' Farinati
> free of person, free of will
> free to buy, witness, sell, testate.

Two texts; two fragments from Ezra Pound. Why should a scholar of Renaissance[2] law and literature be interested in these materials? This paper will argue that Pound's aesthetics are bound up with issues of possession and ownership. Studying the appearance of Cunizza da Romano in Canto VI can

---

[1] Ezra Pound, *Guide to Kulchur* (London: Peter Owen, 1966) 107.
[2] Following Symonds, the Renaissance can be understood as a process that is ongoing and unfinished. In this sense, there is perhaps less reason to be anxious about a periodisation between 'modern' and 'renaissance' literature. See John Addington Symonds, *Renaissance in Italy* (London: Smith, Elder and Co, 1919) 2: "The word Renaissance has of late years received a more extended significance than that which is implied in our English equivalent...[t]he truth is that in many senses we are still in mid-Renaissance."

illuminate both the importance of Renaissance legal and literary materials for Pound and the wider sense in which the Cantos open up possibilities within literary jurisprudence. We will focus on a single issue. Why, in Canto VI, does Pound make reference to manumission, to the granting of freedom to slaves? Why should a reference to this Roman law doctrine appear in the Cantos?[3] The problematic of ownership and possession can draw attention to a key theme in the Cantos: the relationship between law and poetry in the imagining of a vision of law's correct order.

The argument will develop as follows: we will engage with the importance of an idea of persona and dominium for Pound's aesthetics, and find that jurisprudence is intimately linked to a notion of poetic voice. Turning to the Roman law of slavery, we will concern ourselves with the constitution of the doctrine of manumission. These themes will then be brought together in a reading of Canto VI, where Cunizza's kindness in freeing her slaves introduces a theme that will go on to shape the entire development of the Cantos.

2. The Voice of Dominium

The relevance of Roman Jurisprudence to Pound's poetry is indicated by the title of a collection of early poems: *Personae*. With a root meaning of 'mask', persona carries both a poetic or literary signification and a legal meaning. The literary sense is that of the voice the poet borrows to create a dramatic monologue. In law, persona could mean a person (or even a group) capable of having legal rights.[4] We can extend this argument. The legal subject is a possessor of rights over things; a person with dominium.[5] In its broadest sense, dominium describes

---

[3] Manumission is related to "patrimoniale" as part of a nexus of themes that concern inheritance, tradition and language. "Patrimoniale" relates to the English words property or estate. The Latin word on which it is based, "patrimonium" (the paternal estate) thus resonates within patrimoniale; as do links with the Patria, the land one loves; the land of one's birth. "Patrimonio culturale" could be translated into English as meaning one's cultural inheritance; a construction that loses the sense of the word property in English; patrimony perhaps being more related to a private inheritance, and possibly somewhat archaic if used to describe something broader. "Patrimonio lessicale" carries a sense of language's link to the patrio or the father land that is lost in the more neutral English word 'vocabulary'.

[4] William Warwick Buckland, *A Manual of Roman Private Law* (Cambridge: Cambridge University Press 1953) 34.

[5] Dominus can be understood as a person's relationship to a thing (in contrast with potestas, which describes relationships between persons). See Ann Marie Pritchard, *Roman Private Law* (London: Macmillan, 1961) 157. It is "natural" to man, and hence will find its form in the law. Roman law stressed ownership, placing few restrictions on the rights of the owner (158) although it is contended that the term is best understood as a relationship giving rise to a plurality of rights. As has been pointed out, the dominus had manifold entitlements over the res: he could use it, enjoy the products of the res or consume it completely; dominion also

the way in which the subject is born and "positioned in advance"[6] by the structure of the law. Dominium provides the constitution of social being: the basic structure of the subject whose ability to possess things is related to his own possession of his self and his ability to relate to other subjects. To own, to convey; to be located in a kinship structure, where one can inherit property, and leave property to be inherited.[7] In this sense, we might suggest that dominium is the sense of being rooted in a culture, in a set of relationships with others. Identity and authority come out of this social and civic context. Dominium refers, ultimately, to a double figure: one can lay claim to objects because one is born into a culture and a tradition where objects can be owned. Arguably, the *Cantos* bring together the aesthetics and the jurisprudence of dominium; but how could the notion of dominium be related to poetic voice?

In the *Cantos*, dominium is inscribed in a certain tone of voice; a rhythm. This voice is not that of the various characters who speak in the poem; it is a singular voice; a voice that speaks out of a culture and makes a claim to the location of the Cantos within that culture. In Canto VI this voice speaks the opening lines:

---

included the capacity to alienate or dispose of the res. This argument is supported by the claim that classical legal discourse spoke of transferring the thing itself, rather than transferring ownership. Such a conveyance would create a dominus, bringing another's dominium to an end. It is thus important to ask, who was capable of dominium. Dominium was restricted to those who had commercium, or the "capacity to take part in ius civile ceremonies"(23) and, in a later period, to those foreigners who had become specially privileged.

[6] See Pierre Legendre, *L'Empire De la Vérité* (Paris: Fayard, 1983) From Legendre's psychoanalytic perspective, Roman law is to be seen as a "universal structure" laying down a way of 'staging' functions which psychoanalysis considers as necessary to social being: the institution and reproduction of human life. This is a "non –negotiable principle" (116) or a "principle of universal legislation" (116). Identifying this principle means stripping away the discourses on popular rights that have proved obstructive of the truth of Roman law. Roman law has shown itself to be flexible, adapting itself to various historical contexts, from its formal use in the development of the common law tradition to the more concrete way in which it provided the axioms for the law of the Holy See.

[7] For a thorough elaboration of these themes, it would be necessary to return to Hegel's *Philosophy of Right*, and to Marx's critique. See Karl Marx and Frederick Engles, "Contribution to the Critique of Hegel's Philosophy of Law", *Collected Works, Volume 3* (Moscow: Progress Publishers, 1975). Marx observes that it is with the Romans that we find the roots of the law of private property in concepts of civil law. He argues that the Romans based their thinking on sensuous reality: so, underlying the right of private property is the right to control a thing. Roman law operates by classifying relations, and dividing these relations into categories that describe the relationship of subject to object; in other words, which relations are "those of abstract private property" (110). Property is a central element to the composition of the public bond.

"What you have done, Odysseus,
   We know what you have done..."

The voice of dominium grants itself its own right to speak, and to speak to others. It is the legal/aesthetic voice of the Cantos, bestowing on itself the authority to interpret and carry forward the poem. The opening apostrophe to Odysseus assumes this very authority; and, as the Canto develops, the voice directs and orchestrates the way in which the poem is read. In this sense it is capable of owning the poem, and for the Cantos, this means that it can suggest the links between the fragments: it is the voice that knows the law of the poem; the tradition out of which the poem is written.

Although fragments of biography are spoken by the voice of dominium, it may or may not be the voice of Ezra Pound. At times, the voice invites the reader to hear it as such, but it is not necessary to get unduly caught up with this issue, for our primary concern is the voice's operation within the text of the poem. We need to try and define in more detail the particular 'grain' of the voice of dominium. The first time it announces itself is in Canto I, when it interrupts the account of the summoning of Tireseas and draws attention to the act of composition of the poem:

"Lie quiet Divus. I mean, that is Andreas Divus,
In officina Wecheli, 1538, out of Homer."

Asking Divus to lie quiet is the voice that arranges the poem, integrating the Homeric translation into this new field of texts. Canto I is describing a moment of transmission and translation; Divus' translation of the Odyssey. At its broadest this is a concern with the carrying forwards of the classical tradition into the renaissance (as the date suggests). The poem continues, offering comments on its own text:

"Venerandam,
In the Cretan's phrase, with golden crown..."

The translation is finally interrupted with the closing fragment: " so that: ", and the opening of the next Canto:

"Hang it all, Robert Browning..."

Pound is making a reference to Browning's poem *Sordello*. Canto II continues the allusion, making a distinction between Browning's text, the historical figure Sordello and the *Cantos* as a re-reading or re-writing of Browning. In other words, the poetic voice is addressing, at the same time, the composition of the poem and the identity of its antecedents. To acknowledge the importance of Browning's work is to forefront the issue of the tradition and inheritance. *Sordello* suggests the development of the vernacular; a poetic voice that is positioned to the end of the literary periplum that moves from the reception of classical culture to the development of national literatures. Browning's use of Italian forms and concerns repeats and redoubles the borrowings of the Elizabethan 'golden age' from Italianate sources. Browning himself is a figure of the reception and redoubling of the Renaissance itself. These concerns are important elements of dominium, as they delineate the literary inheritance of the *Cantos*, the poem's relations to other cultural forms and periods.

Even when it does not announce itself, the voice of dominium is present (if one accepts that it can be associated with the form of the poem itself). There are many voices that speak in the *Cantos*; but a distinction can be made between the voices speaking in a Canto, and the poetic voice that may or may not draw attention to itself and comment on or forefront the act of writing. Consider the movement of the Canto II. After the opening address, the invoking of Browning, there is an evocation of So-shu that passes into the name of Eleanor of Aquitaine, memories of the Trojan war, and an inter linking of the names of various gods that prepares for the long section of Acoetes' narration of Dionysus and the transformation of the ship. The poem concludes with a lyrical description of night falling. These texts appear to be a diverse body of materials that have simply been brought together with no connection between the various characters, gods or stories. The voice of dominium does not intervene to direct and manage the reader's perceptions. The voice may re-appear at the beginning of Canto III, but with another fragment of biography:

"I sat on the Dogana's steps
For the gondolas cost too much, that year,
And there were not "those girls", there was one face..."

This point can be related back to the extract from the Guide to Kulchur that opens this essay. There is insufficient space in this essay to explore this complex theme, but its contours can be indicated. The voice of dominium is linked to Pound's notion of art itself. Unless the reader has been through the education that Pound recommends, the *Cantos* will remain inert. The reader will not be able to make the links that the voice of dominium demands; perhaps more precisely, unable to hear the tone of words; unable to discriminate. Ultimately, one requires what Pound calls character or virtu. Poetic art requires not only the refining of sensibility, but a moral awakening. Elaborating these ideas takes us to the core of Pound's aesthetics.

For Pound, great art is the foundation of history and philosophy because it presents the world as it is: it operates through "luminous detail"[8] rather than commentary. Whereas history and philosophy are about ideas that are relative and change with time and place, art penetrates into the real. This means that it makes for compression and discrimination. If the artist can achieve "accuracy of sentiment", he can reveal the irrefutable shape of a phenomenon.

The voice of dominium aims to 'speak' in terms of luminous detail and accuracy of sentiment; revealing essential themes through significant fragments. As a poetic voice it unites sound and sense. The troubadours are important for Pound because they exemplify these poetic virtues. The troubadour song carries forward a form of poetry from the classical and pagan traditions to the literatures of Southern Europe, and by implication, into Pound's *Cantos*. Although this broad sweep shows the truth of the poetic corpus, each individual poem contains its "own law". What is this law? Consider Pound's distinction between symptomatic works and donative works. The former are particularly representative of the culture from which they emerge; they are merely representative, a "register" of wider themes. However, donative art explodes out of its time; tearing apart conventions, forming a rupture in the tradition. It is different from what went before, although it is at the same time enabled by its tradition. To return to an earlier term, it is more discriminating; it forces an appreciation of difference: things are not what they might have seemed. The example returns us to a figure of the Renaissance, or, rather to a figure that for Pound makes the triumph of the Renaissance possible: Arnaut Daniel. Writing a century before Dante and Guido, Arnaut both carries forward the classical tradition, and redefines it. As a thesis about poetry, this is also a claim about how one uses language. When language was still lacking in precision, and "prolix", Arnaut discovered "style."[9] The lyric, as a form at it best, produces a correspondence between the rhythmic pulse of words, the music of which language is capable, and the cargo of sense that words carry.

But this can be pushed much further to a notion of character and virtu. It is always someone who speaks and says something. One cannot speak of the lyric

---

[8] See "I Gather the Limbs of Osiris" in Ezra Pound, *Selected Prose 1909-1965*, ed. William Cookson (New York: New Directions, 1973). "Luminous method" is thus an approach to history based on profound moments of vision. To exemplify this theme, Pound cites Burckhardt's history of the Renaissance: " In this year the Venetians refused to make war on the Milanese because they held that any war between buyer and seller must prove to be profitable to neither." This is luminous because it defines a moment, the transition from the middle ages to the modern period. The detail shows that one political and economic order has come to an end, and from its ashes another emerging. There are of course many problems with this theory of interpretation, but to take this at its face value, "luminous method" reveals the "intelligence of a period."(22)

[9] Pound, *Prose* 1973, 27

without speaking of the poet, and this from this relationship it is as if we can derive an entire notion of character, and even an ethics of speaking and acting.

Virtu individuates; allowing us to talk of individual poets as marked by a particular way of using words, a particular way of living. Virtu is also the ability to distinguish and discriminate, to create a world. This process can be described by reference to the great writers. Homer represents man becoming "conscious of the world outside him"; a world of possibilities, of experiences and significances that may remain dark and mysterious. The awareness of the inner world is figured by Dante. Chaucer fuses these positions, so that one can speak of others as like oneself to the extent that they have character and an inner life. However, these great writers merely illustrate a general process of growth towards a maturity where one can say what one means. These issues, then, are not purely ones of poetic technique. There is a wider concept of character implied by Pound's thinking of poetry. How might this relate to the notion of manumission? Why should this be a mark of Cunizza's character and a fit subject for poetry?

3. Poetics, Property and Manumission

Answering the questions posed above makes it necessary to briefly engage with the Roman concept of slavery. To be a slave was to lack civil being, and, perhaps in a Poundian sense, to lack character. To be a slave is be possessed; to fall within a citizen's dominium. In Roman law a slave is a chattel, something that can be owned. Despite Buckland's claim[10] that slavery developed pragmatically as an institution, we need to revise this approach if we are considering slavery as both a concept in property, and as a theme in the *Cantos*. It is necessary to examine the philosophy that underlay slavery. Indeed, Buckland cites Justinian's definition of liberty that can be traced to Florentinus: "Liberty is the natural capacity of doing what we like, except what, by force of law, we are prevented from doing."[11] One might suggest that the Roman law of slavery, if not based on an explicit philosophy, was bound up with a set of assumptions about the nature of civic being and property. If *The Institutes* inform us that men are either free or slaves[12] then we could presume that slavery illuminates the very constitution of the citizen; indeed, the line between slave and freeman suggests a fundamental ontological distinction.

---

[10] William Warwick Buckland, *The Roman Law of Slavery* (Cambridge: Cambridge University Press, 1908) "The Roman law of slavery...was developed by a succession of practical lawyers who were not great philosophers, and as the main purpose of our definition is to help in the elucidation of their writings, it seems unwise to base it on a highly abstract conception which they would hardly have understood and with which they certainly never worked."
[11] Buckland, *Roman* Law 1908, 437.
[12] Buckland, *Roman* Law 1908, 1.

Slavery is brought about by the fundamental intervention in nature by culture. The Ius Naturale made men free by nature. Intervening in this natural state, the Ius Gentium brought about the category of slavery. It is as if one is born again into slavery. Certainly, to be born to a slave mother was definitive of one's status.[13] Capture in war could also make a person a slave. If, in the law of war, a captive could be killed, then to spare a captive's life is to enslave them. A person free by nature is thus reduced to slavery.

It is in this sense that slavery is likened to death; a form of civic death that could be equated with the fact that a slave was a thing: "the point which struck [the Roman writers]...was that a slave was a Res", and for the classical lawyers, the only human *Res*.[14] It is because a slave is a "res" that, by deduction, s/he cannot be a person; in other words, a slave's rightlessness is founded on his or her status as a thing. Slavery, in a more modern idiom, might thus be described as the most profound alienation from one's being as a subject. Indeed, "the Roman slave did not possess the attributes which modern analysis regard as essential to personality."[15] But, we need to be clear on this point. Although a slave lacked legal being, there is evidence that Roman writers still considered a slave to be a human being. Perhaps the closest we can get to the historical sense, then, is that a slave was a human person without rights; at least without those rights and duties that constituted civic being.

To read this jurisprudence through the *Cantos*, we might suggest the following: if to be a person is to have rights, then, the ultimate gesture is to grant those rights to one who has been deprived of legal being.[16] To allow a person to possess his or her self. Manumission is the act of granting freedom to slaves. It can be described as "a release not merely from the owner's control, but from all possibility of being owned."[17] Manumission is the point at which a slave becomes a citizen.[18]

The reference to the *Guide to Kulchur* at the beginning of this essay suggests the emotional dynamic of Pound's approach to Cunizza and manumission. It appears that setting free her slaves was an act of her "kindness" and "old age": " white haired in the House of Cavalcanti"; with Pound speculating that it was Dante himself who heard of the act. Cunizza's act is inspired by "that vigour which is a grace in itself." The point of this observation is not to argue that Pound is concerned with a particular form of manumission[19] but to relate

---

[13] Buckland, *Roman* Law 1908, citing Plautus, 159.
[14] Buckland, *Roman* Law 1908, 3
[15] Buckland, *Roman* Law 1908, 3.
[16] Buckland, *Roman* Law 1908, 42. "Though in principle slavery was lifelong, there was a power of manumission"
[17] Buckland, *Roman* Law 1908, 438.
[18] Buckland, *Roman* Law 1908, 439.
[19] If there is a legal reference here, it might be to manumissio testamento, or at least have its roots in this doctrine.

Cunizza's act to broader field put in place by the Canto. Could it be that, in its fullest sense, Pound associated manumission with a becoming human: the point at which a person enters culture? Manumission relates to a set of concerns that allow the persona to appear as a rights holder, as something capable of possession; as someone who can both inherit and pass on property; a link in a genealogical chain,[20] a "transmission."[21] In the way that the voice of dominium lays claim to the poem by delineating it from other traditions, texts and sources, Cunizza's act of manumission allows slaves to become subjects, delineating their status as citizens from their status as things. Moreover, it is an act that forms an exemplary theme for poetry as it represents for Pound the ultimate moral act. Why else would Dante place Cunizza in paradise? Perhaps this is the clue as to why Cunizza's kindness is so stressed by Pound. But, in what way does this take us back to the law? We need to read Canto VI.

4. Canto VI

The first nine lines of the Canto read as follows:

> "What you have done, Odysseus,
>   We know what you have done....
> And that Guillaume sold out his ground rents
>   (Seventh of Poitiers, Ninth of Aquitain).
> "Tant las fotei com auzirets
>   Cen e quatre vingt et veit vetz..."
> The stone is alive in my hand, the crops
>   will be thick in my death-year..."
> Till Louis is wed with Eleanor

The voice of dominium lies behind Canto VI. It presents linkages between various fragments, an implicit statement about a cultural period. The first movement of the poem, after the apostrophe, introduces a narrative from William of Poitiers,[22] which modulates into a return to the Eleanor of Aquitaine theme, developed with extracts and allusions to troubadour songs, and incidents from the history of the troubadours. This concludes with Cunizza's act of

---

[20] On the idea of genealogy, see Peter Goodrich, *Oedipus Lex* (Berkeley: University of California Press, 1995).
[21] Goodrich, *Oedipus* 1995, 24.
[22] "The first troubadour honorably mentioned is of courtly rank: William IX, Count of Poitiers (1086-1127), a great crusader and most puissant prince...his fame rests rather upon deeds than upon the eight poems that have survived him." See, Ezra Pound *The Spirit of Romance* (London: Peter Owen, 1952) 41.

manumission, and a song from Sordello. How can we link together these concerns; what is the golden thread that makes this poem coherent?

The poem presents, in 'lunminous method', salient details that give the shape of the early Renaissance; it reveals, the "intelligence of a period." The fragments appear disassociated, chaotic, because the poetic method has to work with inherent difficulty, the opacity of facts. The shape of the period will be revealed as the concern that holds these details together. What is the relevance of Odysseus? At least one answer is that Odysseus returned; the Odyssean periplum is the story of the return to the patria. At a different level, Odysseus is a figure for the Cantos themselves. He represents the possibility of a kind of poetic return; a unity between diverse materials, a unity that presupposes a voice, a persona, a point at which the chaos makes sense. It is indeed the voice of dominium that speaks the important lines

> "The stone is alive in my hands, the crops
> will be thick in my death year..."

Other critical approaches to Canto VI suggest that it is Guillaume that speaks these lines. However, they do not appear in quotation marks and Guillaume's voice also seems to be indicated by medieval French diction. It is the voice of dominium that is speaking here; drawing attention to the form of the poem. That the stone is alive in the hands of the sculptor, or that the stone contains a god, is the metaphor for potential and its realization; a description of the art of poetry. The meaning of the poem as a whole is to be found in its arrangement and in the transitions between the various texts and materials of which it is composed.

The Cunizza section has to be understood in this context. Note, first of all, how the opening lines draw attention to inheritance, and an order of law that allows an individual to be given a title:

> "And that Guillaume sold out his ground rents
> Seventh of Poitiers, Ninth of Aquitain"

The Canto goes on to deal with both this notion of lawful genealogy and the points at which that genealogy breaks down and has to be re-established. The law must preserve succession. Consider the Eleanor and Louis narrative:

> "Went over the sea till day's end (he, Louis, with Eleanor)
> Coming at last to Acre....
> And he, Louis, was not at ease in that town,
> And was not at ease by Jordan
> As she rode out to the palm grove
> Her scarf in Saladin's cimier."

The Eleanor narrative contrasts the marriage of Louis and Eleanor with that of Henry. The image of Saladin riding with Eleanor's scarf in his cimier, with Louis unhappy by the Jordan, seems to counterpose images of Eleanor's youthfulness, joyousness and the fact that she is desired by other men, with the hollow man that Louis has become. But, the same year that Saladin wore Eleanor's scarf, she was divorced; indeed, this is the pivotal image in this 'ideogram'. The risk is that a lawful line of inheritance has failed. However, Eleanor marries for a second time to Plantagenet. That a line has been established, that something can now be passed on, is indicated by the extract from a will:

"Nauphal, Vexis, Harry joven
In pledge for all his life and life of all his heirs
Shall have Gisors, and Vexis, Neufchastel
But if no issue Gisors shall revert..."
"Need not wed...Alix in the name
Trinity holy indivisible...Richard's our brother
Need not wed Alix once her father's ward and...
But whomso he choose...for Alix, etc..."

The legal prose is chopped up; phrases are juxtaposed. This editorial decomposition of the text can again be linked to the compositional voice; it is as if the theme has now been established; this inherently unpoetic prose can be abandoned with a perfunctory "etc..."

The next fragment set up an interesting opposition to this presentation of marriage, the disposition of property and legal prose. We have seen that the narrative largely concerns an attempt to found a dynasty, to ensure the perpetuation of a name and property. The law makes an allowance for the problems that might be encountered in the use of a reversion; a legal response to contingency, which here might be the failure of fertility. But, in this cold order, of sex for the sustenance of a family name, of reproduction as the reproduction of property, a new theme appears. The legal sections of this Canto modulate into a text of a letter of a troubadour, Bernart de Ventadour written to Eleanor and asking her to use her influence as his lady had been imprisoned, and could not "shed" her "light in the air". It would seem that poetry, as a celebration of beauty, of something freely given, is being juxtaposed with that which limits and controls succession. The importance of the Cunizza section, is that it brings together both these themes, law and the lyric, a statement of virtu.
Cunizza da Romano:

[That] freed her slaves on a Wednesday
Masnatas er servos, witness
Picus de Farinatis
And Don Elinus and Don Lipus
    Sons of Farianato de' Farinati
"free of person, free of will
free to buy, witness, sell, testate.

This is a celebration of becoming a legal being, of becoming a person; the incidents of which are outlined at the conclusion of this fragment. The listing of names, inherently unpoetic, are here to suggest both verisimilitude, and as figures in a scene that celebrates testimony, and the ability to give testimony as the mark of a freeman. It is set against a Sordello poem:

"Winter and Summer I sing of her grace,
As the rose is fair, so fair is her face,
Both summer and winter I sing of her,
The snow makyth me to remember her."

Suggested here, indicated in outline, is a coming together of the law and poetry. This conjunction is celebrated in this Canto, and is perhaps the key meaning of Cunizza's act. Sordello's "donative" art can re-define the poetic tradition in the same way that her act can suggest a new beginning; a coming together of an objective order of law, and a subjective kindness. Her kindness grants legal being to those who had been considered things. As freemen, her slaves become capable of dominium over things. To acknowledge that a slave is worthy of manumission is to see that they have an inner life, to see that they are subjects rather than objects. Manumission proves Cunizza's character. Cunizza's act is central, because it announces a theme that will be of vast importance to the poem: the composition of the good society.

5. Conclusion

Cunizza does not disappear from the Cantos; indeed, her name and the theme of manumission is repeated in Canto XXIX, the penultimate poem in *A Draft of XXX Cantos*. The reprise of her theme at this significant moment in the poem announces a concern that will increasingly draw Pound's attention as the Cantos develop: what role does the law play in the construction of the good society?
    Canto VI suggests an essential link between the objective order of the law, and the subjective, ethical or even emotional life of the subject. Cunizza exemplifies the integration of these moments, but can this legacy be carried

forward? What is at stake? Is there a risk in asserting such an organic point of origin for the law? Might this be connected with Pound's fascination for Mussolini as the dictator who exemplifies the spirit of his people? If there is to be a literary jurisprudence that has the ambition to engage with one of the most important pieces of modern literature, perhaps these questions of the relationships between aesthetics, politics and jurisprudence might provide a problematic that allows an ongoing and rigorous reading of the fraught text of the Cantos.

APPENDIX

APPENDIX

King James and an Obsession with *The Merchant of Venice*

Peter J. Alscher and Richard H. Weisberg

Cardozo School of Law

1. Introduction

Why did King James insist on seeing *The Merchant of Venice* – uniquely among Shakespeare's plays – twice? And why, for 150 years or so after that under-explored second viewing, did the play virtually disappear from the English boards? This Article combines a close reading of the "legal" scenes in the play with an exploration of the King's fascinating interest in it. The result challenges our readers to engage in a thought experiment about a wrong turn taken, as we believe, by mainstream scholars when they insist (against a complex text) on a simplistic anti-Semitic reading of the play. For it is our position, by now elaborated over 25 years of combined teaching, research and publishing about the play, as well as co-producing the first 21st century philo-Semitic mini-performance of the "legal" sections of Acts II and IV, that the play is most accurately understood and performed as a humane and universalist call for inclusiveness and tolerance. We believe strongly that those full-length productions of *Merchant* that will thrive at the box office in the 21st century, that will engage audiences to new depths of meaning for this seemingly simple comedy, that will convince them from the heart that this playwright is not anti-Semitic, but had the profoundest respect for Jewish values, and specifically those that make a tangible and spiritual contribution to his play, will be those productions that incorporate Portia's defense of Shylock's Jewish integrity and dignity at the climax of the trial scene, thereby ensuring that far from the conflict between these major characters ending in any "victory of Mercy over the law," or triumph of the New Testament over the Old, as has been extolled in academic commentaries on the play for well over 100 years, the only victory lies in Portia's bonding with Shylock over her recognition that male Venice typified by Antonio has unnecessarily provoked a moneylender beyond his human endurance, by directly and indirectly contriving to undermine his humanity, on the Rialto, and by stealing his daughter. We suggest here that – were it not for the forceful intervention of the supercessionalist, fundamentalist King James – Shakespeare would have continued to put on this kind of play, which is sustained both within its text and by Shakespeare's otherwise non-parochial and liberal spirit; but that the King, provoked by the piece as by none other that he had seen performed before or would see thereafter, insisted on a second performance in which the tolerance was drained from the text and after which generations of audiences have become attuned to quite a false vision of an anti-semitic play by an otherwise entirely inclusive playwright.

We appreciate that the vision we are forecasting and promoting as consultants ultimately to both academicians and directors seems radical and even far-fetched, given that we have not a single past production to reference our vision. However we would like to orient our position on a left-right spectrum and argue that our philo-Semitic approach is in reality a centrist even conservative compromise "middle of the road" Shakespearean position, in between two extremes of theatrical possibilities in dealing with this text, between two extremes as well of academic commentary on it over the past century or so. Most of the productions of the past 125 years or so – surprisingly including most post-Holocaust productions – share this common denominator: the climax of the trial can only be read as fulfilling Antonio's shocking conversion demand, with Portia's approval and the Duke's final implementation of it. Academicians strangely hold this conclusion to flow, almost "without interpretation" and as though by divine right, from a text that is every bit as nuanced and ironic as all other Shakespeare plays. To "save" the inescapable texture of this amazing play, some directors (and an increasing number, but still quite small, of academic commentators) go to the other extreme and transform the experience into Shylock's "tragedy". Thus, for approximately 40 years on the London stage (1830-1870), *Merchant* was performed as a four-act social tragedy, not a five-act comedy. Directors perceived Shakespeare's stage directions as requiring Shylock' conversion, but unlike the 18th century tradition preceding them, felt a sympathy for him strongly enough to conclude "he was a man more sinned against than sinning." With that assessment, they hated the combined Antonio Portia Duke conspiracy against him, which forced him to abandon a religion they perfectly respected. So when Shylock exited the court, they took out their vengeance so to speak against Shakespeare himself, by immediately bringing the curtain down! And not raising it again. After Antonio's crime against humanity (complete with its "Alien Statute"), as they saw it, the director didn't care what became of the Bassanio-Portia ring play, the consummation of marriage in Belmont, or Antonio's future. Our reading preserves the comic values of the play while also safeguarding its incredible linguistic and human complexity. Act Five can be fully integrated into a staging or reading that was intended by the playwright to produce ambiguity about the Venetian demand for a conversion, and outright hostility in the audience towards Antonio's cruel legalism in devolving Shylock's property upon the man who stole his daughter and a fair chunk of his coin-box in the bargain. The text's fulness sustained a humane middle-ground staging until – as we argue here – it was forcefully undone, expunged by a royal edict issued between James's first and second viewing of the play.

2. The "Minority Report"

Our middle-ground position has not been without its proponents, both on stage and in the world of reflective analysts of the play. But so dominant has been the insistence on a simplistic reading of the text that these closer readers form a mere minority. Uneasy with the strict intentionalism of the majority, which works from a syllogism based on the alleged expectations of an Elizabethan audience (Shakespeare's viewers craved conversions to Christianity; Antonio insists on Shylock's conversion; the play can only be read as applauding and insisting upon that outcome, since that is what the audience wanted), the Minority reads the text in its fulness and finds ample room for a staging that rejects the merchant's extraordinary and palpably unattractive demands upon his adversary. By "vote" of 95% against 5% (roughly speaking), however, the Majority report insists upon what can only be deemed a "pro-Christian" position from which Shylock's defeat and even humiliation emerge as textual necessities and, somehow, as beneficial to the audience. The Majority report, which most recently appears in Lawrence Danson's book-length treatment of the play, reached its tendentious apogee in the early 20th century proponent E.E.Stoll, who sustained the view that Shylock got what he deserved in the trial scene. For Stoll the stage tradition that deleted Act V showed a complete misunderstanding of Shakespeare's intentions; the only irony concerning Shylock, for the Majority, is that Shakespeare gives him the very legal "victory" he craved, except that it redounds against him, to his own horror.

Blindness had set in already on both sides, left and right, blinkers that obscured the middle. Neither side saw a bond developing between Portia and Shylock that would prevent her from converting him at all! Left and right agreed Shakespearean conversion was necessary and inevitable. So for the (figurative) Left, there was no choice but to "cut", while for the Majority, the play simply could not "mean" anything that might detract from the essentialist, stereotyped Jew, vs. the entirely benevolent Venetians who wish only to do his soul some good despite its evil nature. Guilty of attempted murder, Shylock's conversion baptismally transforms him – offstage, as the scene shifts with the Christian characters back to Belmont– into a good Christian like the kind generous Antonio. Developers of the Majority Report are impatient with any conflicting complexity, even one found literally in the language of the play; they utilize an assumption of Elizabethan abhorrence for usurers and Jews (à la Stoll) and the generic necessity for a bad man transformed to a good, failing again to contemplate that Shakespeare could craft a comedy in which the "villain" is both undone and shown to be better than his persecutors. Majority reporters include Barbara K Lewalski, C.L. Barber, Monica J. Hamill, Maxine Mackay, John P. Sisk, M.C.Bradbrook, Raymond B. Waddington, Herbert Burckhardt, Frank Kermode, Anthony Hecht, Lawrence Danson, Alice Benston, Richard Horwich,

Jan Lawson Hinely, E.M.W.Tillyard, and more recently in a full-length book, succeeding Danson's, Joan Ozark Holmer.

It was Stoll's distinguished countryman, Rudolf von Ihering [1897], who launched the movement of which we are the current proponents. In this Minority Report, Shakespeare scholars and teachers have dissented strongly from the Majority Report by revealing textual intricacies (some of them rendered with Shakespeare's typically fine ear for legal language, to this day often lost on mainstream readers although apparent in the literal text) that make the conversion textually unnecessary and even unlikely, and also by locating the obvious ironies in the very fabric of the play's words, and by insisting that an anti-Semitic Shakespeare is simply not the credible, humane Shakespeare of all the other plays. Those who not only see Shylock "as a man more sinned against than sinning" but also as the porte-parole for a set of positive values deliberately juxtaposed against the loose morality of the Christians include of course von Ihering and more recent analysts such as Ziolkowski [1997] who follow him in part, but also scholars of the distinction of D.D.Moody, H.C.Goddard, H.B. Charleton and more recently, Harold Bloom. Minority Reporters (and there are scores in academia who do not necessarily publish their views) all find the conversion sequence if not also Portia's introduction of the (seemingly) anti-Semitic Alien Statute targeted against Shylock alone, as aesthetically and religiously untenable and totally out of sync with Shakespeare's perceived tolerance everywhere elsewhere in his works.

Our particular contribution to the Minority, in writings (Weisberg, 1992 and 2000; Alscher, 1990, 1993 and 1999) and "pilot" excerpts on the stage (Muncie Indiana, 1997; New York City, 1998; Austin Texas, 2003), has been to integrate Act V – which also has a sustained legal thematic – into the earlier part of the play and to prove that Portia leaves the trial scene utterly disgusted (and continuously threatened) by Antonio. The trial scene has Portia at loggerheads not only with the Shylock she has come to defeat on behalf of her marriage – which cannot begin until this bit of troubling business is resolved – but also and especially with Antonio, the man who constantly seeks to intermeddle between her and her new husband. The tension is palpable, yet it has been largely unremarked and even unstaged.

The Majority Report, which published far more extensively, insists that there can be no compromise on this tension, because they see themselves as the protectors/guardians of Shakespeare's intentions for the scene. Shakespeare's Christianity, which they claim is expressed equally in both Antonio's and Portia's positions, is responsible for the evangelism of unbelievers, and in this case most visibly a Jew who has rejected Christ. It is the 1,000 year old (to Shakespeare, circa 1605) well known– and still upheld in contemporary fundamentalist denominations–doctrine of Christian supersessionism, where the Church replaces the synagogue in the sight of God, believed by the vast majority of educated, church-going Elizabethans, whether still Catholic or then Protestant, and therefore 20th-21st c. audiences *must learn to accommodate themselves to Shakespeare's 16th c. theology*, even when it no longer, or never has been, their own.

Thus the academic Majority Reports repeated and refined through the present day, have dominated the very plot line of "Merchant" productions, ever since the abandonment of the four-act "social tragedy". They say to directors, who are not Shakespeare historians, but want to perform within parameters that are recognizably Shakespearean, even those who still object to the overarching plot formula "bad Jewish usurer and attempted murderer turns converted Christian." "Perform as you will, but to qualify as an authentic Shakespearean play, you must let Antonio and Portia bond, despite all the textual evidence of her increasing antipathy for his baleful influence over her husband. You must ignore her words to him just before he inflicts the conversion and hideous "trust" arrangement on the hapless Jew: 'What mercy can you render him, Antonio?' You must fail to follow the irony in Act V as Antonio still, fantastically, seeks to be his young friend's 'surety', the middle-man even in affairs of the heart between Portia and Bassanio. You must ignore every textual nuance and even some textual words to redeem the Christian message of the play, or – better – to distort it into cruelty above mercy, coercion above choice, interpretive distortion above law and justice." But cracks have appeared in the glistening (but not gold!) edifice of the Majority.

3. King James Changes the Play, but Some Seek to Restore It

3.1. Portia's Sad Duty at Trial: Acting the Part Now (and Back Then)

In the spring of 1996, at the Shakespeare Festival in Stratford, Canada, we saw a Merchant production that we thought might represent a significant variation on the Majority Report. Claude Raines, costumed as a silver haired, bearded gentle looking Jewish businessman, played Shylock. Antonio was more flamboyant, but their Act I chemistry indicated the possibility that they might become projected friends-a Jew and a Christian- on the Rialto, by the play's end. What is relevant to this introduction to our speculation following about how Shakespeare designed the trial resolution, is that in this play, at the end of Act IV, immediately after Portia (Susan Coyne) agrees with Antonio over the conversion and penalties, and "accepts his cross" and Shylock exits, Portia stepped out of her stage role, came two or three steps forward facing the audience directly, then put her hand over her eyes and face, shook her head, as if ashamed of what she had just done. She then turned away and returned to her speaking part. It was an extraordinarily bold move, possibly the first departure for a Portia in one hundred years of performances. (The next day the local critic, also amazed by this boldness and sympathy for the "villain," and Jew at that, remarked that she appeared to be "saying" to the audience, "Has it come to this? Is this what I came to Venice for?")

We took the liberty to find Ms. Coyne after the performance, complimented her, and asked her how she felt about "stepping away" as such a departure from traditional Portia's. She answered quite thoughtfully,

> First I feel Portia is simply unpracticed in a man's world. She seems to be in control until she loses control to Antonio. I feel perfectly wretched standing up there one minute forcing this poor man to give up his religion-for what? I'm sorry, but I find it really all very sad. And then, just minutes later, I'm back in Belmont, having a party, making the audience laugh uproariously! It's just too much. It leaves me feeling like an awful hypocrite.

We explained our position, "We think Shakespeare wanted Portia to feel the way you played it, but the king overruled that. Here is how we think he played it originally. Just the way you'd want it done today! But it's never been tried before." And we briefly described the stage moves. As an actress she got the idea immediately. It was far bolder and extended farther than what the director, Mardi Maraden, had let her do. Ms. Coyne said she liked the idea and wanted to think about it some more.

The *Minority Report* wants to empower potential Portias around the world to take those extra steps. We ask this because of the text, which makes of Portia what Daniela Carpi [1994] calls an "ideal reader" of the contract and – in this Article – we ask it also because we can speculate plausibly that Shakespeare staged the final two Acts with an ear for their irony and not for some simplistic resolution, but that King James would not stand for such complexity when it came to the obvious religious undertone of this play. What King James demanded between Sunday, Feb. 10th 1605 and Tuesday Feb 12th 1605 involved one of the most significant "cleansings" in textual history. And Portias, from then on, were forced (like Ms. Coyne) to battle instincts born of the text they were playing in order to wreak havoc on an undefended outsider's property and religion. This internal struggle only arises because of a long tradition of hating the Jew that goes back not to Shakespeare or his text but to the then-reigning King himself.

3.2. Why King James Demanded a Second Staging

Shakespeare scholars researching James I's role as patron to the King's Men, 1603-1613, have known for over 50 years that the King saw *The Merchant of Venice* twice during this period. [See Appendix I.], as Peter Thomson documents in *Shakespeare's Professional Career* (p. 169). "Between 1 November and 12 February, 1605, they (The King's Men) had plays commanded 11 times. The titles are listed, and offer us as clear a picture of Shakespeare's primacy and record of the period. It is also a useful indication of the company's current repertoire:

1 November	Othello
4 November	The Merry Wives of Windsor
26 December	Measure for Measure
7 January	The Comedy of Errors
8 January	Every Man out of His Humour (Jonson)
c.9 January	Love's Labour's Lost
2 February	Every Man in His Humour (Jonson)
10 February	The Merchant of Venice
12 February	The Merchant of Venice

Why was "Merchant of Venice" performed twice, with only a day's interval? (our emphasis)

It has been assumed since Lelyfeld's first observation of the repeat performance of *Merchant* in 1961 that the probable reason King James I saw Shakespeare's The *Merchant of Venice* two times, while seeing the remaining 36 plays of the canon only once each, was that James, as Head of the Protestant Church of England, had an amicable "meeting of the minds" or an "eye-to-eye" agreement with his talented subject on the theological importance of Supersessionism in his new play. James, a Protestant, subscribed to a more than 1,000-year-old doctrine of Christianity that the Catholic and now Protestant Church had superseded (lit. Latin, "sat upon" or thus " replaced") the Jews, who, though once God's Chosen People, had been themselves rejected and abandoned by God for their national rejection of the Son of God, the Messiah, and as resurrected, the Third Person of the Christian Trinity. Therefore, the only remaining hope for worldwide Jewish salvation was through a radical Jewish conversion to the Church, in and through Jewish submission to the Lordship of Jesus Christ. So for James the only options for still living Jews, including especially fictional yet "anti-Christian" types like Shakespeare's Shylock, was his visibly accepting Christ as savior and Lord, and so abandoning all familial, religious ties to past Judaism.

The alternative to acceptance of Jesus for a Shylock, from the perspective of Church theologians – especially enforcers of the faith, like James – was dying in his corrupt Jewish "flesh" and thus facing God's eternal condemnation for all his many unrepentant sins. In other words, it has been assumed by Merchant historians familiar with the Church's longstanding supersessionist majority belief, that James must have been immediately pleased with Shakespeare's dramatizing and "bringing to life" this long held Christian doctrine through a clear-cut Venetian court scene where the villain Jew decisively loses his blood motivated "pound of flesh" court case. Shakespeare then supposedly "perfects" this resounding legal defeat with "the heroic, the self-sacrificing kind and generous Antonio" demanding the Jew to "presently become a Christian," an option, on this view, that can only ultimately edify the losing Jew. With Shylock then willingly content to accept Christianity, the scholarly assumption has been that the delighted James, seeing church theology suddenly "come to life," insisted upon making a once and only once "recall" of this play that so theologically satisfied him.

In short, the Majority speculates that the first performance Sunday February 10th must therefore have been anti-Semitic in orientation, as were previous pound of flesh plots, only more so, in dramatizing the Jewish Shylock converting to Christianity, instead of (as earlier, merely) fleeing the court to the derisive jeers of the audience, in his unregenerate, still "bloodthirsty" state. Therefore Shakespeare remains, from this Majority scholarly and directorial point of view, theologically an average Elizabethan/Jacobean Christian, certainly Catholic in upbringing but above all – where Shylock is concerned – "evangelical," in intentionally raising his exposed and disgraced Jewish moneylender out of the depths of his hopelessly inferior religion, into a visibly superior one.

On behalf of the Minority, we ask: is there an alternate explanation, more plausibly consistent both with the text of the play and its author's otherwise universal sense of tolerance and respect (even for his villains!), for why James saw *Merchant* twice? Does it not make more sense, we argue, to assume the *opposite* of the Majority report's "meeting of the minds" between king and playwright on the controversial and divisive subject of Christian supersessionalism?

For indeed there existed even then a minority Catholic opposition to the doctrine of supercessionism, articulated fervently by the orthodox Jesuit Robert Parsons, a contemporary of Shakespeare's, who came surprisingly to the defense of Jewish religious freedom, in the context of growing Protestant intolerance toward Catholic freedoms. Parsons thus argued in 1588:

"Surely, as I am now minded I would not for ten thousand worlds, compel a Jew to swear that there were a blessed Trinity. For albeit the thing be never so true, yet should he be damned for swearing against his conscience, and I, for compelling to commit so heinous and grievous a sin."

We contend then that the performance King James saw *first*, on Sunday Feb. 10th, *was Shakespeare's highly ironic and philo-Semitic challenge to the centuries old pound-of-flesh bond plot*, a production (sustainable on a literal reading of the play) meant more as a provocation to than a support of the traditional doctrine of Christian supersessionism. James was likely to have been astounded by Shakespeare's unavoidable philo-Semitism; however the King's Men staged the play that first time before his eyes, here was a Jew with deep-seated ethical values, a moneylender whose sense of family and marital vows predominated over his greed; a practitioner – not only in name – of the 10 commandments who, compared to "the Christian husbands" for whom wedding rings are to be bought and sold cheap, "would not have given it for a wilderness of monkeys " the precious ring he had from his Leah; above all, a Jew doing what Christians are supposed to do best, by showing willingness to be friends with the merchant, his previous enemy and especially to establish a truce with him ("I would be friends with you and have your love") despite the merchant's repeated trespasses against him in the Rialto -all violations framed by Shakespeare against Antonio as violations *against* Christ's Sermon on the Mount and the Lord's Prayer. These structurally unavoidable components of the play, as first performed before the King, disturbed rather than pleased the monarch.

The trial scene only compounds the ethical breaches of the Christian characters, and in Act V Portia finally reveals her awareness of the corruption of her husband's circle of friends, which she has noticed in open court and which stands as a continuing threat to her new marriage. [Weisberg, 1992, 2000] Where James was least prepared for it, Antonio is shown to fail the basic test of Christianity – mercy and love, demanded of the merchant by Portia in rendering a penalty upon the defeated Jew. When James was expecting the fulfillment of Antonio's Act 1, scene 3, "prophecy," ("The Hebrew will turn Christian, he grows kind,") what James actually saw on Sunday evening the 10th was Portia visibly, aggressively and persuasively with the Duke *defending* Shylock's Jewish dignity and integrity against Antonio's demand to convert him. In short the climax of the extended trial scene was Portia's *defense* of Shylock's Jewish integrity against her perception of Antonio's cruel and hypocritical conversion demand. In other words, James saw Portia [as Dr.Balthazar, Dr.of Laws] reject *both* of Antonio's first two demands ["that for this favour (quitting the fine)/He must presently become a Christian;"] and, retroactively, [so he will let me have/ The other half in use, to render it/Upon his death unto the gentleman/ That lately stole his daughter."] The Duke immediately thereafter sides with her no-conversion ruling, thereby confirming or agreeing to only *one*, that is the third and last of Antonio's three demands or "provisions," before he grants his "favour" of quitting the Duke's fine. The Duke explicitly rules, "He [Shylock] shall do *this*, or else I do recant..." He does not say the words "*these*" or "*that*," which might imply complete approval for Antonio's cruel triad of demands. No. The Duke–always far more "merciful" than the supposed essential Christian Antonio– can only tolerate "*this*," namely the third of the merchant's provisions. He apparently agrees only to Antonio's deed of gift for Jessica and Lorenzo, "of all he dies possessed," the only one of the three demands that Shylock can humanly speaking agree to. [Weisberg, 1999; Alscher, 1993] The Duke permits neither the forced conversion, nor, therefore, Antonio's hideous "trust" arrangement, which depended on Shylock's first agreeing to the conversion, and which forces Shylock, for the rest of his life, into a subservient legal partnership with a dominating Antonio whose "trust" arrangement practices a form of interest profiting which he swore to Shylock's face he never engaged in. This is a man who cannot be "trusted!" When therefore Shylock does agree to sign this deed of gift, he decides from the heart as a loving Jewish father, independently of Antonio's attempted usurpation.

The Duke thereby favors Portia's implicit ruling, that Antonio's conversion condition was *not authorized by the Alien Statute*. This intervention was then followed by Shylock's relieved, and credible human response that he was "content" indeed, with Portia's vigorous respect for his religion and person. One last anti-Semitic outburst by Gratiano, a futile attempt to slur the Jew (as though Gratiano had the power to "baptize him by hanging" when there will be no baptism at all), rebounds against him, quashed by a gentle but firm gesture to be silent, from Dr. Balthazar /Portia. Antonio, visibly embarrassed, but with no further room to protest, bids Gratiano to remain silent. When Shylock exits the Venetian court, it is with his Jewish dignity and integrity intact. Yet the play remains a comedy, as Act V permits marriages, but on Portia's revised terms to Bassanio – once she rids herself of Antonio's cloying and threatening intermeddling – terms that derive from the alternative ethical system she saw in the defeated Shylock, defeated on the contingencies of comedy and the needs of her husband but now controlling on Belmont.

This totally unexpected legal defense by Portia, the reaffirmation of Shylock's merciful conscience despite Antonio's condemnation of his "hard Jewish heart," struck James intellectually as posing a theological nightmare. Given his orthodox Protestant theology, his notoriously impulsive temper and his unquestionable power as patron over the playwright, he held his temper only a few more minutes to watch Portia's final Belmont scrutiny of Antonio at V.1.244-25, over his self-serving, arrogant proposal of yet another bond on Bassanio's behalf, this time with Antonio's "*soul* upon the forfeit," to guarantee Bassanio's perpetual fidelity to her- she responds sarcastically, with a full 15 seconds scrutiny of his repeated insistence on standing between husband and wife. "Then you shall be his surety. Give him this [referring to the ring Bassanio had given away after the trial scene] ", emphasizing full well that she alone is capable of assuring her husband's fidelity.

When the king saw this, with Portia once again sharply undermining Antonio's dominion over Bassanio, whom she has yet to bed even once because of Antonio's trial, the king's temper could not be contained. (And here it might be added that King James in particular might have been upset at what today we would call this strongly feminist comedic heroine protecting her interests against the always intermeddling male authority figure, Antonio.) The play, from start to finish, was altogether too equivocal about the Jewish-Christian opposition and the male-female order of things to satisfy this supersessionalist monarch.

3.3. What James Might Have Said to the Bard

It is our speculation that James called "Shaxesberd" (as he called him) to his side with a severe verbal tirade. Requiring the Conversion of the Jews for the hastening of the Second Coming of Christ, questioning the playwright's knowledge of Scripture, challenging his past "softness" with previous villains and criminals like Deputy Lord Angelo in *Measure For Measure* and King Claudius in Hamlet, James decided he would not regain peace or composure until Shaxesberd performed the entire play again this time for his entire pleasure, not his frustration and aggravation. This second time there would be no equivocation. Although no words needed to be changed in the scant time between Sunday and Tuesday, all the obvious philo-Semitic emphases on Sunday were to be expunged. So was set in motion a theological (but hardly a Shakespearean) simple-mindedness that the Majority has kept alive for centuries. Removed (almost) forever were the lawyer lady's defense of the Jew, so the king could have the extreme satisfaction of watching the villain Jew fall to his knees, and kiss the cross of Christ: "But let that lawyer woman hold her tongue, say not a word, and not oppose Antonio's authority!"

> Shaxesberd! Have you gone daft man? Do you not read your scripture? Have you not heard of the Second Coming of Christ? Are you ignorant about the Conversation of the Jews? Surely ye know, you canny have the one without the other?! Or are you a party to that heretic Jesuit, Robert Parsons, who swears he will not commit to a sin by converting the Jew, because it goes against the Jew's conscience? Are you both daft, then? Has there ever been a Jew with a conscience? Damn it man, I'll have none of that heresy in my Palace! The Trinity is the truth and the truth is the Trinity, so let the Jew be damned. Let Parsons wait another 10,000 moons for the Second Coming. I'll not wait that long! And neither will you, Shaxesberd. You have that cur in

the palm of Antonio's hand, man. I say, force him down to his knees. Then let him kiss the cross of Christ, and be content with that! That's where I will see him next, on his knees. Do I make myself plain? Damn it man. I am your patron, not your censor. But I will not have you teach me church theology from a stage! You make it worse, William, with that lawyer woman. Do you think I don't recognize her? I will not have an impudent, interfering woman standing face to face, shaking her head at my Antonio! I will not have it. To defend a godforsaken wretched Jew! Before my very face! Do you hear me, man? I will not stand for it. Your Jew walks into the court with a knife in his hand. He walks out, I say, with a cross around his neck!

Let her do her part, William. Let her, if you will, preach mercy to the villain. He claims a pound, you say, of the good Antonio's flesh? Whatever, I ask you, has our merchant done to him, but kick and spit upon him, as the cur deserved? I say, I see no mercy in the Jew, or from the Jew. But let us hear the rhetoric. For God's sake man you are a master of that! Only do not confuse your story. Give us the full defense of Antonio, and the full prosecution of the Jew. Keep the white the white, and the black the black. Let this kindest man in all Venice have his way in court. The villain Jew follows the kind Antonio in. Then let the convert follow him out, straightaway to church and baptism. Let him be content with that! Are you following my drift man? Hear me out William. I hold things back. But you push me too far. Your Balthazar is a Dr. of Laws, yes? She knows the law, then. Well, I ask you, do you not know the law then? Let me tell you the law then: Apprehend the criminal. Try him. Hang him. Then bury the blackguard!   You do not then resurrect him! You do not pardon him. But you, Shaxberd, are soft on criminals! Soft, I say. I have seen it before at this Palace. Yet have I held my   tongue. For your sake. Because you do have talent, William . When, I have asked myself, will he ever learn? Tonight when you try to teach me, will I teach you: Have I forgotten your Hamlet? I remember your Claudius. Aye, there was a criminal for you for you. Aye, a regicide. Aye, a fratricide. But what does your Prince do to revenge his own murdered father, an anointed king, no less? Who more deserved the sword   swiftly   to his guilty heart? Claudius, I say. But what does your Prince do to him, William? I'll tell you. He cries out "Conscience," like your Jesuit Parsons, and runs away like a trembling schoolgirl! Claudius runs one way, your Prince the other! Do not defend yourself here, Shaxberd. Listen to your king. I'll mark you another example. Always too soft. Take your Measure for Measure. You call it comedy? I call it tragedy. There was yet another criminal exposed for all the world to see. A lecher. The appointed enforcer of the law- "The lord Deputy Angelo", as I recall. Did not your own Duke Vincentio-as I also recall- apprehend him for the virgin violator that he was? Worse, yet the violator of a newly vowed novice, one Isabell? Tell me not that the violation was only with his formerly betrothed. I'll not hear it. The intention was evil. The law is the law. It pertains solely to the intent. You cannot bend it Shaxberd, as you will. What did you do with him, Shaxberd? Apprehend him, try him, hang him? Bury the villain? No, William you did not think of that! No, you pardoned him! The victim pardons the offender! You marry him off to live happily thereafter! What were you thinking, man? I'll answer for you: ye are too soft, man. That is why I am the king who rules, and you the playwright who writes. But tonight I will play the writer this one time. No more of your soft pardons for hard-hearted criminals. Your Jew, I say, is a criminal.

Do not show me the Jew's conscience on stage. Are you telling me, Shaxberd, that your Jew-this Shylock showed our Christian mercy after all? By refraining when no power could have prevented him? I'll not hear it. To whom does he appeal?, I ask:

"Is that the law?" this Shylock asks. He falls to his knees. He looks upward. He appears conscience stricken. Are you telling me, he hears the voice of God? Where? How? He has no heart! Has no one told you, William, that the God of Jacob has long since abandoned him? Abandoned him without hope of redemption? Will not hear him? What are you thinking, man? We are his only conscience, now, and let him thank his God for that!

Your Venetian Duke has ruled more generous than I. I say, he hangs or he converts. That is his only conscience –to kiss the cross or face the gallows. There is no further defense, do you hear me Shaxberd? The gall of that interfering woman! By gods, I thought when she defied Antonio she said "Tis not written in the Statute." I say, Silence that impudent woman! Make her stand back. Make her agree with the good Christian. She will not oppose the will of Christ, and she will not embarrass my Antonio! To his very face! She wants her Bassanio all for herself! She divides my Antonio from his Bassanio. She would have my Antonio alone in Venice with only a Jew for a friend. I will not have it! Not on my stage.

My temper rises, Shaxberd. Enough of my temper. Forgive me, I will settle it. There will be an end to it. Tonight is Sunday. Tomorrow night is Monday. You will play *The Spanish Maze* tomorrow eve, as scheduled. I will wait one more evening to settle this, but not a day more. In my mind's eye William I see your true Merchant already and it gives me great delight after all. I will see the whole of the play again, as I have instructed. Alas William, your plays perplex and exhaust me. But this one now tickles my fancy. I say it whets my appetite after all. I have confidence in you William, do not disappoint me. You are already well rehearsed. My changes will come quickly to your men. Forgive me my temper, young man. Only do as I say, I have only your best interests in mind. The Conversion of the Jews! Your play will hasten the Coming of Christ, William. All will be well. We shall make merry not tonight, but Tuesday night. Tuesday evening The King's Men will bring this *Merchant* back, do you understand? It is a royal command. In 48 hours, that is this Tuesday night, and you will make just these two changes. But first, if you insist on a money lending Jew who dares say sincerely " I would be friends with you" to my dear Antonio, I say that provokes me still, yet I tell you I will stop my ears at that, yet I'll not censor that.

Because he will soon lend under the terms Antonio commands him, and not remain a friendly Jew for long! And we would prefer a hanging, Shaxberd, yet we will settle for a Jewish conversion before our very own eyes. Am I plain enough thus far?

But hear me well. I will not hear the line "Tis not in the Statute." I say it *is* in the statute! The woman will approve the conversion with the nod of her head, and not shake it! I'll have no sympathy whatsoever on stage for the conspiring wretch. Keep all of your own words, William. I ask for no changes, except these, you have heard, let your actors show their meaning in their body motions. Make it so when your Duke declares "He shall do this" your Jew loses everything but his salvation, and my Antonio gains control of a new Christian. Be so kind, William, to give me my handsome Antonio and his handsome Bassanio for a second time. He will meet his Bassanio in Belmont despite his marriage. Ah, William, I will not censor that! But hear me well, and resist me no further: It must be a glorious victory for Antonio, a triumph of our New Testament over the Jew's Old, a victory for our Christian mercy over the Jew's bloodthirsty law. Look not dejected man. Our next performance will bring you the fame you deserve.

And of course, the second change. In Belmont, let the impetuous woman subordinate herself once more in Antonio's presence. Let her welcome with courtesy and affection the kind, longsuffering Antonio, for he has indeed sacrificed all of himself for his beloved Bassanio. Let him embrace his Bassanio as though their friendship had no end. Let not marriage separate and divide these two souls whose affections have bound them together so deeply. Let it be clear to us, that this patient woman thoroughly welcomes and aye, approves this dear merchant's presence in her house, that he may come and go, so to speak, as he wills. Ah, William, I am seeing the improvement already. In my mind's eye William I see the changes in your masterpiece as though you had already performed them. And it delights me as no other comedy I have seen before. Yes, I will see the whole of the play again, as I have instructed. This *Merchant* rejuvenates my fancy. I say it whets my appetite. The Conversion of the Jews! The Second Coming of Christ! I say you will hasten the Coming of Christ, William! All will yet be well. We shall make merry Tuesday night."

As may be discerned from the above reaction, there is a second factor compounding James' intense theological aggravation with Shakespeare's open deviation from theological orthodoxy, re this Jewish character's need for salvation. We will only summarize it here, as it is relevant to our speculation that James bisexual orientation made him at first aroused by, then disappointed by Shakespeare's Sunday evening detour from James' own unique romantic expectations, that is between Antonio and Bassanio, not repeated again in Shakespeare's dramatic canon. Our speculation is that James identified sexually with the Antonio's homoerotic affection for his dearest friend, as James perceived their relationship and from the second act anticipated an Act V ménage a trois where the victorious merchant and married young friend would enjoy constant access to one another.

King James was, according to one of his most reliable literary biographers, a bisexual, and notoriously so. Alvin Kernan relates two contemporary examples, one from 1605, the same year of our Whitehall performances, that lets us see how James' bisexuality may have been aroused by the unique Antonio-Bassanio homoerotic friendship. So that James would not tolerate any "currish, rotten, villain" Jew as he saw him-exclusively through Antonio's eyes- in acts I.3 and III.3, nor any domineering wife-as he saw Portia– come in between the future, and perpetuating friendship of the two most important characters in this play— the only two characters he would have been sexually engaged by. In other words, given his bisexual predisposition James wants the visibly heterosexual and to the king, repulsive, Shylock completely removed from the plot picture, if not hanged, then silently submissive as a "new Christian" under Antonio's tutelage, as if as a character he no longer existed, so that the merchant may continue his perpetual access with the adoring Bassanio, long after his marriage, much as James himself had perpetual access to his handsome courtiers even while his Queen Anne looked on helplessly. [Kernan,116 and see Appendix II.]

What is anathema to James is the implication that Shakespeare is suggesting, on our reading, that Portia in Belmont – after the exhausting trial, where she sees for herself how Antonio's influence over Bassanio threatens her marriage and how Antonio bids fair to continue his control over Bassanio in the ring exchange despite Bassanio's marriage betrothal – has no more room whatever for him in her marriage. She wants no Antonio between her man and herself, perhaps better advising the merchant to return to Venice where mature friendship has been offered him by the now-disgraced Shylock. That she may in her expansive and feminist vision foresee a reconciliation through a non-erotic male friendship between prior enemies in lieu of the older man's questionable manipulation of her new husband – all of this was too much for James. The king needed the Bard's guarantee that from then on no production would equivocate on who was in charge [see also Appendix III] and by what means. The merchant, and not the maid –Venice and not Belmont, Christian manipulation and not a Judaeo-feminist ethic – the primacy of the king's own values had to be ensconced in the performance of this most complex of comedies.

4. Why it Makes Sense to Assume James's Wroth Against the Sunday Performance

4.1. *Merchant* disappears after the Tuesday revision

An advantage of our censorship theory of *Merchant*, is that it explains perhaps for the first time the otherwise inexplicable fact, observed by all our scholars, that *Merchant* disappeared from the English stage immediately after the second royal performance on Tuesday. For surely if king and playwright had met "eye to eye" the prior Sunday, if Shakespeare had presented any version of the conversion sequence we have seen variations of for the past 250 years, hoping to impress the new king, the delighted James would have used his kingly influence to promote his favorite play often and soon after he himself gorged his appetite for it through a second staging at court. Had their been bravos from James on Sunday night, with the playwright, as it were, basking in that praise for the first time in two years at Whitehall, wouldn't the king's applause have been heard in London by that next Tuesday night? Or the next Tuesday in March? April? And on throughout the next century-and-a-half?

We have already speculated an entirely different scenario. After the tirade, the king was confident his short but decisive new stage directions would more than satisfy him. Antonio would be palpably victorious legally and religiously. He would assert his stature once again over a groveling Jew. And he soon would re- assert his intimacy with Bassanio in Belmont, in the very midst of a quiescent Portia's new marriage. But although the king had the power to coerce such changes over the 48 hours that separated his two viewings, he did not have the power to alter the playwright's vision of the text.

Shakespeare was not delighted. James had left him no room to maneuver. Without having to be told this in writing, he knew James, as both his king, and his patron, would not permit his performing his philo-Semitic Merchant anywhere else in England. From now on it would have to be performed as the King James Version or not at all.

Shakespeare pondered the power of majesty. James was not asking him to discuss the implications of his play. They had not become friends in the past two years, and it was less likely that they ever would after this. He had not before been so much as criticized for his work, and suddenly there's a royal reaction against it! Shakespeare would not go down without a fight, but he knew better than to engage this arrogant pedant verbally, not in this court where they would attract any more attention than they might already have.

He thought about the Second Coming of Christ. Yes, there was a point where he agreed with his king! He longed for the coming of Christ but not on the king's timetable! He recalled [the Apostle] Paul's enthusiam for Christ's return, in his own lifetime! Paul was wrong about that. It was the expectation that counted, not the fact. The Lord had tarried another 1,600 years with the Second Coming. "I'll die," thought Shakespeare, "long before his return, yet I'll meet him then face to face. It's only a wretched night like this, with a petty Protestant to please that I'd call for my Saviour's return. What have the Jews to do with it?"

Shakespeare recalled a scripture that inspired his reversing the blame against the Jew in all those nasty pound-of-flesh plots he had come to scorn. Jesus called on Peter to become his friend, to walk with him throughout the countryside, to become "fisherman of men". And this impetuous fisherman gladly left his fishing boats to hear out this mesmerizing Jewish preacher. There was never any coercion from the master. When Jesus asked his disciples years later, "but whom say ye that I am?" Peter boldly replied, "Thou art the Christ, the Son of the living God." Shakespeare recalled vividly Jesus's spontaneous reply to Peter's joyful identification: "Blessed art thou Simon Barjona: for flesh and blood hath not revealed it unto thee, but *my Father which is in heaven.*" (our emphasis) [Mathew 16,17] Shakespeare may well have pondered the question: "If Peter would not have recognized the Christ, no Jew would have. And then where would we Gentiles be? The Father revealed his Son only to those Jews whom He chose. There were two covenants that intersected, not one only for the Gentiles that was suddenly forced on the Jews-not after a 3,000-year-old covenant between God and Abraham that spoke nothing of His Son! And that covenant was never broken no matter how oft God punished his Chosen people. No wonder the nation did not accept him as their Messiah. He was no military man. They had had their Moses. There was a leader. How could they all recognize Him. How did we Gentiles? We killed him! And now I have my James! How many times did He warn them not to bow their knees before any king ruler who claimed to be a God? So why has England, to whom Christ has been revealed to some as that humble loving Son who forced no one to follow Him, whom we could never have found by ourselves, but only by those few Jews of scripture, why are we forcing all their ancestors against their will and God's as well? To become like us?! No, it goes against my conscience. I'll follow my own Shylock's example, and not bow down on my knees before this James who calls out the name of Christ only to intimidate me and arouse his sexual fantasies."

Shakespeare pondered his only face saving option in the face of arbitrary royal power, one that would retain his personal integrity and dignity as a Christian without threatening his career with the King's Men. If the Jews whom he knew, including his own Shylock, would not bow their knee to the name of Jesus, a mortal man, a Jew himself whom they could not recognize as God's Messiah, whose cross the Gentiles turned into a sword to beat them, and alienate them, even while they did not retaliate, did not become anti-Christian in actual practice, then Shakespeare decided he would not bow his knee either before James. He would not change his written stage directions to read "Shylock kneels," at Antonio's-and now James's- insistence. He would perform the play once again on Tuesday night, and once only for the king's benefit, without his heart in it. The king would see what he wanted, a Jew on his knees, kissing Antonio's cross. But with no energy, heart or identity left in him. Shakespeare would then take his version out of his repertoire, and not perform the king's version until the king left the throne. James could keep the playwright from performing the now censored original, but he wouldn't force him to perform the king's alternative again if he did not choose to. So Shakespeare, whom we are treating as a profound Christian with great respect for the Hebrews' long struggles under the direction of the God of Abraham, and with a strong conscience of his own, did not himself kneel to the king's directive. Nothing in King James tirades changed his mind about the loving nature of Abraham's God as he knew it from the Hebrew Scriptures. Nor was he about to publicly destroy corrupt or mock the Jewish identity of his uniquely created character, whatever his momentary and understandable temptation to cut out the heart of Antonio, as the Christian had almost done to him.

So as not to impugn his entire career over a single play, he regrouped with his men, explaining the extreme pressure they were all under, re-rehearsed the disputed Act IV 22 lines, and then visibly omitted by way of body language alone Portia's 15 second scrutiny of Antonio in Belmont when the merchant again – ludicrously and even obscenely, from her perspective – offers himself as "surety" to Bassanio [Weisberg, 1992], that had so personally offended James. Shakespeare did not alter his written quarto or folio stage directions to bow to James's supersessionist theology. He did not change his crucial state direction after Antonio's conversion demand to read, "Shylock kneels."

King James and an Obsession with The Merchant of Venice 213

The King's Men performed James' anti-Semitic *Merchant*, with Antonio's "victory of Mercy over Justice," with the "Triumph of the New Testament over the Old" etc. On Tuesday night the 12th just that once for the king's pleasure, but never again during Shakespeare's lifetime. As fate would have it, James outlived Shakespeare by some 10 years, so the playwright's sacrifice proved a real one. To his regret, Shakespeare did not see his uncensored play again in his lifetime. And neither did any other audience in England get to see it until well into the 18th century!

4.2. The Sunday Production Re-Captured

Thanks to a generous production grant from the University of Texas Law Dept. (Austin, Texas) and the English Dept. Graduate Program in Theater and Dance, we have (March, 2002) performed a 42 minute version of our Philo-Semitic resolution, developing the trajectory of our argument from the I, iii bond formation scene, through the Act IV trial scene culmination in Shylock's exit with his Jewish identity and integrity intact, to the final Belmont scene where Portia "wins Bassanio back" from Antonio, and the merchant is left with nowhere to go in Venice but with the Jew who still would be friends with him.

Thanks to the University of Texas Law Dept. Moot Court Videotaping Facility and the many talents of our extraordinarily imaginative director, Charles Siegel, we have captured our 42 minute long performance on both VHS and DVD copies formats.

Feb. 10th, 2005 will mark the 400th anniversary of the Sunday Feb. 10th, 1605 performance we have been defending as philo-Semitic. Unless decisive and conclusive historical evidence is found to support the anachronistic intentionalist view that no Shakespearean audience would have tolerated a comedic critique of their own religion – or that the otherwise tolerant and liberal spirit of Shakespeare [see Appendix IV] could not possibly have directed his players as we have speculated – we hope to encourage future directors to perform the first complete, five-act philo-Semitic performance – the very one James saw on Sunday but then prevented the rest of the world from savoring.

5. Appendix I

These are the five known scholarly documentations: by Toby Lelyfeld, in her book *Shylock on the Stage* (1961); M.M. Mahood, editor, in her introduction to the New Cambridge Shakespeare edition of *The Merchant of Venice* (1987); John Gross, in his book, *Shylock: A Legend And Its Legacy* (1990); Peter Thomson in his book, Shakespeare's Professional Career (1992); and Alvin

Kernan in his book *Shakespeare, the King's Playwright: Theater in the Stuart Court*, 1603 –1613 (1995). Whitehall Palace documentary records, uncovered by Thomson's and Kernan's independent and exhaustive dating of all the plays at Whitehall, 1603-13, confirm that not only does the king see *Merchant* "twice" but also that there is no other play performed of all 37 that the King sees twice, before or after *Merchant*. We also draw attention to the fact that nowhere else in these scholars' writings do they offer specific *explanations* for the very significant observation, made by Lelyfeld, Mahood and Cross, concerning the "disappearance of *Merchant* from the English stage for almost 150 years," immediately after the king's second or "command performance", on Tues. Feb. 12th, 1605. All underlined emphasis in Appendices I-IV is our own.

Toby Lelyfeld writes:

> The early state history of *The Merchant of Venice* is meager. The first reference to a state presentation is to be found in a list, probably forged, but undoubtedly based on a genuine document used by Malone, [Edmond Malone, an Historical Account of the English Stage, London, 1793] of the plays given at Court in 1604-5. According to this, the *Merchant of Venice* was *witnessed by James in a production by the King's Men on February 10, 1605, and the king admired it sufficiently to order its reshowing two days later. Unhappily the Court Revels Account tells us nothing more of that command performance at Whitehall by "Shaxberd."* The play, of course, could not have been new at this time. The earliest probable date we can set for it is 1594—the year of Lopez' hanging. Bearing in mind the steady demand for new additions to the dramatic repertory of the day, it is not likely that *The Merchant of Venice* languished for want of production between the years of its completion and the 1605 entry, *but we have nothing with which to document its history from that date to the closing of the theaters by the Puritans in 1642.*

M.M. Mahood writes:

> But in the past *The Merchant of Venice* has been highly vulnerable to changing theatrical and social pressures, some of which have distorted it so much that several rescue operations in this century have been needed to get it back to some semblance of the play Shakespeare wrote. Its stage history has been rich, but it has not always been happy.
>
> *The play in fact had virtually no stage history for its first hundred and fifty years. After two performances before James I at Shrovetide,*

King James and an Obsession with The Merchant of Venice

1605, it vanished from the English stage though actors who emigrated to Germany kept a few of its lines alive in German in a chaotic comedy called Der Jud Von Venedig...By 1741, Shakespeare's reputation stood high enough for Charles Macklin to restore the original play.

John Gross writes:

Very little is known about the early stage history of the *Merchant of Venice*. Possibly the part of Shylock was created by Richard Burbage, possibly (though it seems less likely) by the low-comedy actor Will Kemp. By 1600, according to the title page of the First Quarto, the play had already been acted "divers times" by The Lord Chamberlaine's Servants. *In February 1605, on Shrove Tuesday, the King's Servants, in the presence of James I, performed it at Whitehall. It must have been a success, since they were ordered to perform it again two days later. But beyond this, no details of early performances have survived—nothing at all from the entire period between 1605 and 1642, when the theaters were closed down.* Nor have any comments on the play survived from the same period.

Alvin Kernan, in his 1995 study *Shakespeare, The King's Playwright: Theater in the Stuart Court*, 1603-1613, analyses in depth six Shakespeare tragedies (and also *Measure for Measure*) – but *not Merchant* –, all performed by Shakespeare under King James' patronage, and also publishes as an Appendix the exhaustive calendar of all known plays performed at Whitehall Palace during this creative ten year period, including other contemporary playwrights such as Ben Jonson, Beaumont and Fletcher, Cyril Tourneur and many others. He writes:

They (The Kings Men) came back to the palace on Feb. 2, Candlemas, with the other Jonson humor play, *Every Man In*. On the following night they were ready to perform still again, but for some reason their performance was put off until Shrove Sunday, when they appeared for the first of three nights in a row opening with *The Merchant of Venice*. *For the only time on record the king commanded one of their plays to be repeated, and Merchant was on the boards again on the night of the twelfth. Did the king fall asleep at the performance? Did he so like the clever courtroom arguments of Portia and Shylock, which were just his kind of thing that he wanted to hear them again?* Years later he would go back to see for a second time a Cambridge play, Ignoramus, that tickled his fancy, with its satiric portrait of the lawyer who had been his prosecutor in the Raleigh trial, Edward Coke.

6. Appendix II

This is one example Kernan gives of the king's ostentatious flirtations:

> "The Earl of Pembroke, a handsome youth, who is always with the King and always joking with him, actually kissed his Majesty's face, whereupon the King laughed and gave him a little cuff" (*Calendar of State Papers* [Venetian], X, 77). Later James took up with Pembroke's younger brother, the even more handsome Philip, who as a result of this intimacy was made Earl of Montgomery in 1605. Later, Robert Carr (or Kerr), a strikingly beautiful but not strikingly intelligent Scot whom James nursed after he broke his leg at a tournament, became the major favorite, and in time, the all-powerful earl of Somerset.[Kernan publishes a photo of the handsome Somerset] James' need for the open affection of these men was not in his control. He toyed constantly with his own codpiece, fondled his lovers openly, nibbled their cheeks and wrote passionate love letters to them. [Kernan, p. 118]

Given this homoerotic disposition on the king's part, here is another example from *Merchant* of how an ambiguously homoerotic line may have uniquely engaged the king, again triggering expectations in the play of a developing, more fulfilling Antonio-Bassanio romantic relationship to come. Salarino is describing to Solanio Antonio's tearful departing words to Bassanio as he left Venice Belmont:

> ...His [Antonio's] eye being big with tears,
> Turning his face, he put his hands behind him,
> And with affection wondrous sensible
> He wrung Bassanio's hand, and so they parted.
> Solanio: *I think he only loves the world for him.*
> I pray thee let us go out and find him out
> And quicken his embraced heaviness
> With some delight or other. [2.8.48-54, our emphasis]

Relevant perhaps to this passage is Kernan's description of the courtier George Villiers, who became "the great love of James' life." In December 1623, after Shakespeare's death, James writes a letter to the strikingly handsome Villiers expressing his love for him, using the almost identical intimate love language he heard in *Merchant*:

"I cannot content myself without sending you this present, praying God that I meeting with you and that this Christmas a new marriage [sic] ever to be kept hereafter, *as I desire only to live in this world for your sake*, and that I had rather live banished in any part of earth with you than live a sorrowful widow's life without you..." [Kernan, p. 118, our emphasis]

It is as though James still remembered Antonio's intimate love language with Bassanio. Shakespeare had of course written these Solarino-to-Solanio lines at least 3 years, if not as many as 7, before James came to the throne, under Elizabeth's reign. Yet when James hears them, we are speculating, he immediately becomes aroused and engaged by the possibility of Shakespeare's transforming this Act ii parting into an Act V reuniting of the two friends projected far beyond Bssanio's marriage. But the philo-Semitic ending we preview, drawing Antonio back to a new start with Shylock in Venice, puts an abrupt end to that fantasy. And so the king is doubly provoked, incensed, to have Shakespeare perform the play again, this time with Antonio completely dominating the resolution of the trial scene, converting Shylock and asserting control over Bassanio in Belmont all over again. The King James Version of the play.

7. Appendix III

7.1. (Legal) Precedent for James's Interventionist Predilection

It may reasonably be objected to our speculation that James single-handedly overruled Shakespeare's defense of his Jew's integrity and dignity, that there is no historic evidence available to prove this, and in all probability never will be given the current state of James' scholarship. Yet data does exist of a precedent situation in which James overruled the verdict of an actual (as opposed to literary) court of law, where his opinion, much less, final decision, had not been asked for, and then went on to impose a sentence, including a death penalty that he passionately believed was not only legally, but theologically correct. We refer to the sensational case of the Witches of Lothian, which took place in Edinburgh, in August of 1593, approximately 11 ½ years prior to the Merchant case, when James was then King James the Sixth of Scotland. I will quote Kernan's account, itself based on Godfrey Watson's narrative in full, because Kernan's narrative is written without any attempt to support James' intervention in the *Merchant* play (which, as we have pointed out he has yet to consider as a case of intervention or overruling), but which we believe does nevertheless support our contention that any monarch who would so boldly dominate a court of law already committed to acquittal, would have no compunctions about overruling a similarly committed playwright:

"This was not the first time [Kernan, p85], where James was outraged and wrote the archbishop at once, telling him his theology was in error and that he should read Demonologies to bring himself up to date."] that Stuart politics and witchcraft came close together. In a sensational case in Edinburgh in August 1593, a coven known as the Witches of Lothian (which included Agnes Sampson, Gillie Duncan, Margaret Thomson, and five others, led by A schoolmaster, Dr.Fran), was charged with having conspired to keep James from returning from Denmark with his new bride, Queen Anne, in 1590, when the royal couple had been forced to wait in Kronenberg-Elsinore for months for a favorable wind from Denmark to Scotland. Under torture the witches revealed that they had practiced against the king's life as well. Pieces of dead bodies had been tied to cats, who were thrown into the sea; threads were prepared and unknotted to raise tempests; a black toad had been roasted, hung up for three days and the juice collected in an oyster shell. Eventually, as the demonic coup, a handkerchief of the king's was obtained and an image made which was passed to the Devil at a Witches' Sabbath with the ominous words, "This is King James the Sixth, ordained to be consumed at the instance of a nobleman, Francis Earl of Bothwell (Kernan's reference to Godfrey Watson, *Bothwell and the Witches*, London, 1975).

This sounds more like magistrate's language than the spell of a witch, but the name of a Bothwell brought James himself scuttling down to the dungeons at once to sift the witches between torture sessions about what they knew of his feared and dangerous enemy, the earl of Bothwell. The witches didn't know much, but in time they implicated another conspirator, the warlock Richard Graham, and he revealed, again under torture, that he had been approached by Bothwell to cast a spell over James. *The court of law, however, had some doubts and refused to convict the witches, at which James assembled the jury and lectured them to the effect that he knew witchcraft to be "a thing grown common among us. I know it to be a most abominable sin; and I have been occupied these three quarters of a year for the sifting out of them that are guilty therein. As for them who think these witchcrafts to be but fantasies, I remit them to be catechized and instructed in these most evident points" [Kernan reference to Watson, p141] The king had his way, and Graham, after dreadful torments, recanted and was burned alive, as were five of the Witches of Lothian."* [Kernan, p85-86]

Our point is simply that if a king would not hesitate to lecture an already sworn jury over their theological ignorance and then overrule their verdict he would not have hesitated to overrule his playwright once his temper had been aroused. Shakespeare's consolation was that he would not have to perform before James for another 8 months, not until the fall of the 1605-6 season. It may be merely coincidental but beginning with that next theatrical season, Shakespeare offers no more uplifting romantic comedies to James, but beginning with *Macbeth*, (1606), then *Antony and Cleopatra*, (1606), then *Timon of Athens* (1607-8) and *Coriolanus*, (1608), several years dwelling on the arrogance and tragic vulnerabilities of rulers who abuse their power.

Since it is crucial to our argument that our philo-Semitic performance of *Merchant* is also Shakespearean, i.e. could have been written by Shakespeare given his own knowledge and interpretation of the *New* and *Old Testaments*, (and even if his interpretation was certainly a minority one circa 1596-1600), and not our 21st imposition of non-supersessionist theology on a 16th c. text, we too want to promote the fact that James did see *Merchant* twice—the first time a philo-Semitic trial resolution which he would not approve; the second time, just 48 hours later, an anti-Semitic resolution redirected for the first time by Shakespeare, a sequence that would establish that he (the playwright) *had been performing Merchant for a least the previous five years (since 1600, possibly earlier) philo-Semitically*, before arriving, so to speak, at Whitehall, and before that earlier direction was radically undermined and effectively censored by the king. We would not conjecture the possibility that Shakespeare had been performing, as the Lord Chamberlain's men, and under Queen Elizabeth's reign, anti-Semitic productions of this play, and then suddenly changed this pattern for the very fist time before the new king, as if to deliberately provoke him. We are assuming, rather, based on the king's apparent passive indifference to what Shakespeare presented in the very high quality of material preceding *Merchant* (*cf. Hamlet, Measure for Measure, Comedy of Errors, and Henry V*), that the king might not have become any more engaged in the plot of Merchant than he had been in the plots of those. As it turned out, for all the reasons behind the king's tirade, Shakespeare had underestimated his combined theological and sexual sensitivities.

8. Appendix IV

Shakespeare's generally tolerant and liberal spirit apparent everywhere else in his work, is not contradicted in *Merchant*, as we have attempted to show throughout this article. Furthermore it is shockingly simplistic and counter-intuitive to assume (as the Majority does) that this play can be read one way to make it the sole exception to the Shakespearean rule. Even his villains treated with a compassion and three-dimensionality that the Majority report -but not the text of the play- violates in its account of Shylock. Indeed one way of opening up the Merchant is to compare Shylock not to the "villain" category at all, but to the stature of the more complex fully human and thus highly fallible Prosecutor figures, such as Deputy Angelo in *Measure for Measure* and King Leontes in *The Winter's Tale* both of whom also initiate aggressive legal actions against perfectly well-meaning defendants (Claudio in *MM* and Queen Hermione in *WT*) only to find themselves, like Shylock, exposed in the very process of prosecution, and by female defense "lawyers" (Isabel in *MM* and Paulina in *WT*) like Portia, of committing potential more serious crimes themselves. Shakespeare's liberality in *MM* and *WT* shows in forgiving his court prosecutors, Angelo and Leontes, precisely because they ultimately repent their sins publicly, as Shakespeare's text gives Shylock the same opportunity –at "Is that the law?" If Shakespeare's Shylock repents his impulse to kill Antonio, before the God of Abraham, as a God-fearing Jew, Shakespearean liberality would be to defend him against Antonio's impulse to forcibly convert him, when he Antonio—who has never repented his abuses against the moneylender—should be instead grateful for Shylock's Jewish mercy toward him!

Sadly the Majority stereotyping of the play has had its influence on the European Economic Community.

When in 1997, a committee appointed by the Euro Economic Commission voted for the portrait of William Shakespeare to adorn the first Euro Currency as their first choice above all other European artists it was an extraordinarily appropriate perspicacious selection. The committee was recognizing the universality of a literary giant, a humanitarian and literary genius, a poet and dramatist who was not only still extremely popular on stage, almost 400 years after his death in his own country -a status not equaled by any other playwrights performing anywhere in Europe in the early 17th century, but one whose plays are still popular in all the European countries served by the new Euro currency, and are performed as regularly as the most popular contemporary playwrights of those countries.

His plays moreover are studied in both the high schools and universities of these countries, not to mention the rest of the educated world. His portrait is recognized with pride by the vast majority of Europeans approvingly, because he is the creator (as Charles Dickens later was in novel form) of so many memorable human beings (in the words of one American critic, Harold Bloom); and a man of abounding generosity who poured his creative spirit into literally scores of unforgettable characters, who seem in so many instances to have acquired in the popular imagination "a life of their own." Here was a man, not just of his own age, as Ben Jonson so accurately praised and prophesied of him in the early 17th c., but for "our age" too. Any student who read a Shakespeare comedy, or history, or tragedy, would surely have been impressed enough with just one of his many characters, so that seeing the poet's portrait on a daily basis of the face of his own currency, would have given her or him the pleasure of recalling that one fictional face, or that one memorable line.

And serious Shakespeare lovers would take solace that here was at least one international writer whose breadth of human interests and diversity of characters would continue to transcend the national borders of the Europe he set his plays in fore centuries ago, countries who in the 20th and 21st centuries have not until recently been on mutually cooperative economic terms. So here is an Englishman known for his breadth and height of his spirit, not for his narrow-mindedness, nor his bigotry, who championed the potential of both religious and personal freedom, not the beaurocratic and artificial limitations on it; of artistic experiment over dogma; of mercy and tolerance, not cruelly and exclusiveness. His bold and invariably more intelligent daring female heroines affectionately, and sometimes not so affectionately, expose the very worst traits in their men, only to bring about the very best in them in the end.

Why, then, did a second EEC jury overrule, and ultimately veto, the first committee's nomination of Shakespeare's portrait? The nomination and veto were not widely publicized either in England or the European press. There was a single-line explanation, printed in only a paragraph length article by the New York newspaper, "The Jewish Forward", 1997: "Because of his anti-Semitism shown in his play *The Merchant of Venice*." If we of the Minority report were convinced that the jury's allegation accurately described Shakespeare's religious prejudice we would disband this project immediately, when it in facts predates their decision by more than 25 years! But we do not think their allegation is true, and want to take this opportunity to state our opposition. The EEC jury was not condemning Shakespeare personally for the several admittedly anti-Jewish slur against Shylock that occur in almost all the 4 acts Shylock is on stage, e.g. the nasty cutting jeers from Solanio and Solerio in Act III. Because while there are many of these, as long as Shylock hears them Shakespeare gives him in turn perfectly philo-Semitic replies, coming from the depths of his struggling, persecuted soul, revealing his hidden Jewish values as often superior [sic] to those of his tormentors. As e.g.:

> Out upon her! Thou torturest me, Tubal: I had it of Leah when I was a bachelor. I would not have given it for a wilderness of monkeys!

Shakespeare the philo-Semite, who treats Shylock, even when he is furious with his own daughter, with profound respect, gives his beleaguered Jew this extraordinarily sensitive and profound exclamation, whose wisdom Bassanio the romantic hero could benefit from when he gives away his wife's ring to his great regret, his fiancé Portia's wedding ring at the bidding of Shylock's tormentor

Antonio, the "designated" superior Christian! Thus we feel that Shakespeare's Shylock intelligent, sensitive, energetic and verbally gifted as he is created, can hold his own against all Gentile comers in the play, except for the climax of the trial scene, when all his antagonists, including Portia, appear to "gang up" on him simultaneously. And it is in these 22 lines, (beginning with Portia's "What mercy can you show him, Antonio?") that the jury focused on, in delivering their charge of Shakespearean anti-Semitism.

What we believe the EEC jury was condemning, and with the best of intentions, and reinforced without a doubt by the official Catholic Church repudiation, detailed in the 1965 Vatican policy statement "Nostre Aetate," of all expressions of anti-Semitism and supersessionalism in worldwide church teaching, the *very teaching King James fervently believed in, but which Shakespeare did not*. The jury not seeing the many textual ironies leading up to this crucial turning point, and assuming as has been taught for centuries that Portia's "quality of mercy " speech must be exclusively "pro-Antonio" and therefore "anti-Shylock," perceived this one "unanswerable" anti-Semitic blow against this admittedly vulnerable Jew, as inflicted by Antonio with no prior warning in the courtroom. Then -as they read the text or recalled past performances, any one of which performed anywhere in the world would have incorporated some variation on this painful forced conversion sequence—against a man, as they in the late 20th century *again* saw him, a man "more sinned against, than sinning," they would have deplored Portia's approval of it, the Duke's finalizing it, and finally held it against Shakespeare himself that in the end he became so cruelly callous as to cut out his own character's heart.

The committee's bold public decision that Shakespeare himself was a heartless Semite – based on no extra-literary sources or corroborating evidence of any kind – as opposed to one of his main characters, Antonio, and so to be denied a coveted privilege- was the first of its kind in the 20th century. It is misguided, but it at least reflects the widespread change of attitude toward the very idea of the conversion of the Jews, which can no longer be tolerated or pursued according to the 1965 Vatican decree, "Nostre Aetate." Regrettably, however, this negative EEC decision against Shakespeare and the play has contributed to an increasing reluctance by widespread theater audiences to sit through a predictably coercive, religiously strained and patently unmerciful resolution when they can enjoy perfectly uplifting, inclusive comic resolutions in *Midsummer Night's Dream, As You Like It, Twelfth Night and Much Ado About Nothing*. It may also have discouraged imaginative directors such as Kenneth Branagh (with whom we have been in touch, and whose staff expressed great interest in our interpretation, in a letter on file with us), from producing liberal versions of the play for mass audiences.

And yet our Minority report believes that the EEC decision may yet be redeemed to the benefit of William Shakespeare. Because we still have his text, which does not read "Shylock kneels." We understand for the first time, how the original staging might have been crucially altered to propound precisely the contemptuous attitudes against Jews, that Shakespeare's liberal imagination opposed, and the EEC ironically mistaking the King James I theology for the playwright's, courageously condemned. What we are advocating is, that having learned from the Euro jury that the world will reject anti-Semitic Merchants, that courageous directors, innovative actors and challenging teachers will eventually surprise their audiences with the philo-Semitic *Merchant* we are content the King saw on Sunday, February 10th, 1605, a performance for our age!

List of Sources
The Majority Report

Barber, Cesar Lombardi, *Shakespeare's Festive Comedy: A Study of Dramatic Form and Its Relation to Social Custom* (Princeton, New Jersey: Princeton University Press, 1959)163-186.

Baron, Salon, *A Social and Religious History of the Jews,* 16 vols. (New York and London: Columbia University Press, 1973; The Jewish Publication Society of America, Philadelphia, 5733).

Benston, Alice N., "Portia, the Law and the Tripartite Structure of *The Merchant of Venice,*" *Shakespeare Quarterly,* 30,(1979) 367-385.

Bradbrook, Muriel C., "Polyphonic Music: *All's Well That Ends Well— TheMerchant of Venice—Much Ado About Nothing*" *Shakespeare and Elizabethan Poetry* (New York: Oxford University Press, 1952) 167-188.

Burckhardt, Sigurd, "*The Merchant of Venice*: The Gentle Bond," *English Language History,* vol 29, no.3, Sept. (1962) 239-262.

Danson, Lawrence, *The Harmonies of The Merchant of Venice* (New Haven and London: Yale University Press, 1978)

Gross, John, *Shylock: A Legend And Its Legacy,* (New York: Simon and Schuster, 1990) 105.

Hamill, Monica J., "Poetry, Law and the Pursuit of Perfection: Portia's Role in *The Merchant of* Venice", *Studies in English Literature,* 18, (1978) 229-242

Hecht, Anthony, "*The Merchant of Venice*: A Venture in Hermemeutics" *Obligatti: Essays in Criticism* (Atheneum, New York, 1986) 140-229

Hinely, Jan Lawson, "Bond Priorities in *The Merchant of Venice*," *Studies in English Literature*, 20, (1980) 217-39

Holmer, Joan Ozark, *The Merchant of Venice: Choice, Hazards, Consequences.* (New York: St. Martin's Press,1995). *Contains an excellent Bibliography with an abundance of additional Majority Reporter sources.

Horwich, Richard, "Riddle and Dilemma in *The Merchant of Venice*", *Studies in English Literature*, Spring (1977):pp. 191-200

Kermode, Frank, "The Mature Comedies," *Early Shakespeare* (Stratford-Upon-Avon Studies, 3, London, 1961): p. 224

Kernan, Alvin, *Shakespeare, the King's Playwright: Theater in the Stuart Court, 1603-1613,* (Yale University Press, 1995) 70

Lelyfeld, Toby, *Shylock on the Stage*, (London and New York: Routledge and Kegan Paul, 1961) 9

Lewalski, Barbara, "Biblical Allusion and Allegory in *The Merchant of Venice, Shakespeare Quarterly*, 13, (1962) 327-343

Mackay, Maxine, "*The Merchant of Venice*: A Reflection of the Early Conflict Between Courts of Law and Courts of Equity," *Shakespeare Quarterly*, (1982) 371-375

Mahood, Molly M. The New Cambridge Shakespeare *Merchant of Venice*, (Cambridge University Press, 1987), 42

Sisk, John P., "Bondage and Release in *The Merchant of Venice*" *Shakespeare Quarterly* (1982) 217-223

Stoll, Elmer Edgar, "Shylock", *Shakespeare Studies: Historical and Comparative in Method* (New York: Macmillan, 1927).

Thomson, Peter, *Shakespeare's Professional Career*, (Cambridge University Press, 1992) 169.

Tillyard, Eustace Mandeville W., "*The Merchant of Venice*" *Early Comedies* (New York: Barnes and Noble Inc., 1965) 183-84.

Waddington, Raymond B., "Blind Gods: Fortune, Justice and Cupid in *The Merchant of Venice*" *English Language History* (1977) 458-477.

The Minority Report

Alscher, Peter J., " *Shakespeare's Merchant of Venice: Toward a Radical Reconciliation and a Final Solution to Venice's Jewish Problem"*. Unpublished Dissertation, Washington University, St. Louis, Mo. 1990.

Alscher, Peter J., "I would be friends with you..." Staging Directions for a Balanced Resolution to "*The Merchant of Venice*" Trial Scene.(*Cardozo Studies in Law and Literature*, vol. 5, no.1, Spring 1993.

Alscher, Peter J. "Shylock on Appeal" Chapter 18, *Law and the Arts,* ed. Susan Tiefenbrun, under auspices of Hofstra University, Contributions in Legal Studies (New York: Greenwood Press, 1999)

Bloom, Harold, *Shakespeare: The Invention of the Human* (New York: Riverhead Books, 1998)

Charleton, Henry B., "Shakespeare's Jew" from *Shakespearean Comedy* (New York: The Macmillan Company, 1938) 123-60.

Goddard, Harold C. "*The Merchant of Venice*" from *The Meaning of Shakespeare* (Chicago University Press, 1951) 81-116

Kornstein, Daniel J, *Kill All The Lawyers? Shakespeare's Legal Appeal* (New Jersey:Princeton University Press, 1994)

Moody, Anthony D. *Shakespeare: The Merchant of Venice* (London: Edward Arnold Ltd, 1964)

Watson, Godfrey, *Bothwell and the Witches* (London: Robert Dale, 1975).

Weisberg, Richard, "*Poethics and Other Strategies of Literature*" (New York: Columbia U. Press, 1992)

Weisberg, Richard, "Antonio's Legal Cruelty: Interdisciplinarity and "The Merchant of Venice,"* in Myrsiades, Linda ed., "Undisciplining Literature:

Literature, Law and Culture" (New York: Peter Lang, 1999), [reproduced from 25 College Literature, pages 12-20.

DVD (42 minutes); "Three Scenes From The *Merchant of Venice"* (University of Texas School of Law Production Grant, with the Graduate Dept of English, Theater and Dance Contributing the talents of MFA acting students, and under the direction of Charles Siegel. Staged before a live audience, as a contribution to the Law and Fine Arts Joint Symposium: "From Text to Performance" Performed March 8, 2002.

This pathbreaking pilot DVD, showing how Shylock in good faith overcomes his past anger with Antonio, how Portia can defend Shylock from Antonio's conversion demand so that he may exit the Venetian court with his Jewish dignity and integrity intact, and Portia win back Bassanio in Belmont, is available from Peter J. Alscher, 6337 Clearair Drive, Mentor Ohio 44060 (440-257-7900) or through pjalscher@msn.com.

ANGLO-AMERIKANISCHE STUDIEN - ANGLO-AMERICAN STUDIES

Herausgegeben von
Rüdiger Ahrens (Würzburg) und Kevin Cope (Baton Rouge)

Band 1 Hedwig Kiesel: Martin Luther - ein Held John Osbornes. *Luther* - Kontext und historischer Hintergrund. 1986.

Band 2 Monika Hoffarth: Martin Luther King und die amerikanische Rassenfrage. Stereotypenkorrektur und humanitäre Erziehung durch literarische Rezeption. 1990.

Band 3 Peter Erlebach / Thomas Michael Stein (eds.): Graham Greene in Perspective. A Critical Symposium. 1992.

Band 4 Kevin L. Cope (Ed.): Compendious Conversations. The Method of Dialogue in the Early Enlightenment. 1992.

Band 5 Zaixin Zhang: Voices of the Self in Daniel Defoe's Fiction. An Alternative Marxist Approach. 1993.

Band 6 Berthold Schoene: The Making of Orcadia. Narrative Identity in the Prose Work of George Mackay Brown. 1995.

Band 7 Wolfgang Gehring: Schülernahe Lebensbereiche in Englischbüchern für die 7. Jahrgangsstufe. Ein Beitrag zur landeskundlichen Lehrwerkkritik. 1996.

Band 8 Klaus Stierstorfer: John Oxenford (1812-1877) as Farceur and Critic of Comedy. 1996.

Band 9 Beth Swan: Fictions of Law. An Investigation of the Law in Eighteenth-Century English Fiction. 1997.

Band 10 Catharina Boerckel: Weibliche Entwicklungsprozesse bei Jane Austen, Elizabeth Gaskell und George Eliot. 1997.

Band 11 Rosamaria Loretelli / Roberto De Romanis (Eds.): Narrating Transgression. Representations of the Criminal in Early Modern England. 1999.

Band 12 Nic Panagopoulos: The Fiction of Joseph Conrad. The Influence of Schopenhauer and Nietzsche. 1998.

Band 13 Roland Kofer: Historische Mehrdimensionalität in den Dramen Christopher Frys. Eine hermeneutische Analyse der thematischen Struktur der einzelnen Dramen. 1999.

Band 14 Anke S. Herling: Phantastische Elemente im postmodernen Roman. Formen und Funktionen non-mimetischer Darstellungsweisen in ausgewählten Werken der englischsprachigen Literatur. 1999.

Band 15 Christian J. Ganter: Hoffnung wider die Hoffnungslosigkeit – Das Irlandbild im Erzählwerk Bernard MacLavertys. Ein imagologischer Beitrag zur englischen Literaturdidaktik. 1999.

Band 16 Claudia Orażem: Political Economy and Fiction in the Early Works of Harriet Martineau. 1999.

Band 17 Kwok-kan Tam / Andrew Parkin / Terry Siu-han Yip (eds.): Shakespeare Global / Local. The Hong Kong Imaginary in Transcultural Production. 2002.

Band 18 Matthias Merkl: Kulturgeographische Inhalte in deutschen Lehrbüchern für den Englischunterricht der 8. Jahrgangsstufe. Ein Beitrag zur landeskundlichen Lehrwerkkritik. 2002.

Band 19 Martina Engel: Außenseiter und Gemeinschaft. Zur Funktion von Interaktion, Kommunikation und sozialem Handeln in den Romanen George Eliots. 2002.

Band 20 Bárbara Arizti: *Textuality as Striptease*: The Discourses of Intimacy in David Lodge's *Changing Places* and *Small World*. 2002.

Band 21 Andrew Parkin: The Rendez-Vous. Poems of Multicultural Experience. 2003.

Band 22 Götz Ahrendt: *For our father's sake, and mother's care*. Zur Eltern-Kind-Beziehung in den Dramen Shakespeares unter Berücksichtigung zeitgenössischer Traktatliteratur und Porträts. 2003.

Band 23 Brian Hooper: Voices in the Heart. Postcolonialism and Identity in Hong Kong Literature. 2003.

Band 24 Alexander Bidell: Das Konzept des Bösen in *Paradise Lost*. Analyse und Interpretation. 2003.

Band 25 Isolde Schmidt: Skaespeare im Leistungskurs Englisch. Eine empirische Untersuchung. 2004.

Band 26 Claudia Schemberg: Achieving 'At-one-ment'. Storytelling and the Concept of the *Self* in Ian McEwan's *The Child in Time, Black Dogs, Enduring Love,* and *Atonement.* 2004.

Band 27 Wing-chi Ki: Jane Austen and the Dialectic of Misrecognition. 2005.

Band 28 Daniela Carpi (ed.): Property Law in Renaissance Literature. 2005.

www.peterlang.de